PRINCIPIA ETHICA

" Everything is what it is,
and not another thing"
                    BISHOP BUTLER

PRINCIPIA ETHICA

GEORGE EDWARD MOORE

Cardinal Beran Library
St. Mary's Seminary
9845 Memorial Drive
Houston, Texas 77024

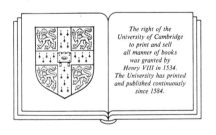

The right of the
University of Cambridge
to print and sell
all manner of books
was granted by
Henry VIII in 1534.
The University has printed
and published continuously
since 1584.*

CAMBRIDGE UNIVERSITY PRESS

CAMBRIDGE

LONDON   NEW YORK   NEW ROCHELLE

MELBOURNE   SYDNEY

41283

Published by the Press Syndicate of the University of Cambridge
The Pitt Building, Trumpington Street, Cambridge CB2 1RP
32 East 57th Street, New York, NY 10022, USA
10 Stamford Road, Oakleigh, Melbourne 3166, Australia

ISBN 0 521 05753 1 hard covers
ISBN 0 521 09114 4 paperback

First published 1903
Reprinted 1922 1929 1948
1951 1954 1956 1959
First paperback edition 1959
Reprinted 1960 1962 1965
1966 1968 1971 1976 1978 1980 1982 1984

Printed in Great Britain at the
University Press, Cambridge

DOCTORIBUS AMICISQUE CANTABRIGIENSIBUS

DISCIPULUS AMICUS CANTABRIGIENSIS

PRIMITIAS

D. D. D.

AUCTOR

PREFACE.

IT appears to me that in Ethics, as in all other philosophical studies, the difficulties and disagreements, of which its history is full, are mainly due to a very simple cause: namely to the attempt to answer questions, without first discovering precisely *what* question it is which you desire to answer. I do not know how far this source of error would be done away, if philosophers would *try* to discover what question they were asking, before they set about to answer it; for the work of analysis and distinction is often very difficult: we may often fail to make the necessary discovery, even though we make a definite attempt to do so. But I am inclined to think that in many cases a resolute attempt would be sufficient to ensure success; so that, if only this attempt were made, many of the most glaring difficulties and disagreements in philosophy would disappear. At all events, philosophers seem, in general, not to make the attempt; and, whether in consequence of this omission or not, they are constantly endeavouring to prove that 'Yes' or 'No' will answer questions, to which *neither* answer is correct, owing to the fact that what they have before their minds is not one question, but several, to some of which the true answer is 'No,' to others 'Yes.'

I have tried in this book to distinguish clearly two kinds of question, which moral philosophers have always professed to answer, but which, as I have tried to shew, they have almost always confused both with one another and with other questions. These two questions may be expressed, the first in the form: What kind of things ought to exist for their own sakes? the second in the form: What kind of actions ought we to perform? I have tried to shew exactly what it is that we ask about a thing, when we ask whether it ought to exist for its own sake, is good in itself or has intrinsic value; and exactly what it is that we ask about an action, when we ask whether we ought to do it, whether it is a right action or a duty.

But from a clear insight into the nature of these two questions, there appears to me to follow a second most important result: namely, what is the nature of the evidence, by which alone any ethical proposition can be proved or disproved, confirmed or rendered doubtful. Once we recognise the exact meaning of the two questions, I think it also becomes plain exactly what kind of reasons are relevant as arguments for or against any particular answer to them. It becomes plain that, for answers to the *first* question, no relevant evidence whatever can be adduced: from no other truth, except themselves alone, can it be inferred that they are either true or false. We can guard against error only by taking care, that, when we try to answer a question of this kind, we have before our minds that question only, and not some other or others; but that there is great danger of such errors of confusion I have tried to shew, and also what are the chief precautions by the use of which we may guard against them. As for the *second* question, it becomes equally plain, that any answer to it *is* capable of proof or disproof—that, indeed, so many different considerations are relevant to its truth or falsehood, as to make the attainment of probability very difficult, and the attainment of certainty impossible. Nevertheless the *kind* of evidence, which is both necessary and alone relevant to such proof and disproof, is capable of exact definition. Such evidence must contain propositions of two kinds and of two kinds only : it must consist, in the first place, of truths with regard to the results of the action in question— of *causal* truths—but it must *also* contain ethical truths of our first or self-evident class. Many truths of both kinds are necessary to the proof that any action ought to be done; and any other kind of evidence is wholly irrelevant. It follows that, if any ethical philosopher offers for propositions of the first kind any evidence whatever, or if, for propositions of the second kind, he either fails to adduce both causal and ethical truths, or adduces truths that are neither, his reasoning has not the least tendency to establish his conclusions. But not only are his conclusions totally devoid of weight : we have, moreover, reason to suspect him of the error of confusion ; since the offering of irrelevant evidence generally indicates that the philosopher who offers it has had before his mind, not the question which he professes to answer, but some other entirely different one. Ethical discussion, hitherto, has perhaps consisted chiefly in reasoning of this totally irrelevant kind.

One main object of this book may, then, be expressed by slightly changing one of Kant's famous titles. I have endeavoured to write 'Prolegomena to any future Ethics that can possibly pretend to be scientific.' In other words, I have endeavoured to discover what are the fundamental principles of ethical reasoning; and the establishment of these principles, rather than of any conclusions which may be attained by their use, may be regarded as my main object. I have, however, also attempted, in Chapter VI, to present some conclusions, with regard to the proper answer of the question 'What is good in itself?' which are very different from any which have commonly been advocated by philosophers. I have tried to define the classes within which all great goods and evils fall; and I have maintained that very many different things are good and evil in themselves, and that neither class of things possesses any other property which is both common to all its members and peculiar to them.

In order to express the fact that ethical propositions of my *first* class are incapable of proof or disproof, I have sometimes followed Sidgwick's usage in calling them 'Intuitions.' But I beg it may be noticed that I am not an 'Intuitionist,' in the ordinary sense of the term. Sidgwick himself seems never to have been clearly aware of the immense importance of the difference which distinguishes his Intuitionism from the common doctrine, which has generally been called by that name. The Intuitionist proper is distinguished by maintaining that propositions of my *second* class—propositions which assert that a certain action is *right* or a *duty*—are incapable of proof or disproof by any enquiry into the results of such actions. I, on the contrary, am no less anxious to maintain that propositions of *this* kind are *not* 'Intuitions,' than to maintain that propositions of my *first* class *are* Intuitions.

Again, I would wish it observed that, when I call such propositions 'Intuitions,' I mean *merely* to assert that they are incapable of proof; I imply nothing whatever as to the manner or origin of our cognition of them. Still less do I imply (as most Intuitionists have done) that any proposition whatever is true, *because* we cognise it in a particular way or by the exercise of any particular faculty: I hold, on the contrary, that in every way in which it is possible to cognise a true proposition, it is also possible to cognise a false one.

When this book had been already completed, I found, in Brentano's 'Origin of the Knowledge of Right and Wrong[1],'

[1] 'The Origin of the Knowledge of Right and Wrong.' By Franz Brentano. English Translation by Cecil Hague. Constable, 1902.—I have written a review of this book, which will, I hope, appear in the *International Journal of Ethics* for October, 1903. I may refer to this review for a fuller account of my reasons for disagreeing with Brentano.

opinions far more closely resembling my own, than those of any
other ethical writer with whom I am acquainted. Brentano
appears to agree with me completely (1) in regarding all ethical
propositions as defined by the fact that they predicate a single
unique objective concept; (2) in dividing such propositions
sharply into the same two kinds; (3) in holding that the first
kind are incapable of proof; and (4) with regard to the kind of
evidence which is necessary and relevant to the proof of the
second kind. But he regards the fundamental ethical concept
as being, not the simple one which I denote by 'good,' but the
complex one which I have taken to define 'beautiful'; and he
does not recognise, but even denies by implication, the principle
which I have called *the principle of organic unities*. In consequence of these two differences, his conclusions as to what
things are good in themselves, also differ very materially from
mine. He agrees, however, that there are many different goods,
and that the love of good and beautiful objects constitutes an
important class among them.

I wish to refer to one oversight, of which I became aware
only when it was too late to correct it, and which may, I am
afraid, cause unnecessary trouble to some readers. I have
omitted to discuss directly the mutual relations of the several
different notions, which are all expressed by the word 'end.'
The consequences of this omission may perhaps be partially
avoided by a reference to my article on 'Teleology' in Baldwin's
Dictionary of Philosophy and Psychology.

If I were to rewrite my work now, I should make a very
different, and I believe that I could make a much better book.
But it may be doubted whether, in attempting to satisfy myself,
I might not merely render more obscure the ideas which I am
most anxious to convey, without a corresponding gain in completeness and accuracy. However that may be, my belief that

to publish the book as it stands was probably the best thing I
could do, does not prevent me from being painfully aware that
it is full of defects.

TRINITY COLLEGE, CAMBRIDGE.
    August, 1903.

[This book is now reprinted without any alteration whatever,
except that a few misprints and grammatical mistakes have been
corrected. It is reprinted, because I am still in agreement with
its main tendency and conclusions; and it is reprinted without
alteration, because I found that, if I were to begin correcting
what in it seemed to me to need correction, I could not stop
short of rewriting the whole book.

                                        G. E. M.]

CAMBRIDGE, 1922.

TABLE OF CONTENTS.

CHAPTER I.

THE SUBJECT-MATTER OF ETHICS.

A.

CHAPTER II.

NATURALISTIC ETHICS.

CHAPTER III.

HEDONISM.

C.

CHAPTER IV.

METAPHYSICAL ETHICS.

A.

D.

CHAPTER V.

ETHICS IN RELATION TO CONDUCT.

CHAPTER VI.

THE IDEAL.

CHAPTER I.

THE SUBJECT-MATTER OF ETHICS.

1. IT is very easy to point out some among our every-day judgments, with the truth of which Ethics is undoubtedly concerned. Whenever we say, 'So and so is a good man,' or 'That fellow is a villain'; whenever we ask, 'What ought I to do?' or 'Is it wrong for me to do like this?'; whenever we hazard such remarks as 'Temperance is a virtue and drunkenness a vice'—it is undoubtedly the business of Ethics to discuss such questions and such statements; to argue what is the true answer when we ask what it is right to do, and to give reasons for thinking that our statements about the character of persons or the morality of actions are true or false. In the vast majority of cases, where we make statements involving any of the terms 'virtue,' 'vice,' 'duty,' 'right,' 'ought,' 'good,' 'bad,' we are making ethical judgments; and if we wish to discuss their truth, we shall be discussing a point of Ethics.

So much as this is not disputed; but it falls very far short of defining the province of Ethics. That province may indeed be defined as the whole truth about that which is at the same time common to all such judgments and peculiar to them. But we have still to ask the question: What is it that is thus common and peculiar? And this is a question to which very different answers have been given by ethical philosophers of acknowledged reputation, and none of them, perhaps, completely satisfactory.

2. If we take such examples as those given above, we shall not be far wrong in saying that they are all of them concerned with the question of 'conduct'—with the question, what, in the conduct of us, human beings, is good, and what is bad, what is right, and what is wrong. For when we say that a man is good, we commonly mean that he acts rightly; when we say that drunkenness is a vice, we commonly mean that to get drunk is a wrong or wicked action. And this discussion of human conduct is, in fact, that with which the name 'Ethics' is most intimately associated. It is so associated by derivation; and conduct is undoubtedly by far the commonest and most generally interesting object of ethical judgments.

Accordingly, we find that many ethical philosophers are disposed to accept as an adequate definition of 'Ethics' the statement that it deals with the question what is good or bad in human conduct. They hold that its enquiries are properly confined to 'conduct' or to 'practice'; they hold that the name 'practical philosophy' covers all the matter with which it has to do. Now, without discussing the proper meaning of the word (for verbal questions are properly left to the writers of dictionaries and other persons interested in literature; philosophy, as we shall see, has no concern with them), I may say that I intend to use 'Ethics' to cover more than this—a usage, for which there is, I think, quite sufficient authority. I am using it to cover an enquiry for which, at all events, there is no other word: the general enquiry into what is good.

Ethics is undoubtedly concerned with the question what good conduct is; but, being concerned with this, it obviously does not start at the beginning, unless it is prepared to tell us what is good as well as what is conduct. For 'good conduct' is a complex notion: all conduct is not good; for some is certainly bad and some may be indifferent. And on the other hand, other things, beside conduct, may be good; and if they are so, then, 'good' denotes some property, that is common to them and conduct; and if we examine good conduct alone of all good things, then we shall be in danger of mistaking for this property, some property which is not shared by those other things: and thus we shall have made a mistake about Ethics even in this limited sense; for we shall not know what good conduct really is. This is a mistake which many writers have actually made,

from limiting their enquiry to conduct. And hence I shall try
to avoid it by considering first what is good in general; hoping,
that if we can arrive at any certainty about this, it will be much
easier to settle the question of good conduct: for we all know
pretty well what 'conduct' is. This, then, is our first question:
What is good? and What is bad? and to the discussion of this
question (or these questions) I give the name of Ethics, since
that science must, at all events, include it.

3.   But this is a question which may have many meanings.
If, for example, each of us were to say 'I am doing good now'
or 'I had a good dinner yesterday,' these statements would each
of them be some sort of answer to our question, although
perhaps a false one. So, too, when A asks B what school he
ought to send his son to, B's answer will certainly be an ethical
judgment. And similarly all distribution of praise or blame to
any personage or thing that has existed, now exists, or will
exist, does give some answer to the question 'What is good?'
In all such cases some particular thing is judged to be good or
bad: the question 'What?' is answered by 'This.' But this is
not the sense in which a scientific Ethics asks the question. Not
one, of all the many million answers of this kind, which must be
true, can form a part of an ethical system; although that science
must contain reasons and principles sufficient for deciding on
the truth of all of them. There are far too many persons, things
and events in the world, past, present, or to come, for a discussion of their individual merits to be embraced in any science.
Ethics, therefore, does not deal at all with facts of this nature,
facts that are unique, individual, absolutely particular; facts
with which such studies as history, geography, astronomy, are
compelled, in part at least, to deal. And, for this reason, it is
not the business of the ethical philosopher to give personal
advice or exhortation.

4.   But there is another meaning which may be given to
the question 'What is good?' 'Books are good' would be an
answer to it, though an answer obviously false; for some books
are very bad indeed. And ethical judgments of this kind do
indeed belong to Ethics; though I shall not deal with many of
them. Such is the judgment 'Pleasure is good'—a judgment,

of which Ethics should discuss the truth, although it is not
nearly as important as that other judgment, with which we shall
be much occupied presently—'Pleasure *alone* is good.' It is
judgments of this sort, which are made in such books on Ethics
as contain a list of 'virtues'—in Aristotle's 'Ethics' for example.
But it is judgments of precisely the same kind, which form the
substance of what is commonly supposed to be a study different
from Ethics, and one much less respectable—the study of
Casuistry. We may be told that Casuistry differs from Ethics,
in that it is much more detailed and particular, Ethics much
more general. But it is most important to notice that Casuistry
does not deal with anything that is absolutely particular—
particular in the only sense in which a perfectly precise line can
be drawn between it and what is general. It is not particular
in the sense just noticed, the sense in which this book is a
particular book, and A's friend's advice particular advice.
Casuistry may indeed be *more* particular and Ethics *more*
general; but that means that they differ only in degree and
not in kind. And this is universally true of 'particular' and
'general,' when used in this common, but inaccurate, sense. So
far as Ethics allows itself to give lists of virtues or even to name
constituents of the Ideal, it is indistinguishable from Casuistry.
Both alike deal with what is general, in the sense in which
physics and chemistry deal with what is general. Just as
chemistry aims at discovering what are the properties of oxygen,
wherever it occurs, and not only of this or that particular speci-
men of oxygen; so Casuistry aims at discovering what actions
are good, *whenever they occur.* In this respect Ethics and
Casuistry alike are to be classed with such sciences as physics,
chemistry and physiology, in their absolute distinction from
those of which history and geography are instances. And it is
to be noted that, owing to their detailed nature, casuistical investigations are actually nearer to physics and to chemistry
than are the investigations usually assigned to Ethics. For just
as physics cannot rest content with the discovery that light is
propagated by waves of ether, but must go on to discover the
particular nature of the ether-waves corresponding to each
several colour; so Casuistry, not content with the general law

that charity is a virtue must attempt to discover the relative merits of every different form of charity. Casuistry forms, therefore, part of the ideal of ethical science: Ethics cannot be complete without it. The defects of Casuistry are not defects of principle; no objection can be taken to its aim and object. It has failed only because it is far too difficult a subject to be treated adequately in our present state of knowledge. The casuist has been unable to distinguish, in the cases which he treats, those elements upon which their value depends. Hence he often thinks two cases to be alike in respect of value, when in reality they are alike only in some other respect. It is to mistakes of this kind that the pernicious influence of such investigations has been due. For Casuistry is the goal of ethical investigation. It cannot be safely attempted at the beginning of our studies, but only at the end.

5. But our question 'What is good?' may have still another meaning. We may, in the third place, mean to ask, not what thing or things are good, but how 'good' is to be defined. This is an enquiry which belongs only to Ethics, not to Casuistry; and this is the enquiry which will occupy us first.

It is an enquiry to which most special attention should be directed; since this question, how 'good' is to be defined, is the most fundamental question in all Ethics. That which is meant by 'good' is, in fact, except its converse 'bad,' the *only* simple object of thought which is peculiar to Ethics. Its definition is, therefore, the most essential point in the definition of Ethics; and moreover a mistake with regard to it entails a far larger number of erroneous ethical judgments than any other. Unless this first question be fully understood, and its true answer clearly recognised, the rest of Ethics is as good as useless from the point of view of systematic knowledge. True ethical judgments, of the two kinds last dealt with, may indeed be made by those who do not know the answer to this question as well as by those who do; and it goes without saying that the two classes of people may lead equally good lives. But it is extremely unlikely that the *most general* ethical judgments will be equally valid, in the absence of a true answer to this question: I shall presently try to shew that the gravest errors have been largely due to beliefs in a false answer. And, in any case, it is impossible that, till the answer to this question be known, any one should know *what is the evidence* for any ethical judgment whatsoever. But the main object of Ethics, as a systematic science, is to give correct *reasons* for thinking that this or that is good; and, unless this question be answered, such reasons cannot be given. Even, therefore, apart from the fact that a false answer leads to false conclusions, the present enquiry is a most necessary and important part of the science of Ethics.

6. What, then, is good? How is good to be defined? Now, it may be thought that this is a verbal question. A definition does indeed often mean the expressing of one word's meaning in other words. But this is not the sort of definition I am asking for. Such a definition can never be of ultimate importance in any study except lexicography. If I wanted that kind of definition I should have to consider in the first place how people generally used the word 'good'; but my business is not with its proper usage, as established by custom. I should, indeed, be foolish, if I tried to use it for something which it did not usually denote: if, for instance, I were to announce that, whenever I used the word 'good,' I must be understood to be thinking of that object which is usually denoted by the word 'table.' I shall, therefore, use the word in the sense in which I think it is ordinarily used; but at the same time I am not anxious to discuss whether I am right in thinking that it is so used. My business is solely with that object or idea, which I hold, rightly or wrongly, that the word is generally used to stand for. What I want to discover is the nature of that object or idea, and about this I am extremely anxious to arrive at an agreement.

But, if we understand the question in this sense, my answer to it may seem a very disappointing one. If I am asked 'What is good?' my answer is that good is good, and that is the end of the matter. Or if I am asked 'How is good to be defined?' my answer is that it cannot be defined, and that is all I have to say about it. But disappointing as these answers may appear, they are of the very last importance. To readers who are familiar with philosophic terminology, I can express their importance by saying that they amount to this: That propositions about the good are all of them synthetic and never analytic; and that is plainly no trivial matter. And the same thing may be expressed more popularly, by saying that, if I am right, then nobody can foist upon us such an axiom as that 'Pleasure is the only good' or that 'The good is the desired' on the pretence that this is 'the very meaning of the word.'

7. Let us, then, consider this position. My point is that 'good' is a simple notion, just as 'yellow' is a simple notion; that, just as you cannot, by any manner of means, explain to any one who does not already know it, what yellow is, so you cannot explain what good is. Definitions of the kind that I was asking for, definitions which describe the real nature of the object or notion denoted by a word, and which do not merely tell us what the word is used to mean, are only possible when the object or notion in question is something complex. You can give a definition of a horse, because a horse has many different properties and qualities, all of which you can enumerate. But when you have enumerated them all, when you have reduced a horse to his simplest terms, then you can no longer define those terms. They are simply something which you think of or perceive, and to any one who cannot think of or perceive them, you can never, by any definition, make their nature known. It may perhaps be objected to this that we are able to describe to others, objects which they have never seen or thought of. We can, for instance, make a man understand what a chimaera is, although he has never heard of one or seen one. You can tell him that it is an animal with a lioness's head and body, with a goat's head growing from the middle of its back, and with a snake in place of a tail. But here the object which you are describing is a complex object; it is entirely composed of parts, with which we are all perfectly familiar—a snake, a goat, a lioness; and we know, too, the manner in which those parts are to be put together, because we know what is meant by the middle of a lioness's back, and where her tail is wont to grow. And so it is with all objects, not previously known, which we are able to define: they are all complex; all composed of parts, which may themselves, in the

first instance, be capable of similar definition, but which must in the end be reducible to simplest parts, which can no longer be defined. But yellow and good, we say, are not complex: they are notions of that simple kind, out of which definitions are composed and with which the power of further defining ceases.

8. When we say, as Webster says, 'The definition of horse is "A hoofed quadruped of the genus Equus,"' we may, in fact, mean three different things. (1) We may mean merely: 'When I say "horse," you are to understand that I am talking about a hoofed quadruped of the genus Equus.' This might be called the arbitrary verbal definition: and I do not mean that good is indefinable in that sense. (2) We may mean, as Webster ought to mean: 'When most English people say "horse," they mean a hoofed quadruped of the genus Equus.' This may be called the verbal definition proper, and I do not say that good is indefinable in this sense either; for it is certainly possible to discover how people use a word: otherwise, we could never have known that 'good' may be translated by 'gut' in German and by 'bon' in French. But (3) we may, when we define horse, mean something much more important. ' We may mean that a certain object, which we all of us know, is composed in a certain manner: that it has four legs, a head, a heart, a liver, etc., etc., all of them arranged in definite relations to one another. It is in this sense that I deny good to be definable. I say that it is not composed of any parts, which we can sub- stitute for it in our minds when we are thinking of it. We might think just as clearly and correctly about a horse, if we thought of all its parts and their arrangement instead of thinking of the whole: we could, I say, think how a horse differed from a donkey just as well, just as truly, in this way, as now we do, only not so easily; but there is nothing whatsoever which we could so substitute for good; and that is what I mean, when I say that good is indefinable.

9. But I am afraid I have still not removed the chief difficulty which may prevent acceptance of the proposition that good is indefinable. I do not mean to say that *the* good, that which is good, is thus indefinable; if I did think so, I should not

be writing on Ethics, for my main object is to help towards
discovering that definition. It is just because I think there
will be less risk of error in our search for a definition of 'the
good,' that I am now insisting that *good* is indefinable. I must
try to explain the difference between these two. I suppose it
may be granted that 'good' is an adjective. Well 'the good,
'that which is good,' must therefore be the substantive to which
the adjective 'good' will apply: it must be the whole of that to
which the adjective will apply, and the adjective must *always*
truly apply to it. But if it is that to which the adjective will
apply, it must be something different from that adjective itself;
and the whole of that something different, whatever it is, will
be our definition of *the* good. Now it may be that this something will have other adjectives, beside 'good,' that will apply
to it. It may be full of pleasure, for example; it may be
intelligent: and if these two adjectives are really part of its
definition, then it will certainly be true, that pleasure and intelligence are good. And many people appear to think that,
if we say 'Pleasure and intelligence are good,' or if we say
'Only pleasure and intelligence are good,' we are defining 'good.'
Well, I cannot deny that propositions of this nature may sometimes be called definitions; I do not know well enough how
the word is generally used to decide upon this point. I only
wish it to be understood that that is not what I mean when
I say there is no possible definition of good, and that I shall
not mean this if I use the word again. I do most fully believe
that some true proposition of the form 'Intelligence is good
and intelligence alone is good' can be found; if none could be
found. our definition of *the* good would be impossible. As it is,
I believe *the* good to be definable; and yet I still say that good
itself is indefinable.

10. 'Good,' then, if we mean by it that quality which we
assert to belong to a thing, when we say that the thing is good,
is incapable of any definition, in the most important sense of
that word. The most important sense of 'definition' is that in
which a definition states what are the parts which invariably
compose a certain whole; and in this sense 'good' has no
definition because it is simple and has no parts. It is one of

those innumerable objects of thought which are themselves incapable of definition, because they are the ultimate terms by reference to which whatever *is* capable of definition must be defined. That there must be an indefinite number of such terms is obvious, on reflection; since we cannot define anything except by an analysis, which, when carried as far as it will go, refers us to something, which is simply different from anything else, and which by that ultimate difference explains the peculiarity of the whole which we are defining: for every whole contains some parts which are common to other wholes also. There is, therefore, no intrinsic difficulty in the contention that 'good' denotes a simple and indefinable quality. There are many other instances of such qualities.

Consider yellow, for example. We may try to define it, by describing its physical equivalent; we may state what kind of light-vibrations must stimulate the normal eye, in order that we may perceive it. But a moment's reflection is sufficient to shew that those light-vibrations are not themselves what we mean by yellow. *They* are not what we perceive. Indeed we should never have been able to discover their existence, unless we had first been struck by the patent difference of quality between the different colours. The most we can be entitled to say of those vibrations is that they are what corresponds in space to the yellow which we actually perceive.

Yet a mistake of this simple kind has commonly been made about 'good.' It may be true that all things which are good are *also* something else, just as it is true that all things which are yellow produce a certain kind of vibration in the light. And it is a fact, that Ethics aims at discovering what are those other properties belonging to all things which are good. But far too many philosophers have thought that when they named those other properties they were actually defining good; that these properties, in fact, were simply not 'other,' but absolutely and entirely the same with goodness. This view I propose to call the 'naturalistic fallacy' and of it I shall now endeavour to dispose.

11. Let us consider what it is such philosophers say. And first it is to be noticed that they do not agree among themselves.

They not only say that they are right as to what good is, but
they endeavour to prove that other people who say that it is
something else, are wrong. One, for instance, will affirm that
good is pleasure, another, perhaps, that good is that which is
desired; and each of these will argue eagerly to prove that the
other is wrong. But how is that possible? One of them says
that good is nothing but the object of desire, and at the same
time tries to prove that it is not pleasure. But from his first
assertion, that good just means the object of desire, one of two
things must follow as regards his proof:

(1) He may be trying to prove that the object of desire is
not pleasure. But, if this be all, where is his Ethics? The
position he is maintaining is merely a psychological one. Desire
is something which occurs in our minds, and pleasure is something else which so occurs; and our would-be ethical philosopher
is merely holding that the latter is not the object of the former.
But what has that to do with the question in dispute? His
opponent held the ethical proposition that pleasure was the
good, and although he should prove a million times over the
psychological proposition that pleasure is not the object of desire,
he is no nearer proving his opponent to be wrong. The position
is like this. One man says a triangle is a circle: another replies
'A triangle is a straight line, and I will prove to you that I am
right: *for*' (this is the only argument) 'a straight line is not a
circle.' 'That is quite true,' the other may reply; 'but nevertheless a triangle is a circle, and you have said nothing whatever
to prove the contrary. What is proved is that one of us is
wrong, for we agree that a triangle cannot be both a straight
line and a circle: but which is wrong, there can be no earthly
means of proving, since you define triangle as straight line and
I define it as circle.'—Well, that is one alternative which any
naturalistic Ethics has to face; if good is *defined* as something
else, it is then impossible either to prove that any other
definition is wrong or even to deny such definition.

(2) The other alternative will scarcely be more welcome.
It is that the discussion is after all a verbal one. When A says
'Good means pleasant' and B says 'Good means desired,' they
may merely wish to assert that most people have used the word

for what is pleasant and for what is desired respectively. And this is quite an interesting subject for discussion: only it is not a whit more an ethical discussion than the last was. Nor do I think that any exponent of naturalistic Ethics would be willing to allow that this was all he meant. They are all so anxious to persuade us that what they call the good is what we really ought to do. 'Do, pray, act so, because the word "good" is generally used to denote actions of this nature': such, on this view, would be the substance of their teaching. And in so far as they tell us how we ought to act, their teaching is truly ethical, as they mean it to be. But how perfectly absurd is the reason they would give for it! 'You are to do this, because most people use a certain word to denote conduct such as this.' 'You are to say the thing which is not, because most people call it lying.' That is an argument just as good!—My dear sirs, what we want to know from you as ethical teachers, is not how people use a word; it is not even, what kind of actions they approve, which the use of this word 'good' may certainly imply: what we want to know is simply what *is* good. We may indeed agree that what most people do think good, is actually so; we shall at all events be glad to know their opinions: but when we say their opinions about what *is* good, we do mean what we say; we do not care whether they call that thing which they mean 'horse' or 'table' or 'chair,' 'gut' or 'bon' or '*ἀγαθός*'; we want to know what it is that they so call. When they say 'Pleasure is good,' we cannot believe that they merely mean 'Pleasure is pleasure' and nothing more than that.

12. Suppose a man says 'I am pleased'; and suppose that is not a lie or a mistake but the truth. Well, if it is true, what does that mean? It means that his mind, a certain definite mind, distinguished by certain definite marks from all others, has at this moment a certain definite feeling called pleasure. 'Pleased' *means* nothing but having pleasure, and though we may be more pleased or less pleased, and even, we may admit for the present, have one or another kind of pleasure; yet in so far as it is pleasure we have, whether there be more or less of it, and whether it be of one kind or another, what we have is

one definite thing, absolutely indefinable, some one thing that
is the same in all the various degrees and in all the various
kinds of it that there may be. We may be able to say how it is
related to other things: that, for example, it is in the mind,
that it causes desire, that we are conscious of it, etc., etc. We
can, I say, describe its relations to other things, but define it we
can *not*. And if anybody tried to define pleasure for us as
being any other natural object; if anybody were to say, for
instance, that pleasure *means* the sensation of red, and were to
proceed to deduce from that that pleasure is a colour, we should
be entitled to laugh at him and to distrust his future statements
about pleasure. Well, that would be the same fallacy which I
have called the naturalistic fallacy. That 'pleased' does not
mean 'having the sensation of red,' or anything else whatever,
does not prevent us from understanding what it does mean. It
is enough for us to know that 'pleased' does mean 'having the
sensation of pleasure,' and though pleasure is absolutely indefinable, though pleasure is pleasure and nothing else whatever,
yet we feel no difficulty in saying that we are pleased. The
reason is, of course, that when I say 'I am pleased,' I do *not*
mean that 'I' am the same thing as 'having pleasure.' And
similarly no difficulty need be found in my saying that 'pleasure
is good' and yet not meaning that 'pleasure' is the same thing
as 'good,' that pleasure *means* good, and that good *means*
pleasure. If I were to imagine that when I said 'I am pleased,'
I meant that I was exactly the same thing as 'pleased,' I should
not indeed call that a naturalistic fallacy, although it would be
the same fallacy as I have called naturalistic with reference to
Ethics. The reason of this is obvious enough. When a man
confuses two natural objects with one another, defining the one
by the other, if for instance, he confuses himself, who is one
natural object, with 'pleased' or with 'pleasure' which are
others, then there is no reason to call the fallacy naturalistic.
But if he confuses 'good,' which is not in the same sense a
natural object, with any natural object whatever, then there is
a reason for calling that a naturalistic fallacy; its being made
with regard to 'good' marks it as something quite specific, and
this specific mistake deserves a name because it is so common.

As for the reasons why good is not to be considered a natural object, they may be reserved for discussion in another place. But, for the present, it is sufficient to notice this: Even if it were a natural object, that would not alter the nature of the fallacy nor diminish its importance one whit. All that I have said about it would remain quite equally true: only the name which I have called it would not be so appropriate as I think it is. And I do not care about the name: what I do care about is the fallacy. It does not matter what we call it, provided we recognise it when we meet with it. It is to be met with in almost every book on Ethics; and yet it is not recognised: and that is why it is necessary to multiply illustrations of it, and convenient to give it a name. It is a very simple fallacy indeed. When we say that an orange is yellow, we do not think our statement binds us to hold that 'orange' means nothing else than 'yellow,' or that nothing can be yellow but an orange. Supposing the orange is also sweet! Does that bind us to say that 'sweet' is exactly the same thing as 'yellow,' that 'sweet' must be defined as 'yellow'? And supposing it be recognised that 'yellow' just means 'yellow' and nothing else whatever, does that make it any more difficult to hold that oranges are yellow? Most certainly it does not: on the contrary, it would be absolutely meaningless to say that oranges were yellow, unless yellow did in the end mean just 'yellow' and nothing else whatever—unless it was absolutely indefinable. We should not get any very clear notion about things, which are yellow— we should not get very far with our science, if we were bound to hold that everything which was yellow, *meant* exactly the same thing as yellow. We should find we had to hold that an orange was exactly the same thing as a stool, a piece of paper, a lemon, anything you like. We could prove any number of absurdities; but should we be the nearer to the truth? Why, then, should it be different with 'good'? Why, if good is good and indefinable, should I be held to deny that pleasure is good? Is there any difficulty in holding both to be true at once? On the contrary, there is no meaning in saying that pleasure is good, unless good is something different from pleasure. It is absolutely useless, so far as Ethics is concerned, to prove, as Mr Spencer tries to do, that increase of pleasure coincides with increase of life, unless good *means* something different from either life or pleasure. He might just as well try to prove that an orange is yellow by shewing that it always is wrapped up in paper.

13. In fact, if it is not the case that 'good' denotes something simple and indefinable, only two alternatives are possible: either it is a complex, a given whole, about the correct analysis of which there may be disagreement; or else it means nothing at all, and there is no such subject as Ethics. In general, however, ethical philosophers have attempted to define good, without recognising what such an attempt must mean. They actually use arguments which involve one or both of the absurdities considered in § 11. We are, therefore, justified in concluding that the attempt to define good is chiefly due to want of clearness as to the possible nature of definition. There are, in fact, only two serious alternatives to be considered, in order to establish the conclusion that 'good' does denote a simple and indefinable notion. It might possibly denote a complex, as 'horse' does; or it might have no meaning at all. Neither of these possibilities has, however, been clearly conceived and seriously maintained, as such, by those who presume to define good; and both may be dismissed by a simple appeal to facts.

(1) The hypothesis that disagreement about the meaning of good is disagreement with regard to the correct analysis of a given whole, may be most plainly seen to be incorrect by consideration of the fact that, whatever definition be offered, it may be always asked, with significance, of the complex so defined, whether it is itself good. To take, for instance, one of the more plausible, because one of the more complicated, of such proposed definitions, it may easily be thought, at first sight, that to be good may mean to be that which we desire to desire. Thus if we apply this definition to a particular instance and say 'When we think that A is good, we are thinking that A is one of the things which we desire to desire,' our proposition may seem quite plausible. But, if we carry the investigation further, and ask ourselves 'Is it good to desire to desire A?' it is apparent, on a little reflection, that this question is itself as intelligible, as the original question 'Is A good?'—that we are,

in fact, now asking for exactly the same information about the desire to desire A, for which we formerly asked with regard to A itself. But it is also apparent that the meaning of this second question cannot be correctly analysed into 'Is the desire to desire A one of the things which we desire to desire?': we have not before our minds anything so complicated as the question 'Do we desire to desire to desire A?' Moreover any one can easily convince himself by inspection that the predicate of this proposition—'good'—is positively different from the notion of 'desiring to desire' which enters into its subject: 'That we should desire to desire A is good' is *not* merely equivalent to 'That A should be good is good.' It may indeed be true that what we desire to desire is always also good; perhaps, even the converse may be true: but it is very doubtful whether this is the case, and the mere fact that we understand very well what is meant by doubting it, shews clearly that we have two different notions before our minds.

(2) And the same consideration is sufficient to dismiss the hypothesis that 'good' has no meaning whatsoever. It is very natural to make the mistake of supposing that what is universally true is of such a nature that its negation would be self-contradictory: the importance which has been assigned to analytic propositions in the history of philosophy shews how easy such a mistake is. And thus it is very easy to conclude that what seems to be a universal ethical principle is in fact an identical proposition; that, if, for example, whatever is called 'good' seems to be pleasant, the proposition 'Pleasure is the good' does not assert a connection between two different notions, but involves only one, that of pleasure, which is easily recognised as a distinct entity. But whoever will attentively consider with himself what is actually before his mind when he asks the question 'Is pleasure (or whatever it may be) after all good?' can easily satisfy himself that he is not merely wondering whether pleasure is pleasant. And if he will try this experiment with each suggested definition in succession, he may become expert enough to recognise that in every case he has before his mind a unique object, with regard to the connection of which with any other object, a distinct question may be asked. Every

one does in fact understand the question 'Is this good?' When
he thinks of it, his state of mind is different from what it would
be, were he asked 'Is this pleasant, or desired, or approved?'
It has a distinct meaning for him, even though he may not
recognise in what respect it is distinct. Whenever he thinks of
'intrinsic value,' or 'intrinsic worth,' or says that a thing 'ought
to exist,' he has before his mind the unique object—the unique
property of things—which I mean by 'good.' Everybody is
constantly aware of this notion, although he may never become
aware at all that it is different from other notions of which he
is also aware. But, for correct ethical reasoning, it is extremely
important that he should become aware of this fact; and, as
soon as the nature of the problem is clearly understood, there
should be little difficulty in advancing so far in analysis.

14. 'Good,' then, is indefinable; and yet, so far as I know,
there is only one ethical writer, Prof. Henry Sidgwick, who has
clearly recognised and stated this fact. We shall see, indeed,
how far many of the most reputed ethical systems fall short of
drawing the conclusions which follow from such a recognition.
At present I will only quote one instance, which will serve to
illustrate the meaning and importance of this principle that
'good' is indefinable, or, as Prof. Sidgwick says, an 'unanalysable
notion.' It is an instance to which Prof. Sidgwick himself
refers in a note on the passage, in which he argues that 'ought'
is unanalysable[1].

'Bentham,' says Sidgwick, 'explains that his fundamental
principle "states the greatest happiness of all those whose
interest is in question as being the right and proper end of
human action"'; and yet 'his language in other passages of the
same chapter would seem to imply' that he *means* by the word
"right" "conducive to the general happiness." Prof. Sidgwick
sees that, if you take these two statements together, you get
the absurd result that 'greatest happiness is the end of human
action, which is conducive to the general happiness'; and so
absurd does it seem to him to call this result, as Bentham calls
it, 'the fundamental principle of a moral system,' that he suggests that Bentham cannot have meant it. Yet Prof. Sidgwick

---

[1] *Methods of Ethics*, Bk. I, Chap. iii, § 1 (6th edition).

himself states elsewhere[1] that Psychological Hedonism is 'not seldom confounded with Egoistic Hedonism'; and that confusion, as we shall see, rests chiefly on that same fallacy, the naturalistic fallacy, which is implied in Bentham's statements. Prof. Sidgwick admits therefore that this fallacy is sometimes committed, absurd as it is; and I am inclined to think that Bentham may really have been one of those who committed it. Mill, as we shall see, certainly did commit it. In any case, whether Bentham committed it or not, his doctrine, as above quoted, will serve as a very good illustration of this fallacy, and of the importance of the contrary proposition that good is indefinable.

Let us consider this doctrine. Bentham seems to imply, so Prof. Sidgwick says, that the word 'right' *means* 'conducive to general happiness.' Now this, by itself, need not necessarily involve the naturalistic fallacy. For the word 'right' is very commonly appropriated to actions which lead to the attainment of what is good; which are regarded as *means* to the ideal and not as ends-in-themselves. This use of 'right,' as denoting what is good as a means, whether or not it be also good as an end, is indeed the use to which I shall confine the word. Had Bentham been using 'right' in this sense, it might be perfectly consistent for him to *define* right as 'conducive to the general happiness,' *provided only* (and notice this proviso) he had already proved, or laid down as an axiom, that general happiness was *the* good, or (what is equivalent to this) that general happiness alone was good. For in that case he would have already defined *the* good as general happiness (a position perfectly consistent, as we have seen, with the contention that 'good' is indefinable), and, since right was to be defined as 'conducive to *the* good,' it would actually *mean* 'conducive to general happiness.' But this method of escape from the charge of having committed the naturalistic fallacy has been closed by Bentham himself. For his fundamental principle is, we see, that the greatest happiness of all concerned is the *right* and proper *end* of human action. He applies the word 'right,' therefore, to the end, as such, not only to the means which are

---

[1] *Methods of Ethics*, Bk. i, Chap. iv, § 1.

conducive to it; and, that being so, right can no longer be
defined as 'conducive to the general happiness,' without involving the fallacy in question. For now it is obvious that the
definition of right as conducive to general happiness can be used
by him in support of the fundamental principle that general
happiness is the right end; instead of being itself derived from
that principle. If right, by definition, means conducive to
general happiness, then it is obvious that general happiness
is the right end. It is not necessary now first to prove or
assert that general happiness is the right end, before right
is defined as conducive to general happiness—a perfectly valid
procedure; but on the contrary the definition of right as conducive to general happiness proves general happiness to be the
right end—a perfectly invalid procedure, since in this case the
statement that 'general happiness is the right end of human
action' is not an ethical principle at all, but either, as we have
seen, a proposition about the meaning of words, or else a
proposition about the *nature* of general happiness, not about its
rightness or goodness.

Now, I do not wish the importance I assign to this fallacy
to be misunderstood. The discovery of it does not at all refute
Bentham's contention that greatest happiness is the proper
end of human action, if that be understood as an ethical
proposition, as he undoubtedly intended it. That principle
may be true all the same; we shall consider whether it is so in
succeeding chapters. Bentham might have maintained it, as
Prof. Sidgwick does, even if the fallacy had been pointed
out to him. What I am maintaining is that the *reasons* which
he actually gives for his ethical proposition are fallacious ones
so far as they consist in a definition of right. What I suggest
is that he did not perceive them to be fallacious; that, if
he had done so, he would have been led to seek for other
reasons in support of his Utilitarianism; and that, had he
sought for other reasons, he *might* have found none which he
thought to be sufficient. In that case he would have changed
his whole system—a most important consequence. It is undoubtedly also possible that he would have thought other
reasons to be sufficient, and in that case his ethical system,

in its main results, would still have stood. But, even in this latter case, his use of the fallacy would be a serious objection to him as an ethical philosopher. For it is the business of Ethics, I must insist, not only to obtain true results, but also to find valid reasons for them. The direct object of Ethics is knowledge and not practice; and any one who uses the naturalistic fallacy has certainly not fulfilled this first object, however correct his practical principles may be.

My objections to Naturalism are then, in the first place, that it offers no reason at all, far less any valid reason, for any ethical principle whatever; and in this it already fails to satisfy the requirements of Ethics, as a scientific study. But in the second place I contend that, though it gives a reason for no ethical principle, it is a *cause* of the acceptance of false principles—it deludes the mind into accepting ethical principles, which are false; and in this it is contrary to every aim of Ethics. It is easy to see that if we start with a definition of right conduct as conduct conducive to general happiness; then, knowing that right conduct is universally conduct conducive to the good, we very easily arrive at the result that the good is general happiness. If, on the other hand, we once recognise that we must start our Ethics without a definition, we shall be much more apt to look about us, before we adopt any ethical principle whatever; and the more we look about us, the less likely are we to adopt a false one. It may be replied to this: Yes, but we shall look about us just as much, before we settle on our definition, and are therefore just as likely to be right. But I will try to shew that this is not the case. If we start with the conviction that a definition of good can be found, we start with the conviction that good *can mean* nothing else than some one property of things; and our only business will then be to discover what that property is. But if we recognise that, so far as the meaning of good goes, anything whatever may be good, we start with a much more open mind. Moreover, apart from the fact that, when we think we have a definition, we cannot logically defend our ethical principles in any way whatever, we shall also be much less apt to defend them well, even if illogically. For we shall start with the conviction that good must mean so and so, and shall therefore be inclined either to misunderstand our opponent's arguments or to cut them short with the reply, 'This is not an open question: the very meaning of the word decides it; no one can think otherwise except through confusion.'

15. Our first conclusion as to the subject-matter of Ethics is, then, that there is a simple, indefinable, unanalysable object of thought by reference to which it must be defined. By what name we call this unique object is a matter of indifference, so long as we clearly recognise what it is and that it does differ from other objects. The words which are commonly taken as the signs of ethical judgments all do refer to it; and they are expressions of ethical judgments solely because they do so refer. But they may refer to it in two different ways, which it is very important to distinguish, if we are to have a complete definition of the range of ethical judgments. Before I proceeded to argue that there was such an indefinable notion involved in ethical notions, I stated (§ 4) that it was necessary for Ethics to enumerate all true universal judgments, asserting that such and such a thing was good, whenever it occurred. But, although all such judgments do refer to that unique notion which I have called 'good,' they do not all refer to it in the same way. They may either assert that this unique property does always attach to the thing in question, or else they may assert only that the thing in question is *a cause or necessary condition* for the existence of other things to which this unique property does attach. The nature of these two species of universal ethical judgments is extremely different; and a great part of the difficulties, which are met with in ordinary ethical speculation, are due to the failure to distinguish them clearly. Their difference has, indeed, received expression in ordinary language by the contrast between the terms 'good as means' and 'good in itself,' 'value as a means' and 'intrinsic value.' But these terms are apt to be applied correctly only in the more obvious instances; and this seems to be due to the fact that the distinction between the conceptions which they denote has not been made a separate object of investigation. This distinction may be briefly pointed out as follows.

16. Whenever we judge that a thing is 'good as a means,'
we are making a judgment with regard to its causal relations:
we judge *both* that it will have a particular kind of effect, *and*
that that effect will be good in itself. But to find causal
judgments that are universally true is notoriously a matter
of extreme difficulty. The late date at which most of the
physical sciences became exact, and the comparative fewness
of the laws which they have succeeded in establishing even
now, are sufficient proofs of this difficulty. With regard, then,
to what are the most frequent objects of ethical judgments,
namely actions, it is obvious that we cannot be satisfied that
any of our universal causal judgments are true, even in the
sense in which scientific laws are so. We cannot even discover
hypothetical laws of the form 'Exactly this action will always,
under these conditions, produce exactly that effect.' But for a
correct ethical judgment with regard to the effects of certain
actions we require more than this in two respects. (1) We require
to know that a given action will produce a certain effect, *under
whatever circumstances it occurs.* But this is certainly impossible.
It is certain that in different circumstances the same action may
produce effects which are utterly different in all respects upon
which the value of the effects depends. Hence we can never be
entitled to more than a *generalisation*—to a proposition of the
form 'This result *generally* follows this kind of action'; and
even this generalisation will only be true, if the circumstances
under which the action occurs are generally the same. This is
in fact the case, to a great extent, within any one particular
age and state of society. But, when we take other ages into
account, in many most important cases the normal circumstances of a given kind of action will be so different, that the
generalisation which is true for one will not be true for another.
With regard then to ethical judgments which assert that a
certain kind of action is good as a means to a certain kind
of effect, none will be *universally* true; and many, though
generally true at one period, will be generally false at others.
But (2) we require to know not only that *one* good effect will
be produced, but that, among all subsequent events affected by
the action in question, the balance of good will be greater

than if any other possible action had been performed. In other words, to judge that an action is generally a means to good is to judge not only that it generally does *some* good, but that it generally does the greatest good of which the circumstances admit. In this respect ethical judgments about the effects of action involve a difficulty and a complication far greater than that involved in the establishment of scientific laws. For the latter we need only consider a single effect; for the former it is essential to consider not only this, but the effects of that effect, and so on as far as our view into the future can reach. It is, indeed, obvious that our view can never reach far enough for us to be certain that any action will produce the best possible effects. We must be content, if the greatest possible balance of good seems to be produced within a limited period. But it is important to notice that the whole series of effects within a period of considerable length is actually taken account of in our common judgments that an action is good as a means; and that hence this additional complication, which makes ethical generalisations so far more difficult to establish than scientific laws, is one which is involved in actual ethical discussions, and is of practical importance. The commonest rules of conduct involve such considerations as the balancing of future bad health against immediate gains; and even if we can never settle with any certainty how we shall secure the greatest possible total of good, we try at least to assure ourselves that probable future evils will not be greater than the immediate good.

17. There are, then, judgments which state that certain kinds of things have good effects; and such judgments, for the reasons just given, have the important characteristics (1) that they are unlikely to be true, if they state that the kind of thing in question *always* has good effects, and (2) that, even if they only state that it *generally* has good effects, many of them will only be true of certain periods in the world's history. On the other hand there are judgments which state that certain kinds of things are themselves good; and these differ from the last in that, if true at all, they are all of them universally true. It is, therefore, extremely important to distinguish these two kinds of possible judgments. Both may be expressed in the same language: in both cases we commonly say 'Such and such a thing is good.' But in the one case 'good' will mean 'good as means,' *i.e.* merely that the thing is a means to good—will have good effects: in the other case it will mean 'good as end'—we shall be judging that the thing itself has the property which, in the first case, we asserted only to belong to its effects. It is plain that these are very different assertions to make about a thing; it is plain that either or both of them may be made, both truly and falsely, about all manner of things; and it is certain that unless we are clear as to which of the two we mean to assert, we shall have a very poor chance of deciding rightly whether our assertion is true or false. It is precisely this clearness as to the meaning of the question asked which has hitherto been almost entirely lacking in ethical speculation. Ethics has always been predominantly concerned with the investigation of a limited class of actions. With regard to these we may ask *both* how far they are good in themselves *and* how far they have a general tendency to produce good results. And the arguments brought forward in ethical discussion have always been of both classes—both such as would prove the conduct in question to be good in itself and such as would prove it to be good as a means. But that these are the only questions which any ethical discussion can have to settle, and that to settle the one is *not* the same thing as to settle the other—these two fundamental facts have in general escaped the notice of ethical philosophers. Ethical questions are commonly asked in an ambiguous form. It is asked 'What is a man's duty under these circumstances?' or 'Is it right to act in this way?' or 'What ought we to aim at securing?' But all these questions are capable of further analysis; a correct answer to any of them involves both judgments of what is good in itself and causal judgments. This is implied even by those who maintain that we have a direct and immediate judgment of absolute rights and duties. Such a judgment can only mean that the course of action in question is *the* best thing to do; that, by acting so, every good that *can* be secured will have been secured. Now we are not concerned with the question whether such a judgment will ever be true.

The question is: What does it imply, if it is true? And the only possible answer is that, whether true or false, it implies both a proposition as to the degree of goodness of the action in question, as compared with other things, and a number of causal propositions. For it cannot be denied that the action will have consequences: and to deny that the consequences matter is to make a judgment of their intrinsic value, as compared with the action itself. In asserting that the action is *the* best thing to do, we assert that it together with its consequences presents a greater sum of intrinsic value than any possible alternative. And this condition may be realised by any of the three cases:— (*a*) If the action itself has greater intrinsic value than any alternative, whereas both its consequences and those of the alternatives are absolutely devoid either of intrinsic merit or intrinsic demerit; or (*b*) if, though its consequences are intrinsically bad, the balance of intrinsic value is greater than would be produced by any alternative; or (*c*) if, its consequences being intrinsically good, the degree of value belonging to them and it conjointly is greater than that of any alternative series. In short, to assert that a certain line of conduct is, at a given time, absolutely right or obligatory, is obviously to assert that more good or less evil will exist in the world, if it be adopted than if anything else be done instead. But this implies a judgment as to the value both of its own consequences and of those of any possible alternative. And that an action will have such and such consequences involves a number of causal judgments.

Similarly, in answering the question 'What ought we to aim at securing?' causal judgments are again involved, but in a somewhat different way. We are liable to forget, because it is so obvious, that this question can never be answered correctly except by naming something which *can* be secured. Not everything can be secured; and, even if we judge that nothing which cannot be obtained would be of equal value with that which can, the possibility of the latter, as well as its value, is essential to its being a proper end of action. Accordingly neither our judgments as to what actions we ought to perform, nor even our judgments as to the ends which they ought to produce, are pure judgments of intrinsic value. With regard to the former, an action which is absolutely obligatory *may* have no intrinsic value whatsoever; that it is perfectly virtuous may mean merely that it causes the best possible effects. And with regard to the latter, these best possible results which justify our action can, in any case, have only so much of intrinsic value as the laws of nature allow us to secure; and they in their turn *may* have no intrinsic value whatsoever, but may merely be a means to the attainment (in a still further future) of something that has such value. Whenever, therefore, we ask 'What ought we to do?' or 'What ought we to try to get?' we are asking questions which involve a correct answer to two others, completely different in kind from one another. We must know *both* what degree of intrinsic value different things have, *and* how these different things may be obtained. But the vast majority of questions which have actually been discussed in Ethics—*all* practical questions, indeed—involve this double knowledge; and they have been discussed without any clear separation of the two distinct questions involved. A great part of the vast disagreements prevalent in Ethics is to be attributed to this failure in analysis. By the use of conceptions which involve both that of intrinsic value and that of causal relation, as if they involved intrinsic value only, two different errors have been rendered almost universal. Either it is assumed that nothing has intrinsic value which is not possible, or else it is assumed that what is necessary must have intrinsic value. Hence the primary and peculiar business of Ethics, the determination what things have intrinsic value and in what degrees, has received no adequate treatment at all. And on the other hand a *thorough* discussion of means has been also largely neglected, owing to an obscure perception of the truth that it is perfectly irrelevant to the question of intrinsic values. But however this may be, and however strongly any particular reader may be convinced that some one of the mutually contradictory systems which hold the field has given a correct answer either to the question what has intrinsic value, or to the question what we ought to do, or to both, it must at least be admitted that the questions what is best in itself and what will bring about the best possible, are

utterly distinct; that both belong to the actual subject-matter
of Ethics; and that the more clearly distinct questions are
distinguished, the better is our chance of answering both
correctly.

18. There remains one point which must not be omitted
in a complete description of the kind of questions which Ethics
has to answer. The main division of those questions is, as
I have said, into two; the question what things are good in
themselves, and the question to what other things these are
related as effects. The first of these, which is the primary
ethical question and is presupposed by the other, includes a
correct comparison of the various things which have intrinsic
value (if there are many such) in respect of the degree of value
which they have; and such comparison involves a difficulty of
principle which has greatly aided the confusion of intrinsic
value with mere 'goodness as a means.' It has been pointed out
that one difference between a judgment which asserts that a
thing is good in itself, and a judgment which asserts that it is
a means to good, consists in the fact that the first, if true of
one instance of the thing in question, is necessarily true of all;
whereas a thing which has good effects under some circumstances
may have bad ones under others. Now it is certainly true that
all judgments of intrinsic value are in this sense universal; but
the principle which I have now to enunciate may easily make
it appear as if they were not so but resembled the judgment
of means in being merely general. There is, as will presently
be maintained, a vast number of different things, each of which
has intrinsic value; there are also very many which are positively
bad; and there is a still larger class of things, which appear
to be indifferent. But a thing belonging to any of these three
classes may occur as part of a whole, which includes among
its other parts other things belonging both to the same and to
the other two classes; and these wholes, as such, may also have
intrinsic value. The paradox, to which it is necessary to call
attention, is that *the value of such a whole bears no regular pro-*
portion to the sum of the values of its parts. It is certain that a
good thing may exist in such a relation to another good thing
that the value of the whole thus formed is immensely greater

than the sum of the values of the two good things. It is certain
that a whole formed of a good thing and an indifferent thing
may have immensely greater value than that good thing itself
possesses. It is certain that two bad things or a bad thing and
an indifferent thing may form a whole much worse than the
sum of badness of its parts. And it seems as if indifferent
things may also be the sole constituents of a whole which has
great value, either positive or negative. Whether the addition
of a bad thing to a good whole may increase the positive value
of the whole, or the addition of a bad thing to a bad may
produce a whole having positive value, may seem more doubtful; but it is, at least, possible, and this possibility must be
taken into account in our ethical investigations. However we
may decide particular questions, the principle is clear. *The
value of a whole must not be assumed to be the same as the sum
of the values of its parts.*

A single instance will suffice to illustrate the kind of relation
in question. It seems to be true that to be conscious of a
beautiful object is a thing of great intrinsic value; whereas
the same object, if no one be conscious of it, has certainly comparatively little value, and is commonly held to have none at all.
But the consciousness of a beautiful object is certainly a whole
of some sort in which we can distinguish as parts the object on
the one hand and the being conscious on the other. Now this
latter factor occurs as part of a different whole, whenever we
are conscious of anything; and it would seem that some of these
wholes have at all events very little value, and may even be
indifferent or positively bad. Yet we cannot always attribute
the slightness of their value to any positive demerit in the object
which differentiates them from the consciousness of beauty;
the object itself may approach as near as possible to absolute
neutrality. Since, therefore, mere consciousness does not always
confer great value upon the whole of which it forms a part, even
though its object may have no great demerit, we cannot attribute the great superiority of the consciousness of a beautiful
thing over the beautiful thing itself to the mere addition of the
value of consciousness to that of the beautiful thing. Whatever
the intrinsic value of consciousness may be, it does not give to

the whole of which it forms a part a value proportioned to the sum of its value and that of its object. If this be so, we have here an instance of a whole possessing a different intrinsic value from the sum of that of its parts; and whether it be so or not, what is meant by such a difference is illustrated by this case.

19. There are, then, wholes which possess the property that their value is different from the sum of the values of their parts; and the relations which subsist between such parts and the whole of which they form a part have not hitherto been distinctly recognised or received a separate name. Two points are especially worthy of notice. (1) It is plain that the existence of any such part is a necessary condition for the existence of that good which is constituted by the whole. And exactly the same language will also express the relation between a means and the good thing which is its effect. But yet there is a most important difference between the two cases, constituted by the fact that the part is, whereas the means is not, a part of the good thing for the existence of which its existence is a necessary condition. The necessity by which, if the good in question is to exist, the means to it must exist is merely a natural or causal necessity. If the laws of nature were different, exactly the same good might exist, although what is now a necessary condition of its existence did not exist. The existence of the means has no intrinsic value; and its utter annihilation would leave the value of that which it is now necessary to secure entirely unchanged. But in the case of a part of such a whole as we are now considering, it is otherwise. In this case the good in question cannot conceivably exist, unless the part exist also. The necessity which connects the two is quite independent of natural law. What is asserted to have intrinsic value is the existence of the whole; and the existence of the whole includes the existence of its part. Suppose the part removed, and what remains is *not* what was asserted to have intrinsic value; but if we suppose a means removed, what remains is just what *was* asserted to have intrinsic value. And yet (2) the existence of the part may *itself* have no more intrinsic value than that of the means. It is this fact which constitutes the paradox of the relation which we are discussing.

It has just been said that what has intrinsic value is the existence of the whole, and that this includes the existence of the part; and from this it would seem a natural inference that the existence of the part has intrinsic value. But the inference would be as false as if we were to conclude that, because the number of two stones was two, each of the stones was also two. The part of a valuable whole retains exactly the same value when it is, as when it is not, a part of that whole. If it had value under other circumstances, its value is not any greater, when it is part of a far more valuable whole; and if it had no value by itself, it has none still, however great be that of the whole of which it now forms a part. We are not then justified in asserting that one and the same thing is under some circumstances intrinsically good, and under others not so; as we are justified in asserting of a means that it sometimes does and sometimes does not produce good results. And yet we are justified in asserting that it is far more desirable that a certain thing should exist under some circumstances than under others; namely when other things will exist in such relations to it as to form a more valuable whole. *It* will not have more intrinsic value under these circumstances than under others; *it* will not necessarily even be a means to the existence of things having more intrinsic value: but it will, like a means, be a necessary condition for the existence of that which *has* greater intrinsic value, although, unlike a means, it will itself form a part of this more valuable existent.

20.   I have said that the peculiar relation between part and whole which I have just been trying to define is one which has received no separate name. It would, however, be useful that it should have one; and there is a name, which might well be appropriated to it, if only it could be divorced from its present unfortunate usage. Philosophers, especially those who profess to have derived great benefit from the writings of Hegel, have latterly made much use of the terms 'organic whole,' 'organic unity,' 'organic relation.' The reason why these terms might well be appropriated to the use suggested is that the peculiar relation of parts to whole, just defined, is one of the properties which distinguishes the wholes to which they are actually applied with the greatest frequency. And the reason why it is desirable that they should be divorced from their present usage is that, as at present used, they have no distinct sense and, on the contrary, both imply and propagate errors of confusion.

To say that a thing is an 'organic whole' is generally understood to imply that its parts are related to one another and to itself as means to end; it is also understood to imply that they have a property described in some such phrase as that they have 'no meaning or significance apart from the whole'; and finally such a whole is also treated as if it had the property to which I am proposing that the name should be confined. But those who use the term give us, in general, no hint as to how they suppose these three properties to be related to one another. It seems generally to be assumed that they are identical; and always, at least, that they are necessarily connected with one another. That they are not identical I have already tried to shew; to suppose them so is to neglect the very distinctions pointed out in the last paragraph; and the usage might well be discontinued merely because it encourages such neglect. But a still more cogent reason for its discontinuance is that, so far from being necessarily connected, the second is a property which can attach to nothing, being a self-contradictory conception; whereas the first, if we insist on its most important sense, applies to many cases, to which we have no reason to think that the third applies also, and the third certainly applies to many to which the first does not apply.

21. These relations between the three properties just distinguished may be illustrated by reference to a whole of the kind from which the name 'organic' was derived—a whole which is an organism in the scientific sense—namely the human body.

(1) There exists between many parts of our body (though not between all) a relation which has been familiarised by the fable, attributed to Menenius Agrippa, concerning the belly and its members. We can find in it parts such that the continued existence of the one is a necessary condition for the continued existence of the other; while the continued existence of this latter is also a necessary condition for the continued existence of the former. This amounts to no more than saying

that in the body we have instances of two things, both enduring for some time, which have a relation of mutual causal dependence on one another—a relation of 'reciprocity.' Frequently no more than this is meant by saying that the parts of the body form an 'organic unity,' or that they are mutually means and ends to one another. And we certainly have here a striking characteristic of living things. But it would be extremely rash to assert that this relation of mutual causal dependence was only exhibited by living things and hence was sufficient to define their peculiarity. And it is obvious that of two things which have this relation of mutual dependence, neither may have intrinsic value, or one may have it and the other lack it. They are not necessarily 'ends' to one another in any sense except that in which 'end' means 'effect.' And moreover it is plain that in this sense the whole cannot be an end to any of its parts. We are apt to talk of 'the whole' in contrast to one of its parts, when in fact we mean only *the rest* of the parts. But strictly the whole must include all its parts and no part can be a cause of the whole, because it cannot be a cause of itself. It is plain, therefore, that this relation of mutual causal dependence implies nothing with regard to the value of either of the objects which have it; and that, even if both of them happen also to have value, this relation between them is one which cannot hold between part and whole.

But (2) it may also be the case that our body as a whole has a value greater than the sum of values of its parts; and this may be what is meant when it is said that the parts are means to the whole. It is obvious that if we ask the question 'Why *should* the parts be such as they are?' a proper answer may be 'Because the whole they form has so much value.' But it is equally obvious that the relation which we thus assert to exist between part and whole is quite different from that which we assert to exist between part and part when we say 'This part exists, because that one could not exist without it.' In the latter case we assert the two parts to be causally connected; but, in the former, part and whole cannot be causally connected, and the relation which we assert to exist between them may exist even though the parts are not causally connected either.

All the parts of a picture do not have that relation of mutual causal dependence, which certain parts of the body have, and yet the existence of those which do not have it may be absolutely essential to the value of the whole. The two relations are quite distinct in kind, and we cannot infer the existence of the one from that of the other. It can, therefore, serve no useful purpose to include them both under the same name; and if we are to say that a whole is organic because its parts are (in this sense) 'means' to the whole, we must *not* say that it is organic because its parts are causally dependent on one another.

22. But finally (3) the sense which has been most prominent in recent uses of the term 'organic whole' is one whereby it asserts the parts of such a whole to have a property which the parts of no whole can possibly have. It is supposed that just as the whole would not be what it is but for the existence of the parts, so the parts would not be what they are but for the existence of the whole; and this is understood to mean not merely that any particular part could not exist unless the others existed too (which is the case where relation (1) exists between the parts), but actually that the part is no distinct object of thought—that the whole, of which it is a part, is in its turn a part of it. That this supposition is self-contradictory a very little reflection should be sufficient to shew. We may admit, indeed, that when a particular thing is a part of a whole, it does possess a predicate which it would not otherwise possess —namely that it is a part of that whole. But what cannot be admitted is that this predicate alters the nature or enters into the definition of the thing which has it. When we think of the part *itself*, we mean just *that which* we assert, in this case, to *have* the predicate that it is part of the whole; and the mere assertion that *it* is a part of the whole involves that it should itself be distinct from that which we assert of it. Otherwise we contradict ourselves since we assert that, not *it*, but something else—namely it together with that which we assert of it —has the predicate which we assert of it. In short, it is obvious that no part contains analytically the whole to which it belongs, or any other parts of that whole. The relation of part to whole is *not* the same as that of whole to part; and the very definition

of the latter is that it does contain analytically that which is said to be its part. And yet this very self-contradictory doctrine is the chief mark which shews the influence of Hegel upon modern philosophy—an influence which pervades almost the whole of orthodox philosophy. This is what is generally implied by the cry against falsification by abstraction: that a whole is always a part of its part! 'If you want to know the truth about a part,' we are told, 'you must consider *not* that part, but something else—namely the whole: *nothing* is true of the part, but only of the whole.' Yet plainly it must be true of the part at least that it is a part of the whole; and it is obvious that when we say it is, we do *not* mean merely that the whole is a part of itself. This doctrine, therefore, that a part can have 'no meaning or significance apart from its whole' must be utterly rejected. It implies itself that the statement 'This is a part of that whole' has a meaning; and in order that this may have one, both subject and predicate must have a distinct meaning. And it is easy to see how this false doctrine has arisen by confusion with the two relations (1) and (2) which may really be properties of wholes.

(*a*)   The *existence* of a part may be connected by a natural or causal necessity with the existence of the other parts of its whole; and further what is a part of a whole and what has ceased to be such a part, although differing intrinsically from one another, may be called by one and the same name. Thus, to take a typical example, if an arm be cut off from the human body, we still call it an arm. Yet an arm, when it is a part of the body, undoubtedly differs from a dead arm: and hence we may easily be led to say 'The arm which is a part of the body would not be what it is, if it were not such a part,' and to think that the contradiction thus expressed is in reality a characteristic of things. But, in fact, the dead arm never was a part of the body; it is only *partially* identical with the living arm. Those parts of it which are identical with parts of the living arm are exactly the same, whether they belong to the body or not; and in them we have an undeniable instance of one and the same thing at one time forming a part, and at another not forming a part of the presumed 'organic whole.'

On the other hand those properties which *are* possessed by the living, and *not* by the dead, arm, do not exist in a changed form in the latter: they simply do not exist there *at all*. By a causal necessity their existence depends on their having that relation to the other parts of the body which we express by saying that they form part of it. Yet, most certainly, *if* they ever did not form part of the body, they *would* be exactly what they are when they do. That they differ intrinsically from the properties of the dead arm and that they form part of the body are propositions not analytically related to one another. There is no contradiction in supposing them to retain such intrinsic differences and yet not to form part of the body.

But (*b*) when we are told that a living arm has no *meaning* or *significance* apart from the body to which it belongs, a different fallacy is also suggested. 'To have meaning or significance' is commonly used in the sense of 'to have importance'; and this again means 'to have value either as a means or as an end.' Now it is quite possible that even a living arm, apart from its body, would have no intrinsic value whatever; although the whole of which it is a part has great intrinsic value owing to its presence. Thus we may easily come to say that, *as* a part of the body, it has great value, whereas *by itself* it would have none; and thus that its whole 'meaning' lies in its relation to the body. But in fact the value in question obviously does not belong to *it* at all. To have value merely as a part is equivalent to having no value at all, but merely being a part of that which has it. Owing, however, to neglect of this distinction, the assertion that a part has value, *as a part*, which it would not otherwise have, easily leads to the assumption that it is also different, as a part, from what it would otherwise be; for it is, in fact, true that two things which have a different value must also differ in other respects. Hence the assumption that one and the same thing, because it is a part of a more valuable whole at one time than at another, therefore has more intrinsic value at one time than at another, has encouraged the self-contradictory belief that one and the same thing may be two different things, and that only in one of its forms is it truly what it is.

For these reasons, I shall, where it seems convenient, take

the liberty to use the term 'organic' with a special sense. I shall use it to denote the fact that a whole has an intrinsic value different in amount from the sum of the values of its parts. I shall use it to denote this and only this. The term will not imply any causal relation whatever between the parts of the whole in question. And it will not imply either, that the parts are inconceivable except as parts of that whole, or that, when they form parts of such a whole, they have a value different from that which they would have if they did not. Understood in this special and perfectly definite sense the relation of an organic whole to its parts is one of the most important which Ethics has to recognise. A chief part of that science should be occupied in comparing the relative values of various goods; and the grossest errors will be committed in such comparison if it be assumed that wherever two things form a whole, the value of that whole is merely the sum of the values of those two things. With this question of 'organic wholes,' then, we complete the enumeration of the kind of problems, with which it is the business of Ethics to deal.

23. In this chapter I have endeavoured to enforce the following conclusions. (1) The peculiarity of Ethics is not that it investigates assertions about human conduct, but that it investigates assertions about that property of things which is denoted by the term 'good,' and the converse property denoted by the term 'bad.' It must, in order to establish its conclusions, investigate the truth of *all* such assertions, *except* those which assert the relation of this property only to a single existent (1—4). (2) This property, by reference to which the subject-matter of Ethics must be defined, is itself simple and indefinable (5—14). And (3) all assertions about its relation to other things are of two, and only two, kinds: they either assert in what degree things themselves possess this property, or else they assert causal relations between other things and those which possess it (15—17). Finally, (4) in considering the different degrees in which things themselves possess this property, we have to take account of the fact that a whole may possess it in a degree different from that which is obtained by summing the degrees in which its parts possess it (18—22).

CHAPTER II.

24. IT results from the conclusions of Chapter I, that all ethical questions fall under one or other of three classes. The first class contains but one question—the question What is the nature of that peculiar predicate, the relation of which to other things constitutes the object of all other ethical investigations? or, in other words, What is *meant* by good? This first question I have already attempted to answer. The peculiar predicate, by reference to which the sphere of Ethics must be defined, is simple, unanalysable, indefinable. There remain two classes of questions with regard to the relation of this predicate to other things. We may ask either (1) To what things and in what degree does this predicate directly attach? What things are good in themselves? or (2) By what means shall we be able to make what exists in the world as good as possible? What causal relations hold between what is best in itself and other things?

In this and the two following chapters, I propose to discuss certain theories, which offer us an answer to the question What is good in itself? I say advisedly—*an* answer: for these theories are all characterised by the fact that, if true, they would simplify the study of Ethics very much. They all hold that there is only *one* kind of fact, of which the existence has any value at all. But they all also possess another characteristic, which is my reason for grouping them together and treating them first: namely that the main reason why the single kind of fact they name has been held to define the sole good, is that it has been

3   M

held to define what is meant by 'good' itself. In other words
they are all theories of the end or ideal, the adoption of which
has been chiefly caused by the commission of what I have called
the naturalistic fallacy: they all confuse the first and second of
the three possible questions which Ethics can ask. It is, indeed,
this fact which explains their contention that only a single kind
of thing is good. That a thing should be good, it has been
thought, *means* that it possesses this single property: and hence
(it is thought) only what possesses this property is good. The
inference seems very natural; and yet what is meant by it is
self-contradictory. For those who make it fail to perceive that
their conclusion 'what possesses this property is good' is a
significant proposition: that it does not mean either 'what
possesses this property, possesses this property' or 'the word
"good" denotes that a thing possesses this property.' And yet,
if it does *not* mean one or other of these two things, the inference
contradicts its own premise.

I propose, therefore, to discuss certain theories of what is
good in itself, which are *based* on the naturalistic fallacy, in the
sense that the commission of this fallacy has been the main
cause of their wide acceptance. The discussion will be designed
both (1) further to illustrate the fact that the naturalistic
fallacy is a fallacy, or, in other words, that we are all aware of a
certain simple quality, which (and not anything else) is what we
mainly mean by the term 'good'; and (2) to shew that not one,
but many different things, possess this property. For I cannot
hope to recommend the doctrine that things which are good do
not owe their goodness to their common possession of any other
property, without a criticism of the main doctrines, opposed to
this, whose power to recommend themselves is proved by their
wide prevalence.

25. The theories I propose to discuss may be conveniently
divided into two groups. The naturalistic fallacy always implies
that when we think 'This is good,' what we are thinking is that
the thing in question bears a definite relation to some one other
thing. But this one thing, by reference to which good is defined,
may be either what I may call a natural object—something of
which the existence is admittedly an object of experience—or

else it may be an object which is only inferred to exist in a supersensible real world. These two types of ethical theory I propose to treat separately. Theories of the second type may conveniently be called 'metaphysical,' and I shall postpone consideration of them till Chapter IV. In this and the following chapter, on the other hand, I shall deal with theories which owe their prevalence to the supposition that good can be defined by reference to a *natural object*; and these are what I mean by the name, which gives the title to this chapter, 'Naturalistic Ethics.' It should be observed that the fallacy, by reference to which I define 'Metaphysical Ethics,' is the same in kind; and I give it but one name, the naturalistic fallacy. But when we regard the ethical theories recommended by this fallacy, it seems convenient to distinguish those which consider goodness to consist in a relation to something which exists here and now, from those which do not. According to the former, Ethics is an empirical or positive science: its conclusions could be all established by means of empirical observation and induction. But this is not the case with Metaphysical Ethics. There is, therefore, a marked distinction between these two groups of ethical theories based on the same fallacy. And within Naturalistic theories, too, a convenient division may also be made. There is one natural object, namely pleasure, which has perhaps been as frequently held to be the sole good as all the rest put together. And there is, moreover, a further reason for treating Hedonism separately. That doctrine has, I think, as plainly as any other, owed its prevalence to the naturalistic fallacy; but it has had a singular fate in that the writer, who first clearly exposed the fallacy of the naturalistic arguments by which it had been attempted to *prove* that pleasure was the sole good, has maintained that nevertheless it *is* the sole good. I propose, therefore, to divide my discussion of Hedonism from that of other Naturalistic theories; treating of Naturalistic Ethics in general in this chapter, and of Hedonism, in particular, in the next.

26. The subject of the present chapter is, then, ethical theories which declare that no intrinsic value is to be found except in the possession of some one *natural* property, other than pleasure; and which declare this because it is supposed that to

be 'good' *means* to possess the property in question. Such
theories I call 'Naturalistic.' I have thus appropriated the
name Naturalism to a particular method of approaching Ethics—
a method which, strictly understood, is inconsistent with the
possibility of any Ethics whatsoever. This method consists in
substituting for 'good' some one property of a natural object or
of a collection of natural objects; and in thus replacing Ethics
by some one of the natural sciences. In general, the science
thus substituted is one of the sciences specially concerned with
man, owing to the general mistake (for such I hold it to be) of
regarding the matter of Ethics as confined to human conduct.
In general, Psychology has been the science substituted, as by
J. S. Mill; or Sociology, as by Professor Clifford, and other modern
writers. But any other science might equally well be substituted. It is the same fallacy which is implied, when Professor
Tyndall recommends us to 'conform to the laws of matter': and
here the science which it is proposed to substitute for Ethics is
simply Physics. The name then is perfectly general; for, no
matter what the something is that good is held to mean, the
theory is still Naturalism. Whether good be defined as yellow
or green or blue, as loud or soft, as round or square, as sweet or
bitter, as productive of life or productive of pleasure, as willed or
desired or felt: whichever of these or of any other object in the
world, good may be held to *mean*, the theory, which holds it to
mean them, will be a naturalistic theory. I have called such
theories naturalistic because all of these terms denote properties,
simple or complex, of some simple or complex natural object;
and, before I proceed to consider them, it will be well to define
what is meant by 'nature' and by 'natural objects.'

By 'nature,' then, I do mean and have meant that which is
the subject-matter of the natural sciences and also of psychology.
It may be said to include all that has existed, does exist, or will
exist in time. If we consider whether any object is of such a
nature that it may be said to exist now, to have existed, or to
be about to exist, then we may know that that object is a
natural object, and that nothing, of which this is not true, is a
natural object. Thus, for instance, of our minds we should say
that they did exist yesterday, that they do exist to-day, and

probably will exist in a minute or two. We shall say that we had thoughts yesterday, which have ceased to exist now, although their effects may remain: and in so far as those thoughts did exist, they too are natural objects.

There is, indeed, no difficulty about the 'objects' themselves, in the sense in which I have just used the term. It is easy to say which of them are natural, and which (if any) are not natural. But when we begin to consider the properties of objects, then I fear the problem is more difficult. Which among the properties of natural objects are natural properties and which are not? For I do not deny that good is a property of certain natural objects: certain of them, I think, are good; and yet I have said that 'good' itself is not a natural property. Well, my test for these too also concerns their existence in time. Can we imagine 'good' as existing by itself in time, and not merely as a property of some natural object? For myself, I cannot so imagine it, whereas with the greater number of properties of objects—those which I call the natural properties—their existence does seem to me to be independent of the existence of those objects. They are, in fact, rather parts of which the object is made up than mere predicates which attach to it. If they were all taken away, no object would be left, not even a bare substance: for they are in themselves substantial and give to the object all the substance that it has. But this is not so with good. If indeed good were a feeling, as some would have us believe, then it would exist in time. But that is why to call it so is to commit the naturalistic fallacy. It will always remain pertinent to ask, whether the feeling itself is good; and if so, then good cannot itself be identical with any feeling.

27. Those theories of Ethics, then, are 'naturalistic' which declare the sole good to consist in some one property of things, which exists in time; and which do so because they suppose that 'good' itself can be defined by reference to such a property. And we may now proceed to consider such theories.

And, first of all, one of the most famous of ethical maxims is that which recommends a 'life according to nature.' That was the principle of the Stoic Ethics; but, since their Ethics has some claim to be called metaphysical, I shall not attempt to deal with it here. But the same phrase reappears in Rousseau; and it is not unfrequently maintained even now that what we ought to do is to live naturally. Now let us examine this contention in its general form. It is obvious, in the first place, that we cannot say that everything natural is good, except perhaps in virtue of some metaphysical theory, such as I shall deal with later. If everything natural is equally good, then certainly Ethics, as it is ordinarily understood, disappears: for nothing is more certain, from an ethical point of view, than that some things are bad and others good; the object of Ethics is, indeed, in chief part, to give you general rules whereby you may avoid the one and secure the other. What, then, does 'natural' mean, in this advice to live naturally, since it obviously cannot apply to everything that is natural?

The phrase seems to point to a vague notion that there is some such thing as natural good; to a belief that Nature may be said to fix and decide what shall be good, just as she fixes and decides what shall exist. For instance, it may be supposed that 'health' is susceptible of a natural definition, that Nature has fixed what health shall be: and health, it may be said, is obviously good; hence in this case Nature has decided the matter; we have only to go to her and ask her what health is, and we shall know what is good: we shall have based an ethics upon science. But what is this natural definition of health? I can only conceive that health should be defined in natural terms as the *normal* state of an organism; for undoubtedly disease is also a natural product. To say that health is what is preserved by evolution, and what itself tends to preserve, in the struggle for existence, the organism which possesses it, comes to the same thing: for the point of evolution is that it pretends to give a causal explanation of why some forms of life are normal and others are abnormal; it explains the origin of species. When therefore we are told that health is natural, we may presume that what is meant is that it is normal; and that when we are told to pursue health as a natural end, what is implied is that the normal

must be good. But is it so obvious that the normal must
be good? Is it really obvious that health, for instance, is
good? Was the excellence of Socrates or of Shakespeare
normal? Was it not rather abnormal, extraordinary? It is, I
think, obvious in the first place, that not all that is good is
normal; that, on the contrary, the abnormal is often better
than the normal: peculiar excellence, as well as peculiar
viciousness, must obviously be not normal but abnormal. Yet
it may be said that nevertheless the normal is good; and I
myself am not prepared to dispute that health is good. What
I contend is that this must not be taken to be obvious; that
it must be regarded as an open question. To declare it to be
obvious is to suggest the naturalistic fallacy: just as, in some
recent books, a proof that genius is diseased, abnormal, has
been used in order to suggest that genius ought not to be
encouraged. Such reasoning is fallacious, and dangerously
fallacious. The fact is that in the very words 'health' and
'disease' we do commonly include the notion that the one
is good and the other bad. But, when a so-called scientific
definition of them is attempted, a definition in natural terms,
the only one possible is that by way of 'normal' and 'abnormal.'
Now, it is easy to prove that some things commonly thought
excellent are abnormal; and it follows that they are diseased.
But it does not follow, except by virtue of the naturalistic
fallacy, that those things, commonly thought good, are therefore
bad. All that has really been shewn is that in some cases there
is a conflict between the common judgment that genius is
good, and the common judgment that health is good. It is not
sufficiently recognised that the latter judgment has not a whit
more warrant for its truth than the former; that both are
perfectly open questions. It may be true, indeed, that by
'healthy' we do commonly imply 'good'; but that only shews
that when we so use the word, we do not mean the same thing
by it as the thing which is meant in medical science. That
health, *when* the word is used to denote something good, is
good, goes no way at all to shew that health, when the word is
used to denote something normal, is also good. We might
as well say that, because 'bull' denotes an Irish joke and

also a certain animal, the joke and the animal must be the
same thing. We must not, therefore, be frightened by the
assertion that a thing is natural into the admission that it
is good; good does not, by definition, mean anything that is
natural; and it is therefore always an open question whether
anything that is natural is good.

28. But there is another slightly different sense in which
the word 'natural' is used with an implication that it denotes
something good. This is when we speak of natural affections,
or unnatural crimes and vices. Here the meaning seems to be,
not so much that the action or feeling in question is normal or
abnormal, as that it is necessary. It is in this connection that
we are advised to imitate savages and beasts. Curious advice
certainly; but, of course, there may be something in it. I am
not here concerned to enquire under what circumstances some
of us might with advantage take a lesson from the cow. I have
really no doubt that such exist. What I am concerned with is
a certain kind of reason, which I think is sometimes used to
support this doctrine—a naturalistic reason. The notion sometimes lying at the bottom of the minds of preachers of this
gospel is that we cannot improve on nature. This notion is
certainly true, in the sense that anything we can do, that may
be better than the present state of things, will be a natural
product. But that is not what is meant by this phrase;
nature is again used to mean a mere part of nature; only this
time the part meant is not so much the normal as an arbitrary
minimum of what is necessary for life. And when this minimum is recommended as 'natural'—as the way of life to which
Nature points her finger—then the naturalistic fallacy is used.
Against this position I wish only to point out that though
the performance of certain acts, not in themselves desirable,
may be *excused* as necessary means to the preservation of life,
that is no reason for *praising* them, or advising us to limit
ourselves to those simple actions which are necessary, if it is
possible for us to improve our condition even at the expense
of doing what is in this sense unnecessary. Nature does
indeed set limits to what is possible; she does control the
means we have at our disposal for obtaining what is good;

and of this fact, practical Ethics, as we shall see later, must
certainly take account: but when she is supposed to have a
preference for what is necessary, what is necessary means only
what is necessary to obtain a certain end, presupposed as the
highest good; and what the highest good is Nature cannot
determine. Why should we suppose that what is merely
necessary to life is *ipso facto* better than what is necessary to
the study of metaphysics, useless as that study may appear?
It may be that life is only worth living, because it enables
us to study metaphysics—is a necessary means thereto. The
fallacy of this argument from nature has been discovered as
long ago as Lucian. 'I was almost inclined to laugh,' says
Callicratidas, in one of the dialogues imputed to him[1], 'just
now, when Charicles was praising irrational brutes and the
savagery of the Scythians: in the heat of his argument he was
almost repenting that he was born a Greek. What wonder if
lions and bears and pigs do not act as I was proposing? That
which reasoning would fairly lead a man to choose, cannot be
had by creatures that do not reason, simply because they are so
stupid. If Prometheus or some other god had given each of
them the intelligence of a man, then they would not have lived
in deserts and mountains nor fed on one another. They would
have built temples just as we do, each would have lived in the
centre of his family, and they would have formed a nation
bound by mutual laws. Is it anything surprising that brutes,
who have had the misfortune to be unable to obtain by fore-
thought any of the goods, with which reasoning provides us,
should have missed love too? Lions do not love; but neither
do they philosophise; bears do not love; but the reason is they
do not know the sweets of friendship. It is only men, who, by
their wisdom and their knowledge, after many trials, have
chosen what is best.'

29.   To argue that a thing is good *because* it is 'natural,' or
bad *because* it is 'unnatural,' in these common senses of the
term, is therefore certainly fallacious: and yet such arguments
are very frequently used. But they do not commonly pretend
to give a systematic theory of Ethics. Among attempts to

[1] "Ερωτες, 436—7.

systematise an appeal to nature, that which is now most prevalent is to be found in the application to ethical questions of the term 'Evolution'—in the ethical doctrines which have been called 'Evolutionistic.' These doctrines are those which maintain that the course of 'evolution,' while it shews us the direction in which we *are* developing, thereby and for that reason shews us the direction in which we *ought* to develop. Writers, who maintain such a doctrine, are at present very numerous and very popular; and I propose to take as my example the writer, who is perhaps the best known of them all—Mr Herbert Spencer. Mr Spencer's doctrine, it must be owned, does not offer the *clearest* example of the naturalistic fallacy as used in support of Evolutionistic Ethics. A clearer example might be found in the doctrine of Guyau[1], a writer who has lately had considerable vogue in France, but who is not so well known as Spencer. Guyau might almost be called a disciple of Spencer; he is frankly evolutionistic, and frankly naturalistic; and I may mention that he does not seem to think that he differs from Spencer by reason of his naturalism. The point in which he has criticised Spencer concerns the question how far the ends of 'pleasure' and of 'increased life' coincide as motives and means to the attainment of the ideal: he does not seem to think that he differs from Spencer in the fundamental principle that the ideal is 'Quantity of life, measured in breadth as well as in length,' or, as Guyau says, 'Expansion and intensity of life'; nor in the naturalistic reason which he gives for this principle. And I am not sure that he does differ from Spencer in these points. Spencer does, as I shall shew, use the naturalistic fallacy in details; but with regard to his fundamental principles, the following doubts occur: Is he fundamentally a Hedonist? And, if so, is he a naturalistic Hedonist? In that case he would better have been treated in my next chapter. Does he hold that a tendency to increase quantity of life is merely a *criterion* of good conduct? Or does he hold that such increase of life is marked out by nature as an end at which we ought to aim?

I think his language in various places would give colour to

[1] See *Esquisse d'une Morale sans Obligation ni Sanction*, par M. Guyau. 4ᵐᵉ édition. Paris: F. Alcan, 1896.

all these hypotheses; though some of them are mutually inconsistent. I will try to discuss the main points.

30. The modern vogue of 'Evolution' is chiefly owing to
Darwin's investigations as to the origin of species. Darwin
formed a strictly biological hypothesis as to the manner in which
certain forms of animal life became established, while others
died out and disappeared. His theory was that this might
be accounted for, partly at least, in the following way. When
certain varieties occurred (the cause of their occurrence is still,
in the main, unknown), it might be that some of the points, in
which they varied from their parent species or from other
species then existing, made them better able to persist in the
environment in which they found themselves—less liable to be
killed off. They might, for instance, be better able to endure
the cold or heat or changes of the climate; better able to find
nourishment from what surrounded them; better able to escape
from or resist other species which fed upon them; better fitted
to attract or to master the other sex. Being thus less liable to
die, their numbers relatively to other species would increase;
and that very increase in their numbers might tend towards the
extinction of those other species. This theory, to which Darwin
gave the name 'Natural Selection,' was also called the theory
of survival of the fittest. The natural process which it thus
described was called evolution. It was very natural to suppose
that evolution meant evolution from what was lower into what
was higher; in fact it was observed that at least one species,
commonly called higher—the species man—had so survived, and
among men again it was supposed that the higher races, ourselves for example, had shewn a tendency to survive the lower,
such as the North American Indians. We can kill them more
easily than they can kill us. The doctrine of evolution was
then represented as an explanation of how the higher species
survives the lower. Spencer, for example, constantly uses
'more evolved' as equivalent to 'higher.' But it is to be noted
that this forms no part of Darwin's scientific theory. That
theory will explain, equally well, how by an alteration in the
environment (the gradual cooling of the earth, for example)
quite a different species from man, a species which we think

ınfinitely lower, might survive us. The survival of the fittest
does *not* mean, as one might suppose, the survival of what is
fittest to fulfil a good purpose—best adapted to a good end: at
the last, it means merely the survival of the fittest to survive;
and the value of the scientific theory, and it is a theory of great
value, just consists in shewing what are the causes which produce certain biological effects. Whether these effects are good
or bad, it cannot pretend to judge.

31. But now let us hear what Mr Spencer says about
the application of Evolution to Ethics.

'I recur,' he says[1], 'to the main proposition set forth ın
these two chapters, which has, I think, been fully justified.
Guided by the truth that as the conduct with which Ethics
deals is part of conduct at large, conduct at large must be
generally understood before this part can be specially understood; and guided by the further truth that to understand
conduct at large we must understand the evolution of conduct;
we have been led to see that Ethics has for its subject-matter,
that form which universal conduct assumes during the last
stages of its evolution. We have also concluded that these last
stages in the evolution of conduct are those displayed by
the *highest*[2] type of being when he is forced, by increase of
numbers, to live more and more in presence of his fellows.
And there has followed *the corollary that conduct gains ethical
sanction*[2] in proportion as the activities, becoming less and less
militant and more and more industrial, are such as do not
necessitate mutual injury or hindrance, but consist with, and
are furthered by, co-operation and mutual aid.

'These implications of the Evolution-Hypothesis, we shall
now see harmonize with the leading moral ideas men have
otherwise reached.'

Now, if we are to take the last sentence strictly—if the
propositions which precede it are really thought by Mr Spencer
to be *implications* of the Evolution-Hypothesis—there can be
no doubt that Mr Spencer has committed the naturalistic
fallacy. All that the Evolution-Hypothesis tells us is that
certain kinds of conduct are more evolved than others; and

---

[1] *Data of Ethics*, Chap. ıı, § 7, *ad fin.*   [2] The italics are mine.

this is, in fact, all that Mr Spencer has attempted to prove in the two chapters concerned. Yet he tells us that one of the things it has proved is that *conduct gains ethical sanction* in proportion as it displays certain characteristics. What he has tried to prove is only that, in proportion as it displays those characteristics, it is *more evolved*. It is plain, then, that Mr Spencer *identifies* the gaining of ethical sanction with the being more evolved: this follows strictly from his words. But Mr Spencer's language is extremely loose; and we shall presently see that he seems to regard the view it here implies as false. We cannot, therefore, take it as Mr Spencer's definite view that 'better' means nothing but 'more evolved'; or even that what is 'more evolved' is *therefore* 'better.' But we are entitled to urge that he is influenced by these views, and therefore by the naturalistic fallacy. It is only by the assumption of such influence that we can explain his confusion as to what he has really proved, and the absence of any attempt to prove, what he says he has proved, that conduct which is more evolved is better. We shall look in vain for any attempt to shew that 'ethical sanction' is in proportion to 'evolution,' or that it is the 'highest' type of being which displays the most evolved conduct; yet Mr Spencer concludes that this is the case. It is only fair to assume that he is not sufficiently conscious how much these propositions stand in need of proof—what a very different thing is being 'more evolved' from being 'higher' or 'better.' It may, of course, be true that what is more evolved is also higher and better. But Mr Spencer does not seem aware that to assert the one is in any case not the same thing as to assert the other. He argues at length that certain kinds of conduct are 'more evolved,' and then informs us that he has proved them to gain ethical sanction in proportion, without any warning that he has omitted the most essential step in such a proof. Surely this is sufficient evidence that he does not see how essential that step is.

32. Whatever be the degree of Mr Spencer's own guilt, what has just been said will serve to illustrate the kind of fallacy which is constantly committed by those who profess to 'base' Ethics on Evolution. But we must hasten to add that the view which Mr Spencer elsewhere most emphatically recommends is an utterly different one. It will be useful briefly to deal with this, in order that no injustice may be done to Mr Spencer. The discussion will be instructive partly from the lack of clearness, which Mr Spencer displays, as to the relation of this view to the 'evolutionistic' one just described; and partly because there is reason to suspect that in this view also he is influenced by the naturalistic fallacy.

We have seen that, at the end of his second chapter, Mr Spencer seems to announce that he has already proved certain characteristics of conduct to be a measure of its ethical value. He seems to think that he has proved this merely by considering the evolution of conduct; and he has certainly not given any such proof, unless we are to understand that 'more evolved' is a mere synonym for 'ethically better.' He now promises merely to *confirm* this certain conclusion by shewing that it 'harmonizes with the leading moral ideas men have otherwise reached.' But, when we turn to his third chapter, we find that what he actually does is something quite different. He here asserts that to establish the conclusion 'Conduct is better in proportion as it is more evolved' an entirely new proof is necessary. That conclusion will be *false*, unless a certain proposition, of which we have heard nothing so far, is true—unless it be true that life is *pleasant* on the whole. And the ethical proposition, for which he claims the support of the 'leading moral ideas' of mankind, turns out to be that 'life is good or bad, according as it does, or does not, bring a surplus of agreeable feeling' (§ 10). Here, then, Mr Spencer appears, not as an Evolutionist, but as a Hedonist, in Ethics. No conduct is better, *because* it is more evolved. Degree of evolution can at most be a *criterion* of ethical value; and it will only be that, if we can prove the extremely difficult generalisation that the more evolved is always, on the whole, the pleasanter. It is plain that Mr Spencer here rejects the naturalistic identification of 'better' with 'more evolved'; but it is possible that he is influenced by another naturalistic identification—that of 'good' with 'pleasant.' It is possible that Mr Spencer is a naturalistic Hedonist.

33. Let us examine Mr Spencer's own words. He begins
this third chapter by an attempt to shew that *we call* 'good the
acts conducive to life, in self or others, and bad those which
directly or indirectly tend towards death, special or general'
(§ 9). And then he asks: 'Is there any assumption made' in
so calling them? 'Yes'; he answers, 'an assumption of extreme
significance has been made—an assumption underlying all
moral estimates. The question to be definitely raised and
answered before entering on any ethical discussion, is the
question of late much agitated—Is life worth living? Shall we
take the pessimist view? or shall we take the optimist view?...
On the answer to this question depends every decision concerning the goodness or badness of conduct.' But Mr Spencer
does not immediately proceed to give the answer. Instead of
this, he asks another question: 'But now, have these irrecon-
cilable opinions [pessimist and optimist] anything in common?'
And this question he immediately answers by the statement:
'Yes, there is one postulate in which pessimists and optimists
agree. Both their arguments assume it to be self-evident that
life is good or bad, according as it does, or does not, bring
a surplus of agreeable feeling' (§ 10). It is to the defence
of this statement that the rest of the chapter is devoted; and
at the end Mr Spencer formulates his conclusion in the following
words: 'No school can avoid taking for the ultimate moral
aim a desirable state of feeling called by whatever name—
gratification, enjoyment, happiness. Pleasure somewhere, at
some time, to some being or beings, is an inexpugnable element
of the conception' (§ 16 *ad fin.*).

Now in all this, there are two points to which I wish to call
attention. The first is that Mr Spencer does not, after all, tell
us clearly what he takes to be the relation of Pleasure and
Evolution in ethical theory. Obviously he should mean that
pleasure is the *only* intrinsically desirable thing; that other
good things are 'good' only in the sense that they are means
to its existence. Nothing but this can properly be meant by
asserting it to be '*the* ultimate moral aim,' or, as he subsequently
says (§ 62 *ad fin.*), '*the* ultimately supreme end.' And, if this
were so, it would follow that the more evolved conduct was

better than the less evolved, only because, and in proportion
as, it gave more pleasure. But Mr Spencer tells us that two
conditions are, taken together, *sufficient* to prove the more
evolved conduct better: (1) That it should tend to produce
more life; (2) That life should be worth living or contain
a balance of pleasure. And the point I wish to emphasise is
that if these conditions are sufficient, then pleasure cannot be
the sole good. For though to produce more life is, if the
second of Mr Spencer's propositions be correct, *one way* of
producing more pleasure, it is not the only way. It is quite
possible that a small quantity of life, which was more intensely
and uniformly present, should give a greater quantity of
pleasure than the greatest possible quantity of life that was
only just 'worth living.' And in that case, on the hedonistic
supposition that pleasure is the only thing worth having, we
should have to prefer the smaller quantity of life and therefore,
according to Mr Spencer, the less evolved conduct. Accordingly, if Mr Spencer is a true Hedonist, the fact that life gives
a balance of pleasure is *not*, as he seems to think, sufficient
to prove that the more evolved conduct is the better. If
Mr Spencer means us to understand that it *is* sufficient, then
his view about pleasure can only be, not that it is the sole good
or 'ultimately supreme end,' but that a balance of it is a
necessary constituent of the supreme end. In short, Mr Spencer
seems to maintain that more life is decidedly better than less,
if only it give a balance of pleasure: and that contention is
inconsistent with the position that pleasure is '*the* ultimate
moral aim.' Mr Spencer implies that of two quantities of life,
which gave an equal amount of pleasure, the larger would
nevertheless be preferable to the less. And if this be so, then
he must maintain that quantity of life or degree of evolution is
itself an ultimate condition of value. He leaves us, therefore,
in doubt whether he is not still retaining the Evolutionistic
proposition, that the more evolved is better, simply because
it is more evolved, alongside of the Hedonistic proposition,
that the more pleasant is better, simply because it is more
pleasant.

But the second question which we have to ask is: What

reasons has Mr Spencer for assigning to pleasure the position which he does assign to it? He tells us, we saw, that the 'arguments' both of pessimists and of optimists 'assume it to be self-evident that life is good or bad, according as it does, or does not, bring a surplus of agreeable feeling'; and he betters this later by telling us that 'since avowed or implied pessimists, and optimists of one or other shade, taken together constitute all men, it results that this postulate is universally accepted' (§ 16). That these statements are absolutely false is, of course, quite obvious: but why does Mr Spencer think them true? and, what is more important (a question which Mr Spencer does not distinguish too clearly from the last), why does he think the postulate itself to be true? Mr Spencer himself tells us his 'proof is' that 'reversing the application of the words' good and bad—applying the word 'good' to conduct, the 'aggregate results' of which are painful, and the word 'bad' to conduct, of which the 'aggregate results' are pleasurable—'creates absurdities' (§ 16). He does not say whether this is because it is absurd to think that the quality, which we *mean by the word* 'good,' really applies to what is painful. Even, however, if we assume him to mean this, and if we assume that absurdities are thus created, it is plain he would only prove that what is painful is properly thought to be *so far* bad, and what is pleasant to be *so far* good: it would not prove at all that pleasure is '*the* supreme end.' There is, however, reason to think that part of what Mr Spencer means is the naturalistic fallacy: that he imagines 'pleasant' or 'productive of pleasure' is the very meaning of the word 'good,' and that 'the absurdity' is due to this. It is at all events certain that he does not distinguish this possible meaning from that which would admit that 'good' denotes an unique indefinable quality. The doctrine of naturalistic Hedonism is, indeed, quite strictly implied in his statement that 'virtue' cannot '*be defined* otherwise than in terms of happiness' (§ 13); and, though, as I remarked above, we cannot insist upon Mr Spencer's words as a certain clue to any definite meaning, that is only because he generally expresses by them several inconsistent alternatives—the naturalistic fallacy being, in this case, one such alternative. It is certainly

impossible to find any further reasons given by Mr Spencer for
his conviction that pleasure both is the supreme end, and is
universally admitted to be so. He seems to assume throughout
that we *must* mean by good conduct what is productive of
pleasure, and by bad what is productive of pain. So far,
then, as he is a Hedonist, he would seem to be a naturalistic
Hedonist.

So much for Mr Spencer. It is, of course, quite possible
that his treatment of Ethics contains many interesting and
instructive remarks. It would seem, indeed, that Mr Spencer's
main view, that of which he is most clearly and most often
conscious, is that pleasure is the sole good, and that to consider
the direction of evolution is by far the best *criterion* of the way
in which we shall get most of it: and this theory, *if* he could
establish that amount of pleasure is always in direct proportion
to amount of evolution *and also* that it was plain what conduct
was more evolved, *would* be a very valuable contribution to
the science of Sociology; it would even, if pleasure were the
sole good, be a valuable contribution to Ethics. But the
above discussion should have made it plain that, if what we
want from an ethical philosopher is a scientific and systematic
Ethics, not merely an Ethics professedly 'based on science';
if what we want is a clear discussion of the fundamental
principles of Ethics, and a statement of the ultimate reasons
why one way of acting should be considered better than
another—then Mr Spencer's 'Data of Ethics' is immeasurably
far from satisfying these demands.

34. It remains only to state clearly what is definitely
fallacious in prevalent views as to the relation of Evolution
to Ethics—in those views with regard to which it seems so
uncertain how far Mr Spencer intends to encourage them.
I propose to confine the term 'Evolutionistic Ethics' to the
view that we need only to consider the tendency of 'evolution'
in order to discover the direction in which we *ought* to go.
This view must be carefully distinguished from certain others,
which may be commonly confused with it. (1) It might, for
instance, be held that the direction in which living things have
hitherto developed is, as a matter of fact, the direction of

progress. It might be held that the 'more evolved' is, as
a matter of fact, also better. And in such a view no fallacy is
involved. But, if it is to give us any guidance as to how we
ought to act in the future, it does involve a long and painful
investigation of the exact points in which the superiority of
the more evolved consists. We cannot assume that, because
evolution is progress *on the whole*, therefore every point in
which the more evolved differs from the less is a point in which
it is better than the less. A simple consideration of the course
of evolution will therefore, on this view, by no means suffice to
inform us of the course we ought to pursue. We shall have to
employ all the resources of a strictly ethical discussion in order
to arrive at a correct valuation of the different results of
evolution—to distinguish the more valuable from the less
valuable, and both from those which are no better than their
causes, or perhaps even worse. In fact it is difficult to see how,
on this view—if all that be meant is that evolution has *on the
whole* been a progress—the theory of evolution can give any
assistance to Ethics at all. The judgment that evolution has
been a progress is itself an independent ethical judgment; and
even if we take it to be more certain and obvious than any of the
detailed judgments upon which it must logically depend for
confirmation, we certainly cannot use it as a datum from which
to infer details. It is, at all events, certain that, if this had
been the *only* relation held to exist between Evolution and
Ethics, no such importance would have been attached to the
bearing of Evolution on Ethics as we actually find claimed for
it. (2) The view, which, as I have said, seems to be Mr Spencer's
main view, may also be held without fallacy. It may be held
that the more evolved, though not itself the better, is a *criterion*,
because a concomitant, of the better. But this view also
obviously involves an exhaustive preliminary discussion of the
fundamental ethical question what, after all, is better. That
Mr Spencer entirely dispenses with such a discussion in support
of his contention that pleasure is the sole good, I have pointed
out; and that, if we attempt such a discussion, we shall arrive
at no such simple result, I shall presently try to shew. If
however the good is not simple, it is by no means likely that

we shall be able to discover Evolution to be a criterion of it. We shall have to establish a relation between two highly complicated sets of data; and, moreover, if we had once settled what were goods, and what their comparative values, it is extremely unlikely that we should need to call in the aid of Evolution as a criterion of how to get the most. It is plain, then, again, that if this were the only relation imagined to exist between Evolution and Ethics, it could hardly have been thought to justify the assignment of any importance in Ethics to the theory of Evolution. Finally, (3) it may be held that, though Evolution gives us no help in discovering what results of our efforts will be best, it does give some help in discovering what it is *possible* to attain and what are the means to its attainment. That the theory really may be of service to Ethics in this way cannot be denied. But it is certainly not common to find this humble, ancillary bearing clearly and exclusively assigned to it. In the mere fact, then, that these non-fallacious views of the relation of Evolution to Ethics would give so very little importance to that relation, we have evidence that what is typical in the coupling of the two names is the fallacious view to which I propose to restrict the name 'Evolutionistic Ethics.' This is the view that we ought to move in the direction of evolution simply *because* it is the direction of evolution. That the forces of Nature are working on that side is taken as a presumption that it is the right side. That such a view, apart from metaphysical presuppositions, with which I shall presently deal, is simply fallacious, I have tried to shew. It can only rest on a confused belief that somehow the good simply *means* the side on which Nature is working. And it thus involves another confused belief which is very marked in Mr Spencer's whole treatment of Evolution. For, after all, is Evolution the side on which Nature is working? In the sense, which Mr Spencer gives to the term, and in any sense in which it can be regarded as a fact that the more evolved is higher, Evolution denotes only a *temporary* historical process. That things will permanently continue to evolve in the future, or that they have always evolved in the past, we have not the smallest reason to believe. For Evolution does not, in this sense, denote a natural *law*, like the law of gravity. Darwin's theory of natural selection does indeed state a natural law: it states that, given certain conditions, certain results will always happen. But Evolution, as Mr Spencer understands it and as it is commonly understood, denotes something very different. It denotes only a process which has actually occurred at a given time, because the conditions at the beginning of that time happened to be of a certain nature. That such conditions will always be given, or have always been given, cannot be assumed; and it is only the process which, according to natural law, must follow from *these* conditions and no others, that appears to be also on the whole a progress. Precisely the same natural laws— Darwin's, for instance—would under other conditions render inevitable not Evolution—not a development from lower to higher—but the converse process, which has been called Involution. Yet Mr Spencer constantly speaks of the process which is exemplified in the development of man as if it had all the augustness of a universal Law of Nature: whereas we have no reason to believe it other than a temporary accident, requiring not only certain universal natural laws, but also the existence of a certain state of things at a certain time. The only *laws* concerned in the matter are certainly such as, under other circumstances, would allow us to infer, not the development, but the extinction of man. And that circumstances will always be favourable to further development, that Nature will always work on the side of Evolution, we have no reason whatever to believe. Thus the idea that Evolution throws important light on Ethics seems to be due to a double confusion. Our respect for the process is enlisted by the representation of it as the Law of Nature. But, on the other hand, our respect for Laws of Nature would be speedily diminished, did we not imagine that this desirable process was one of them. To suppose that a Law of Nature is *therefore* respectable, is to commit the naturalistic fallacy; but no one, probably, would be tempted to commit it, unless something which *is* respectable, were represented as a Law of Nature. If it were clearly recognised that there is no evidence for supposing Nature to be on the side of the Good, there would probably be less tendency to hold the opinion, which on other grounds is demonstrably false, that no such evidence is required. And if both false opinions were clearly seen to be false, it would be plain that Evolution has very little indeed to say to Ethics.

35. In this chapter I have begun the criticism of certain ethical views, which seem to owe their influence mainly to the naturalistic fallacy—the fallacy which consists in identifying the simple notion which we mean by ‘good’ with some other notion. They are views which profess to tell us what is good in itself; and my criticism of them is mainly directed (1) to bring out the negative result, that we have no reason to suppose that which they declare to be the sole good, really to be so, (2) to illustrate further the positive result, already established in Chapter I, that the fundamental principles of Ethics must be *synthetic* propositions, declaring what things, and in what degree, possess a simple and unanalysable property which may be called ‘intrinsic value’ or ‘goodness.’ The chapter began (1) by dividing the views to be criticised into (*a*) those which, supposing ‘good’ to be defined by reference to some super-sensible reality, conclude that the sole good is to be found in such a reality, and may therefore be called ‘Metaphysical,’ (*b*) those which assign a similar position to some natural object, and may therefore be called ‘Naturalistic.’ Of naturalistic views, that which regards ‘pleasure’ as the sole good has received far the fullest and most serious treatment and was therefore re-served for Chapter III: all other forms of Naturalism may be first dismissed, by taking typical examples (24—26). (2) As typical of naturalistic views, other than Hedonism, there was first taken the popular commendation of what is ‘natural’: it was pointed out that by ‘natural’ there might here be meant either ‘normal’ or ‘necessary,’ and that neither the ‘normal’ nor the ‘necessary’ could be seriously supposed to be either always good or the only good things (27—28). (3) But a more important type, because one which claims to be capable of system, is to be found in ‘Evolutionistic Ethics.’ The influence of the fallacious opinion that to be ‘better’ *means* to be ‘more evolved’ was illustrated by an examination of Mr Herbert Spencer’s Ethics; and it was pointed out that, but for the in-fluence of this opinion, Evolution could hardly have been supposed to have any important bearing upon Ethics (29—34).

CHAPTER III.

HEDONISM.

36. In this chapter we have to deal with what is perhaps the most famous and the most widely held of all ethical principles—the principle that nothing is good but pleasure. My chief reason for treating of this principle in this place is, as I said, that Hedonism appears in the main to be a form of Naturalistic Ethics: in other words, that pleasure has been so generally held to be the sole good, is almost entirely due to the fact that it has seemed to be somehow involved in the *definition* of 'good'—to be pointed out by the very meaning of the word. If this is so, then the prevalence of Hedonism has been mainly due to what I have called the naturalistic fallacy—the failure to distinguish clearly that unique and indefinable quality which we mean by good. And that it is so, we have very strong evidence in the fact that, of all hedonistic writers, Prof. Sidgwick alone has clearly recognised that by 'good' we do mean something unanalysable, and has alone been led thereby to emphasise the fact that, if Hedonism be true, its claims to be so must be rested solely on its self-evidence—that we must maintain 'Pleasure is the sole good' to be a mere *intuition*. It appeared to Prof. Sidgwick as a new discovery that what he calls the 'method' of Intuitionism must be retained as valid alongside of, and indeed as the foundation of, what he calls the alternative 'methods' of Utilitarianism and Egoism. And that it was a new discovery can hardly be doubted. In previous Hedonists we find no clear and consistent recognition of the fact that their fundamental proposition involves the assumption that a certain unique predicate can be directly seen to belong to pleasure alone among existents: they do not emphasise, as they could hardly have failed to have done had they perceived it, how utterly independent of all other truths this truth must be.

Moreover it is easy to see how this unique position should have been assigned to pleasure without any clear consciousness of the assumption involved. Hedonism is, for a sufficiently obvious reason, the first conclusion at which any one who begins to reflect upon Ethics naturally arrives. It is very easy to notice the fact that we are pleased with things. The things we enjoy and the things we do not, form two unmistakable classes, to which our attention is constantly directed. But it is comparatively difficult to distinguish the fact that we *approve* a thing from the fact that we are pleased with it. Although, if we look at the two states of mind, we must see that they are different, even though they generally go together, it is very difficult to see in *what respect* they are different, or that the difference can in any connection be of more importance than the many other differences, which are so patent and yet so difficult to analyse, between one *kind* of enjoyment and another. It is very difficult to see that by 'approving' of a thing we mean *feeling that it has a certain predicate*—the predicate, namely, which defines the peculiar sphere of Ethics; whereas in the enjoyment of a thing no such unique object of thought is involved. Nothing is more natural than the vulgar mistake, which we find expressed in a recent book on Ethics[1]: 'The primary ethical fact is, we have said, that something is approved or disapproved: that is, in other words, the ideal representation of certain events in the way of sensation, perception, or idea, is attended with a feeling of pleasure or of pain.' In ordinary speech, 'I want this,' 'I like this,' 'I care about this' are constantly used as equivalents for 'I think this good.' And in this way it is very natural to be led to suppose that there is no distinct class of ethical judgments, but only the class 'things enjoyed'; in spite of the fact, which is very clear, if not very common, that we do not always approve what we enjoy. It is,

[1] A. E. Taylor's *Problem of Conduct*, p. 120.

of course, very obvious that from the supposition that 'I think this good' is identical with 'I am pleased with this,' it cannot be *logically* inferred that pleasure alone is good. But, on the other hand, it is very difficult to see what could be logically inferred from such a supposition; and it seems *natural* enough that such an inference should suggest itself. A very little examination of what is commonly written on the subject will suffice to shew that a logical confusion of this nature is very common. Moreover the very commission of the naturalistic fallacy involves that those who commit it should not recognise clearly the meaning of the proposition 'This is good'—that they should not be able to distinguish this from other propositions which seem to resemble it; and, where this is so, it is, of course, impossible that its logical relations should be clearly perceived.

37. There is, therefore, ample reason to suppose that Hedonism is in general a form of Naturalism—that its acceptance is generally due to the naturalistic fallacy. It is, indeed, only when we have detected this fallacy, when we have become clearly aware of the unique object which is meant by 'good,' that we are able to give to Hedonism the precise definition used above, 'Nothing is good but pleasure': and it may, therefore, be objected that, in attacking this doctrine under the name of Hedonism, I am attacking a doctrine which has never really been held. But it is very common to hold a doctrine, without being clearly aware what it is you hold; and though, when Hedonists argue in favour of what they call Hedonism, I admit that, in order to suppose their arguments valid, they must have before their minds something *other* than the doctrine I have defined, yet, in order to draw the conclusions that they draw, it is necessary that they should *also* have before their minds this doctrine. In fact, my justification for supposing that I shall have refuted *historical* Hedonism, if I refute the proposition 'Nothing is good but pleasure, is, that although Hedonists have rarely stated their principle in this form and though its truth, in this form, will certainly not follow from their arguments, yet their ethical *method* will follow logically from nothing else. Any pretence of the hedonistic method, to discover to us practical truths which we should not otherwise have known, is founded on the principle that the course of action which will bring the greatest balance of pleasure is certainly the right one; and, failing an absolute proof that the greatest balance of pleasure *always* coincides with the greatest balance of other goods, which it is not generally attempted to give, this principle can only be justified if pleasure be the sole good. Indeed it can hardly be doubted that Hedonists are distinguished by arguing, in disputed practical questions, *as if* pleasure were the sole good; and that it is justifiable, for this among other reasons, to take this as *the* ethical principle of Hedonism will, I hope, be made further evident by the whole discussion of this chapter.

By Hedonism, then, I mean the doctrine that pleasure *alone* is good as an end—'good' in the sense which I have tried to point out as indefinable. The doctrine that pleasure, *among other things,* is good as an end, is not Hedonism; and I shall not dispute its truth. Nor again is the doctrine that other things, beside pleasure, are good as means, at all inconsistent with Hedonism: the Hedonist is not bound to maintain that 'Pleasure alone is good,' if under good he includes, as we generally do, what is good as means to an end, *as well as* the end itself. In attacking Hedonism, I am therefore simply and solely attacking the doctrine that 'Pleasure *alone* is good as an end or in itself': I am not attacking the doctrine that 'Pleasure *is* good as an end or in itself,' nor am I attacking any doctrine whatever as to what are the best means we can take in order to obtain pleasure or any other end. Hedonists do, in general, recommend a course of conduct which is very similar to that which I should recommend. I do not quarrel with them about most of their practical conclusions, I quarrel only with the reasons by which they seem to think their conclusions can be supported; and I do emphatically deny that the correctness of their conclusions is any ground for inferring the correctness of their principles. A correct conclusion may always be obtained by fallacious reasoning; and the good life or virtuous maxims of a Hedonist afford absolutely no presumption that his ethical philosophy is also good. It is his ethical philosophy alone with which I am concerned: what I dispute is the excellence of his reasoning, not the excellence of his character as a man or even as moral teacher. It may be thought that my contention is unimportant, but that is no ground for thinking that I am not in the right. What I am concerned with is knowledge only— that we should think correctly and so far arrive at some truth, however unimportant: I do not say that such knowledge will make us more useful members of society. If any one does not care for knowledge for its own sake, then I have nothing to say to him: only it should not be thought that a lack of interest in what I have to say is any ground for holding it untrue.

38. Hedonists, then, hold that all other things but pleasure, whether conduct or virtue or knowledge, whether life or nature or beauty, are only good as means to pleasure or for the sake of pleasure, never for their own sakes or as ends in themselves. This view was held by Aristippus, the disciple of Socrates, and by the Cyrenaic school which he founded; it is associated with Epicurus and the Epicureans; and it has been held in modern times, chiefly by those philosophers who call themselves 'Utilitarians'—by Bentham, and by Mill, for instance. Herbert Spencer, as we have seen, also says he holds it; and Professor Sidgwick, as we shall see, holds it too.

Yet all these philosophers, as has been said, differ from one another more or less, both as to what they mean by Hedonism, and as to the reasons for which it is to be accepted as a true doctrine. The matter is therefore obviously not quite so simple as it might at first appear. My own object will be to shew quite clearly what the theory must imply, if it is made precise, if all confusions and inconsistencies are removed from the conception of it; and, when this is done, I think it will appear that all the various reasons given for holding it to be true, are really quite inadequate; that they are not reasons for holding Hedonism, but only for holding some other doctrine which is confused therewith. In order to attain this object I propose to take first Mill's doctrine, as set forth in his book called *Utilitarianism*: we shall find in Mill a conception of Hedonism, and arguments in its favour, which fairly represent those of a large class of hedonistic writers. To these representative

conceptions and arguments grave objections, objections which
appear to me to be conclusive, have been urged by Professor
Sidgwick. These I shall try to give in my own words; and
shall then proceed to consider and refute Professor Sidgwick's
own much more precise conceptions and arguments. With this,
I think, we shall have traversed the whole field of Hedonistic
doctrine. It will appear, from the discussion, that the task of
deciding what is or is not good in itself is by no means an easy
one; and in this way the discussion will afford a good example
of the method which it is necessary to pursue in attempting to
arrive at the truth with regard to this primary class of ethical
principles. In particular it will appear that two principles of
method must be constantly kept in mind: (1) that the naturalistic fallacy must not be committed; (2) that the distinction
between means and ends must be observed.

39. I propose, then, to begin by an examination of Mill's
Utilitarianism. That is a book which contains an admirably
clear and fair discussion of many ethical principles and methods.
Mill exposes not a few simple mistakes which are very likely to
be made by those who approach ethical problems without much
previous reflection. But what I am concerned with is the
mistakes which Mill himself appears to have made, and these
only so far as they concern the Hedonistic principle. Let me
repeat what that principle is. It is, I said, that pleasure is the
only thing at which we ought to aim, the only thing that is
good as an end and for its own sake. And now let us turn to
Mill and see whether he accepts this description of the question
at issue. 'Pleasure,' he says at the outset, 'and freedom from
pain, are the only things desirable as ends' (p. 10[1]); and again,
at the end of his argument, 'To think of an object as desirable
(unless for the sake of its consequences) and to think of it as
pleasant are one and the same thing' (p. 58). These statements,
taken together, and apart from certain confusions which are
obvious in them, seem to imply the principle I have stated;
and if I succeed in shewing that Mill's reasons for them do not
prove them, it must at least be admitted that I have not been
fighting with shadows or demolishing a man of straw.

[1] My references are to the 13th edition, 1897.

It will be observed that Mill adds 'absence of pain' to 'pleasure' in his first statement, though not in his second. There is, in this, a confusion, with which, however, we need not deal. I shall talk of 'pleasure' alone, for the sake of conciseness; but all my arguments will apply *à fortiori* to 'absence of pain': it is easy to make the necessary substitutions.

Mill holds, then, that 'happiness is desirable, and *the only thing desirable*[1], as an end; all other things being only desirable as means to that end' (p. 52). Happiness he has already defined as 'pleasure, and the absence of pain' (p. 10); he does not pretend that this is more than an arbitrary verbal definition; and, as *such*, I have not a word to say against it. His principle, then, is 'pleasure is the only thing desirable,' if I may be allowed, when I say 'pleasure,' to include in that word (so far as necessary) absence of pain. And now what are his reasons for holding that principle to be true? He has already told us (p. 6) that 'Questions of ultimate ends are not amenable to direct proof. Whatever can be proved to be good, must be so by being shewn to be a means to something *admitted to be good without proof.*' With this, I perfectly agree: indeed the chief object of my first chapter was to shew that this is so. Anything which is good as an end must be admitted to be good without proof. We are agreed so far. Mill even uses the same examples which I used in my second chapter. 'How,' he says, 'is it possible to prove that health is good?' 'What proof is it possible to give that pleasure is good?' Well, in Chapter IV, in which he deals with the proof of his Utilitarian principle, Mill repeats the above statement in these words: 'It has already,' he says, 'been remarked, that questions of ultimate ends do not admit of proof, in the ordinary acceptation of the term' (p. 52). 'Questions about ends,' he goes on in this same passage, 'are, in other words, questions what things are desirable.' I am quoting these repetitions, because they make it plain what otherwise might have been doubted, that Mill is using the words 'desirable' or 'desirable as an end' as absolutely and precisely equivalent to the words 'good as an end.' We are,

[1] My italics.

then, now to hear, what reasons he advances for this doctrine
that pleasure alone is good as an end.

40. 'Questions about ends,' he says (pp. 52—3), 'are, in other
words, questions what things are desirable. The utilitarian
doctrine is, that happiness is desirable, and the only thing
desirable, as an end; all other things being only desirable as
means to that end. What ought to be required of this doctrine
—what conditions is it requisite that the doctrine should fulfil—
to make good its claim to be believed?

'The only proof capable of being given that a thing is visible,
is that people actually see it. The only proof that a sound is
audible, is that people hear it; and so of the other sources of
our experience. In like manner, I apprehend, the sole evidence
it is possible to produce that anything is desirable, is that
people do actually desire it. If the end which the utilitarian
doctrine proposes to itself were not, in theory and in practice,
acknowledged to be an end, nothing could ever convince any
person that it was so. No reason can be given why the general
happiness is desirable, except that each person, so far as he
believes it to be attainable, desires his own happiness. This,
however, being the fact, we have not only all the proof which
the case admits of, but all which it is possible to require, that
happiness is a good: that each person's happiness is a good to
that person, and the general happiness, therefore, a good to the
aggregate of all persons. Happiness has made out its title as
one of the ends of conduct, and consequently one of the criteria
of morality.'

There, that is enough. That is my first point. Mill has
made as naïve and artless a use of the naturalistic fallacy as
anybody could desire. 'Good,' he tells us, means 'desirable,'
and you can only find out what is desirable by seeking to find
out what is actually desired. This is, of course, only one step
towards the proof of Hedonism; for it may be, as Mill goes on
to say, that other things beside pleasure are desired. Whether or
not pleasure is the only thing desired is, as Mill himself admits
(p. 58), a psychological question, to which we shall presently
proceed. The important step for Ethics is this one just taken,
the step which pretends to prove that 'good' means 'desired.'

Well, the fallacy in this step is so obvious, that it is quite wonderful how Mill failed to see it. The fact is that 'desirable' does not mean 'able to be desired' as 'visible' means 'able to be seen.' The desirable means simply what *ought* to be desired or *deserves* to be desired; just as the detestable means not what can be but what ought to be detested and the damnable what deserves to be damned. Mill has, then, smuggled in, under cover of the word 'desirable,' the very notion about which he ought to be quite clear. 'Desirable' does indeed mean 'what it is good to desire'; but when this is understood, it is no longer plausible to say that our only test of *that*, is what is actually desired. Is it merely a tautology when the Prayer Book talks of *good* desires? Are not *bad* desires also possible? Nay, we find Mill himself talking of a 'better and nobler object of desire' (p. 10), as if, after all, what is desired were not *ipso facto* good, and good in proportion to the amount it is desired. Moreover, if the desired is *ipso facto* the good; then the good is *ipso facto* the motive of our actions, and there can be no question of finding motives for doing it, as Mill is at such pains to do. If Mill's explanation of 'desirable' be *true*, then his statement (p. 26) that the rule of action may be *confounded* with the motive of it is untrue: for the motive of action will then be according to him *ipso facto* its rule; there can be no distinction between the two, and therefore no confusion, and thus he has contradicted himself flatly. These are specimens of the contradictions, which, as I have tried to shew, must always follow from the use of the naturalistic fallacy; and I hope I need now say no more about the matter.

41. Well, then, the first step by which Mill has attempted to establish his Hedonism is simply fallacious. He has attempted to establish the identity of the good with the desired, by confusing the proper sense of 'desirable,' in which it denotes that which it is good to desire, with the sense which it would bear if it were analogous to such words as 'visible.' If 'desirable' is to be identical with 'good,' then it must bear one sense; and if it is to be identical with 'desired,' then it must bear quite another sense. And yet to Mill's contention that the desired is necessarily good, it is quite essential that these two senses of 'desirable' should be the same. If he holds they are the same, then he has contradicted himself elsewhere; if he holds they are not the same, then the first step in his proof of Hedonism is absolutely worthless.

But now we must deal with the second step. Having proved, as he thinks, that the good means the desired, Mill recognises that, if he is further to maintain that pleasure alone is good, he must prove that pleasure alone is really desired. This doctrine that 'pleasure alone is the object of all our desires' is the doctrine which Prof. Sidgwick has called Psychological Hedonism: and it is a doctrine which most eminent psychologists are now agreed in rejecting. But it is a necessary step in the proof of any such Naturalistic Hedonism as Mill's; and it is so commonly held, by people not expert either in psychology or in philosophy, that I wish to treat it at some length. It will be seen that Mill does not hold it in this bare form. He admits that other things than pleasure are desired; and this admission is at once a contradiction of his Hedonism. One of the shifts by which he seeks to evade this contradiction we shall afterwards consider. But some may think that no such shifts are needed: they may say of Mill, what Callicles says of Polus in the *Gorgias*[1], that he has made this fatal admission through a most unworthy fear of appearing paradoxical; that they, on the other hand, will have the courage of their convictions, and will not be ashamed to go to any lengths of paradox, in defence of what they hold to be the truth.

42. Well, then, we are supposing it held that pleasure is the object of all desire, that it is the universal end of all human activity. Now I suppose it will not be denied that people are commonly said to desire other things: for instance, we usually talk of desiring food and drink, of desiring money, approbation, fame. The question, then, must be of what is meant by desire, and by the object of desire. There is obviously asserted some sort of necessary or universal relation between something which is called desire, and another thing which is called pleasure. The question is of what sort this relation is; whether in conjunction with the naturalistic fallacy above mentioned, it will justify

[1] 481 c—487 b.

Hedonism. Now I am not prepared to deny that there is some universal relation between pleasure and desire; but I hope to shew, that, if there is, it is of such sort as will rather make against than for Hedonism. It is urged that pleasure is always the object of desire, and I am ready to admit that pleasure is always, in part at least, the *cause* of desire. But this distinction is very important. Both views might be expressed in the same language; both might be said to hold that whenever we desire, we always desire *because of* some pleasure: if I asked my supposed Hedonist, ' Why do you desire that?' he might answer, quite consistently with his contention, ' Because there is pleasure there,' and if he asked me the same question, I might answer, equally consistently with my contention, ' Because there is pleasure here.' Only our two answers would not mean the same thing. It is this use of the same language to denote quite different facts, which I believe to be the chief cause why Psychological Hedonism is so often held, just as it was also the cause of Mill's naturalistic fallacy.

Let us try to analyse the psychological state which is called ' desire.' That name is usually confined to a state of mind in which the idea of some object or event, not yet existing, is present to us. Suppose, for instance, I am desiring a glass of port wine. I have the idea of drinking such a glass before my mind, although I am not yet drinking it. Well, how does pleasure enter in to this relation ? My theory is that it enters in, in this way. The *idea* of the drinking causes a feeling of pleasure in my mind, which helps to produce that state of incipient activity, which is called ' desire.' It is, therefore, because of a pleasure, which I already have—the pleasure excited by a mere idea—that I desire the wine, which I have not. And I am ready to admit that a pleasure of this kind, an actual pleasure, is always among the causes of every desire, and not only of every desire, but of every mental activity, whether conscious or sub-conscious. I am ready to *admit* this, I say : I cannot vouch that it is the true psychological doctrine; but, at all events, it is not *primâ facie* quite absurd. And now, what is the other doctrine, the doctrine which I am supposing held, and which is at all events essential to Mill's argument ?

4   M

It is this. That when I desire the wine, it is not the wine which I desire but the pleasure which I expect to get from it. In other words, the doctrine is that the idea of a pleasure *not actual* is always necessary to cause desire; whereas my doctrine was that the *actual* pleasure caused by the idea of something else was always necessary to cause desire. It is these two different theories which I suppose the Psychological Hedonists to confuse: the confusion is, as Mr Bradley puts it[1], between 'a pleasant thought' and 'the thought of a pleasure.' It is in fact only where the latter, the 'thought of a pleasure,' is present, that pleasure can be said to be the *object* of desire, or the *motive* to action. On the other hand, when only a pleasant thought is present, as, I admit, *may* always be the case, then it is the object of the thought—that which we are thinking about—which is the object of desire and the motive to action; and the pleasure, which that thought excites, may, indeed, cause our desire or move us to action, but it is not our end or object nor our motive.

Well, I hope this distinction is sufficiently clear. Now let us see how it bears upon Ethical Hedonism. I assume it to be perfectly obvious that the idea of the object of desire is not always and only the idea of a pleasure. In the first place, plainly, we are not always conscious of expecting pleasure, when we desire a thing. We may be only conscious of the thing which we desire, and may be impelled to make for it at once, without any calculation as to whether it will bring us pleasure or pain. And, in the second place, even when we do expect pleasure, it can certainly be very rarely pleasure *only* which we desire. For instance, granted that, when I desire my glass of port wine, I have also an idea of the pleasure I expect from it, plainly that pleasure cannot be the only object of my desire; the port wine must be included in my object, else I might be led by my desire to take wormwood instead of wine. If the desire were directed *solely* towards the pleasure, it could not lead me to take the wine; if it is to take a definite direction, it is absolutely necessary that the idea of the object, from which the pleasure is expected, should also be present and

<hr>

[1] *Ethical Studies*, p. 232.

should control my activity. The theory then that what is desired is always and only pleasure must break down: it is impossible to prove that pleasure alone is good, by that line of argument. But, if we substitute for this theory, that other, possibly true, theory, that pleasure is always the cause of desire, then all the plausibility of our ethical doctrine that pleasure alone is good straightway disappears. For in this case, pleasure is not what I desire, it is not what I want: it is something which I already have, before I can want anything. And can any one feel inclined to maintain, that that which I already have, while I am still desiring something else, is always and alone the good?

43. But now let us return to consider another of Mill's arguments for his position that 'happiness is the sole end of human action.' Mill admits, as I have said, that pleasure is not the only thing we actually desire. 'The desire of virtue,' he says, 'is not as universal, but it is as authentic a fact, as the desire of happiness[1].' And again, 'Money is, in many cases, desired in and for itself[2].' These admissions are, of course, in naked and glaring contradiction with his argument that pleasure is the only thing desirable, because it is the only thing desired. How then does Mill even attempt to avoid this contradiction? His chief argument seems to be that 'virtue,' 'money' and other such objects, when they are thus desired in and for themselves, are desired only as 'a part of happiness[3].' Now what does this mean? Happiness, as we saw, has been defined by Mill, as 'pleasure and the absence of pain.' Does Mill mean to say that 'money,' these actual coins, which he admits to be desired in and for themselves, are a part either of pleasure or of the absence of pain? Will he maintain that those coins themselves are in my mind, and actually a part of my pleasant feelings? If this is to be said, all words are useless: nothing can possibly be distinguished from anything else; if these two things are not distinct, what on earth is? We shall hear next that this table is really and truly the same thing as this room; that a cab-horse is in fact indistinguishable from St Paul's Cathedral; that this book of Mill's which I hold in

[1] p. 53.   [2] p. 55.   [3] pp. 56—7.

4-2

my hand, because it was his pleasure to produce it, is now and at this moment a part of the happiness which he felt many years ago and which has so long ceased to be. Pray consider a moment what this contemptible nonsense really means. 'Money,' says Mill, 'is only desirable as a means to happiness.' Perhaps so; but what then? 'Why,' says Mill, 'money is undoubtedly desired for its own sake.' 'Yes, go on,' say we. 'Well,' says Mill, 'if money is desired for its own sake, it must be desirable as an end-in-itself: I have said so myself.' 'Oh,' say we, 'but you also said just now that it was only desirable as a means.' 'I own I did,' says Mill, 'but I will try to patch up matters, by saying that what is only a means to an end, is the same thing as a part of that end. I daresay the public won't notice.' And the public haven't noticed. Yet this is certainly what Mill has done. He has broken down the distinction between means and ends, upon the precise observance of which his Hedonism rests. And he has been compelled to do this, because he has failed to distinguish 'end' in the sense of what is desirable, from 'end' in the sense of what is desired: a distinction which, nevertheless, both the present argument and his whole book presupposes. This is a consequence of the naturalistic fallacy.

44. Mill, then, has nothing better to say for himself than this. His two fundamental propositions are, in his own words, 'that to think of an object as desirable (unless for the sake of its consequences), and to think of it as pleasant, are one and the same thing; and that to desire anything except in proportion as the idea of it is pleasant, is a physical and metaphysical impossibility[1].' Both of these statements are, we have seen, merely supported by fallacies. The first seems to rest on the naturalistic fallacy ; the second rests partly on this, partly on the fallacy of confusing ends and means, and partly on the fallacy of confusing a pleasant thought with the thought of a pleasure. His very language shews this. For that the idea of a thing is pleasant, in his second clause, is obviously meant to be the same fact which he denotes by 'thinking of it as pleasant,' in his first.

Accordingly, Mill's arguments for the proposition that pleasure is the sole good, and our refutation of those arguments, may be summed up as follows:

First of all, he takes 'the desirable,' which he uses as a synonym for 'the good,' to *mean* what *can* be desired. The test, again, of what can be desired, is, according to him, what actually is desired: if, therefore, he says, we can find some one thing which is always and alone desired, that thing will necessarily be the only thing that is desirable, the only thing that is good as an end. In this argument the naturalistic fallacy is plainly involved. That fallacy, I explained, consists in the contention that good *means* nothing but some simple or complex notion, that can be defined in terms of natural qualities. In Mill's case, good is thus supposed to *mean* simply what is desired; and what is desired is something which can thus be defined in natural terms. Mill tells us that we ought to desire something (an ethical proposition), because we actually do desire it; but if his contention that 'I ought to desire' means nothing but 'I do desire' were true, then he is only entitled to say, 'We do desire so and so, because we do desire it'; and that is not an ethical proposition at all; it is a mere tautology. The whole object of Mill's book is to help us to discover what we ought to do; but, in fact, by attempting to define the meaning of this 'ought,' he has completely debarred himself from ever fulfilling that object: he has confined himself to telling us what we do do.

Mill's first argument then is that, because good means desired, therefore the desired is good; but having thus arrived at an ethical conclusion, by denying that any ethical conclusion is possible, he still needs another argument to make his conclusion a basis for Hedonism. He has to prove that we always do desire pleasure or freedom from pain, and that we never desire anything else whatever. This second doctrine, which Professor Sidgwick has called Psychological Hedonism, I accordingly discussed. I pointed out how obviously untrue it is that we never desire anything but pleasure; and how there is not a shadow of ground for saying even that, whenever we desire anything, we always desire pleasure *as well as* that thing.

I attributed the obstinate belief in these untruths partly to
a confusion between the cause of desire and the object of desire.
It may, I said, be true that desire can never occur unless it be
preceded by some *actual* pleasure; but even if this is true, it
obviously gives no ground for saying that the object of desire is
always some *future* pleasure. By the object of desire is meant
that, of which the idea causes desire in us; it is some pleasure,
which we anticipate, some pleasure which we have not got,
which is the object of desire, whenever we do desire pleasure.
And any actual pleasure, which may be excited by the idea of
this anticipated pleasure, is obviously not the same pleasure as
that anticipated pleasure, of which only the idea is actual. This
actual pleasure is not what we want; what we want is always
something which we have not got; and to say that pleasure
always causes us to want is quite a different thing from saying
that what we want is always pleasure.

Finally, we saw, Mill admits all this. He insists that we
do *actually* desire other things than pleasure, and yet he says
we do *really* desire nothing else. He tries to explain away this
contradiction, by confusing together two notions, which he has
before carefully distinguished—the notions of means and of end.
He now says that a means to an end is the same thing as a
part of that end. To this last fallacy special attention should
be given, as our ultimate decision with regard to Hedonism will
largely turn upon it.

45.   It is this ultimate decision with regard to Hedonism
at which we must now try to arrive. So far I have been
only occupied with refuting Mill's naturalistic arguments for
Hedonism; but the doctrine that pleasure alone is desirable
may still be true, although Mill's fallacies cannot prove it
so. This is the question which we have now to face. This
proposition, 'pleasure alone is good or desirable,' belongs undoubtedly to that class of propositions, to which Mill at first
rightly pretended it belonged, the class of first principles, which
are not amenable to direct proof. But in this case, as he
also rightly says, 'considerations may be presented capable of
determining the intellect either to give or withhold its assent to
the doctrine' (p. 7). It is such considerations that Professor

Sidgwick presents, and such also that I shall try to present
for the opposite view.   This proposition that 'pleasure alone
is good as an end,' the fundamental proposition of Ethical
Hedonism, will then appear, in Professor Sidgwick's language,
as an object of intuition. I shall try to shew you why my
intuition denies it, just as his intuition affirms it. It *may*
always be true notwithstanding; neither intuition can *prove*
whether it is true or not; I am bound to be satisfied, if I can
'present considerations capable of determining the intellect' to
reject it.

Now it may be said that this is a very unsatisfactory state
of things. It is indeed; but it is important to make a distinction between two different reasons, which may be given
for calling it unsatisfactory. Is it unsatisfactory because our
principle cannot be proved? or is it unsatisfactory merely
because we do not agree with one another about it? I am
inclined to think that the latter is the chief reason. For the
mere fact that in certain cases proof is impossible does not
usually give us the least uneasiness. For instance, nobody can
prove that this is a chair beside me; yet I do not suppose
that any one is much dissatisfied for that reason. We all agree
that it is a chair, and that is enough to content us, although
it is quite possible we may be wrong. A madman, of course,
might come in and say that it is not a chair but an elephant.
We could not prove that he was wrong, and the fact that he
did not agree with us might then begin to make us uneasy.
Much more, then, shall we be uneasy, if some one, whom we
do not think to be mad, disagrees with us. We shall try to
argue with him, and we shall probably be content if we lead
him to agree with us, although we shall not have proved our
point. We can only persuade him by shewing him that our
view is consistent with something else which he holds to be
true, whereas his original view is contradictory to it. But it
will be impossible to prove that that something else, which
we both agree to be true, is really so; we shall be satisfied
to have settled the matter in dispute by means of it, merely
because we are agreed on it. In short, our dissatisfaction in these
cases is almost always of the type felt by the poor lunatic in

the story. 'I said the world was mad,' says he, 'and the
world said that I was mad; and, confound it, they outvoted
me.' It is, I say, almost always such a disagreement, and not
the impossibility of proof, which makes us call the state of
things unsatisfactory. For, indeed, who can prove that proof
itself is a warrant of truth? We are all agreed that the laws
of logic are true and therefore we accept a result which is
proved by their means; but such a proof is satisfactory to us
only because we are all so fully agreed that it is a warrant
of truth. And yet we cannot, by the nature of the case, prove
that we are right in being so agreed.

Accordingly, I do not think we need be much distressed
by our admission that we cannot prove whether pleasure alone
is good or not. We may be able to arrive at an agreement
notwithstanding; and if so, I think it will be satisfactory.
And yet I am not very sanguine about our prospects of such
satisfaction. Ethics, and philosophy in general, have always
been in a peculiarly unsatisfactory state. There has been no
agreement about them, as there is about the existence of chairs
and lights and benches. I should therefore be a fool if I
hoped to settle one great point of controversy, now and once
for all. It is extremely improbable I shall convince. It would
be highly presumptuous even to hope that in the end, say
two or three centuries hence, it will be agreed that pleasure
is not the sole good. Philosophical questions are so difficult,
the problems they raise are so complex, that no one can fairly
expect, now, any more than in the past, to win more than a
very limited assent. And yet I confess that the considerations
which I am about to present appear to me to be absolutely
convincing. I do think that they *ought* to convince, if only I
can put them well. In any case, I can but try. I *shall* try
now to put an end to that unsatisfactory state of things, of
which I have been speaking. I shall try to produce an agreement that the fundamental principle of Hedonism is very like
an absurdity, by shewing what it must mean, if it is clearly
thought out, and how that clear meaning is in conflict with
other beliefs, which will, I hope, not be so easily given up.

46. Well, then, we now proceed to discuss Intuitionistic

Hedonism. And the beginning of this discussion marks, it is to be observed, a turning-point in my ethical method. The point I have been labouring hitherto, the point that 'good is indefinable,' and that to deny this involves a fallacy, is a point capable of strict proof: for to deny it involves contradictions. But now we are coming to the question, for the sake of answering which Ethics exists, the question what things or qualities are good. Of any answer to *this* question no direct proof is possible, and that, just because of our former answer, as to the meaning of good, direct proof *was* possible. We are now confined to the hope of what Mill calls 'indirect proof,' the hope of determining one another's intellect; and we are now so confined, just because, in the matter of the former question we are not so confined. Here, then, is an intuition to be submitted to our verdict—the intuition that 'pleasure alone is good as an end—good in and for itself.'

47. Well, in this connection it seems first desirable to touch on another doctrine of Mill's—another doctrine which, in the interest of Hedonism, Professor Sidgwick has done very wisely to reject. This is the doctrine of 'difference of quality in pleasures.' 'If I am asked,' says Mill[1], 'what I mean by difference of quality in pleasures, or what makes one pleasure more valuable than another, merely as a pleasure, except its being greater in amount, there is but one possible answer. Of two pleasures, if there be one to which all or almost all who have experience of both give a decided preference, irrespective of any feeling of moral obligation to prefer it, that is the more desirable pleasure. If one of the two is, by those who are competently acquainted with both, placed so far above the other that they prefer it, even though knowing it to be attended with a greater amount of discontent, and would not resign it for any quantity of the other pleasure which their nature is capable of, we are justified in ascribing to the preferred enjoyment a superiority in quality, so far outweighing quantity as to render it, in comparison, of small account.'

Now it is well known that Bentham rested his case for Hedonism on 'quantity of pleasure' alone. It was his maxim,

[1] p. 12.

that 'quantity of pleasure being equal, pushpin is as good as poetry.' And Mill apparently considers Bentham to have proved that nevertheless poetry is better than pushpin; that poetry does produce a greater quantity of pleasure. But yet, says Mill, the Utilitarians 'might have taken the other and, as it may be called, higher ground, with entire consistency' (p. 11). Now we see from this that Mill acknowledges 'quality of pleasure' to be another or different ground for estimating pleasures, than Bentham's quantity; and moreover, by that question-begging 'higher,' which he afterwards translates into 'superior,' he seems to betray an uncomfortable feeling, that, after all, if you take quantity of pleasure for your only standard, something may be wrong and you may deserve to be called a pig. And it may presently appear that you very likely would deserve that name. But, meanwhile, I only wish to shew that Mill's admissions as to quality of pleasure are either inconsistent with his Hedonism, or else afford no other ground for it than would be given by mere quantity of pleasure.

It will be seen that Mill's test for one pleasure's superiority in quality over another is the preference of most people who have experienced both. A pleasure so preferred, he holds, is more desirable. But then, as we have seen, he holds that 'to think of an object as desirable and to think of it as pleasant are one and the same thing' (p. 58). He holds, therefore, that the preference of experts merely proves that one pleasure is pleasanter than another. But if that is so, how can he distinguish this standard from the standard of quantity of pleasure? Can one pleasure be pleasanter than another, except in the sense that it gives *more* pleasure? 'Pleasant' must, if words are to have any meaning at all, denote some one quality common to all the things that are pleasant; and, if so, then one thing can only be more pleasant than another, according as it has more or less of this one quality. But, then, let us try the other alternative, and suppose that Mill does not seriously mean that this preference of experts merely proves one pleasure to be pleasanter than another. Well, in this case what does 'preferred' mean? It cannot mean 'more desired,' since, as we know, the degree of desire is always, according to Mill, in exact proportion to the degree of pleasantness. But, in that case, the basis of Mill's Hedonism collapses, for he is admitting that one thing may be preferred over another, and thus proved more desirable, although it is not more desired. In this case Mill's judgment of preference is just a judgment of that intuitional kind which I have been contending to be necessary to establish the hedonistic or any other principle. It is a direct judgment that one thing is more desirable, or better than another; a judgment utterly independent of all considerations as to whether one thing is more desired or pleasanter than another. This is to admit that good is good and indefinable.

48. And note another point that is brought out by this discussion. Mill's judgment of preference, so far from establishing the principle that pleasure alone is good, is obviously inconsistent with it. He admits that experts can judge whether one pleasure is more desirable than another, because pleasures differ in quality. But what does this mean? If one pleasure can differ from another in quality, that means, that *a* pleasure is something complex, something composed, in fact, of pleasure *in addition to* that which produces pleasure. For instance, Mill speaks of 'sensual indulgences' as 'lower pleasures.' But what is a sensual indulgence? It is surely a certain excitement of some sense *together with* the pleasure caused by such excitement. Mill, therefore, in admitting that a sensual indulgence can be directly judged to be lower than another pleasure, in which the degree of pleasure involved may be the same, is admitting that other things may be good, or bad, quite independently of the pleasure which accompanies them. *A* pleasure is, in fact, merely a misleading term which conceals the fact that what we are dealing with is not pleasure but something else, which may indeed necessarily produce pleasure, but is nevertheless quite distinct from it.

Mill, therefore, in thinking that to estimate quality of pleasure is quite consistent with his hedonistic principle that pleasure and absence of pain alone are desirable as ends, has again committed the fallacy of confusing ends and means. For take even the most favourable supposition of his meaning; let

us suppose that by a pleasure he does not mean, as his words
imply, that which produces pleasure and the pleasure produced.
Let us suppose him to mean that there are various kinds of
pleasure, in the sense in which there are various kinds of
colour—blue, red, green, etc. Even in this case, if we are to
say that our end is colour alone, then, although it is impossible
we should have colour without having some particular colour,
yet the particular colour we must have, is only a *means* to our
having colour, if colour is really our end. And if colour is our
only possible end, as Mill says pleasure is, then there can be
no possible reason for preferring one colour to another, red, for
instance, to blue, except that the one is more of a colour than
the other. Yet the opposite of this is what Mill is attempting
to hold with regard to pleasures.

Accordingly a consideration of Mill's view that some pleasures
are superior to others *in quality* brings out one point which
may 'help to determine the intellect' with regard to the
intuition 'Pleasure is the only good.' For it brings out the fact
that if you say 'pleasure,' you must mean 'pleasure': you must
mean some one thing common to all different 'pleasures,' some
one thing, which may exist in different degrees, but which
cannot differ in *kind*. I have pointed out that, if you say, as
Mill does, that quality of pleasure is to be taken into account,
then you are no longer holding that pleasure *alone* is good as an
end, since you imply that something else, something which
is *not* present in all pleasures, is *also* good as an end. The
illustration I have given from colour expresses this point in its
most acute form. It is plain that if you say 'Colour alone is
good as an end,' then you can give no possible reason for
preferring one colour to another. Your only standard of good
and bad will then be 'colour'; and since red and blue both
conform equally to this, the only standard, you can have no
other whereby to judge whether red is better than blue. It is
true that you cannot have colour unless you also have one or all
of the particular colours: they, therefore, if colour is the end,
will all be good as means, but none of them can be better than
another even as a means, far less can any one of them be
regarded as an end in itself. Just so with pleasure: If we do

really mean 'Pleasure alone is good as an end,' then we must agree with Bentham that 'Quantity of pleasure being equal, pushpin is as good as poetry.' To have thus dismissed Mill's reference to quality of pleasure, is therefore to have made one step in the desired direction. The reader will now no longer be prevented from agreeing with me, by any idea that the hedonistic principle 'Pleasure alone is good as an end' is consistent with the view that one pleasure may be of a better quality than another. These two views, we have seen, are contradictory to one another. We must choose between them : and if we choose the latter, then we must give up the principle of Hedonism.

49. But, as I said, Professor Sidgwick has seen that they are inconsistent. He has seen that he must choose between them. He has chosen. He has rejected the test by quality of pleasure, and has accepted the hedonistic principle. He still maintains that 'Pleasure alone is good as an end.' I propose therefore to discuss the considerations which he has offered in order to convince us. I shall hope by that discussion to remove some more of such prejudices and misunderstandings as might prevent agreement with me. If I can shew that some of the considerations which Professor Sidgwick urges are such as we need by no means agree with, and that others are actually rather in my favour than in his, we may have again advanced a few steps nearer to the unanimity which we desire.

50. The passages in the *Methods of Ethics* to which I shall now invite attention are to be found in I. IX. 4 and in III. XIV. 4—5.

The first of these two passages runs as follows :

"I think that if we consider carefully such permanent results as are commonly judged to be good, other than qualities of human beings, we can find nothing that, on reflection, appears to possess this quality of goodness out of relation to human existence, or at least to some consciousness or feeling.

"For example, we commonly judge some inanimate objects, scenes, etc. to be good as possessing beauty, and others bad from ugliness: still no one would consider it rational to aim at the production of beauty in external nature, apart from any

possible contemplation of it by human beings. In fact when
beauty is maintained to be objective, it is not commonly meant
that it exists as beauty out of relation to any mind whatsoever:
but only that there is some standard of beauty valid for all minds.

"It may, however, be said that beauty and other results
commonly judged to be good, though we do not conceive them
to exist out of relation to human beings (or at least minds of
some kind), are yet so far separable as ends from the human
beings on whom their existence depends, that their realization
may conceivably come into competition with the perfection
or happiness of these beings. Thus, though beautiful things
cannot be thought worth producing except as possible objects
of contemplation, still a man may devote himself to their
production without any consideration of the persons who are
to contemplate them. Similarly knowledge is a good which
cannot exist except in minds; and yet one may be more
interested in the development of knowledge than in its possession
by any particular minds; and may take the former as an
ultimate end without regarding the latter.

"Still, as soon as the alternatives are clearly apprehended,
it will, I think, be generally held that beauty, knowledge, and
other ideal goods, as well as all external material things, are
only reasonably to be sought by men in so far as they conduce
(1) to Happiness or (2) to the Perfection or Excellence of
human existence. I say 'human,' for though most utilitarians
consider the pleasure (and freedom from pain) of the inferior
animals to be included in the Happiness which they take as the
right and proper end of conduct, no one seems to contend that
we ought to aim at perfecting brutes except as a means to our
ends, or at least as objects of scientific or æsthetic contemplation
for us. Nor, again, can we include, as a practical end, the
existence of beings above the human. We certainly apply the
idea of Good to the Divine Existence, just as we do to His
work, and indeed in a preeminent manner: and when it is said
that, 'we should do all things to the glory of God,' it may seem
to be implied that the existence of God is made better by our
glorifying Him. Still this inference when explicitly drawn
appears somewhat impious; and theologians generally recoil from

it, and refrain from using the notion of a possible addition to the Goodness of the Divine Existence as a ground of human duty. Nor can the influence of our actions on other extra-human intelligences besides the Divine be at present made matter of scientific discussion.

"I shall therefore confidently lay down, that if there be any Good other than Happiness to be sought by man, as an ultimate practical end, it can only be the Goodness, Perfection, or Excellence of Human Existence. How far this notion includes more than Virtue, what its precise relation to Pleasure is, and to what method we shall be logically led if we accept it as fundamental, are questions which we shall more conveniently discuss after the detailed examination of these two other notions, Pleasure and Virtue, in which we shall be engaged in the two following Books."

It will be observed that in this passage Prof. Sidgwick tries to limit the range of objects among which the ultimate end may be found. He does not yet say what that end is, but he does exclude from it everything but certain characters of Human Existence. And the possible ends, which he thus excludes, do not again come up for consideration. They are put out of court once for all by this passage and by this passage only. Now is this exclusion justified?

I cannot think it is. 'No one,' says Prof. Sidgwick, 'would consider it rational to aim at the production of beauty in external nature, apart from any possible contemplation of it by human beings.' Well, I may say at once, that I, for one, do consider this rational; and let us see if I cannot get any one to agree with me. Consider what this admission really means. It entitles us to put the following case. Let us imagine one world exceedingly beautiful. Imagine it as beautiful as you can; put into it whatever on this earth you most admire— mountains, rivers, the sea; trees, and sunsets, stars and moon. Imagine these all combined in the most exquisite proportions, so that no one thing jars against another, but each contributes to increase the beauty of the whole. And then imagine the ugliest world you can possibly conceive. Imagine it simply one heap of filth, containing everything that is most disgusting to us, for whatever reason, and the whole, as far as may be, without one redeeming feature. Such a pair of worlds we are entitled to compare: they fall within Prof. Sidgwick's meaning, and the comparison is highly relevant to it. The only thing we are not entitled to imagine is that any human being ever has or ever, by any possibility, *can*, live in either, can ever see and enjoy the beauty of the one or hate the foulness of the other. Well, even so, supposing them quite apart from any possible contemplation by human beings; still, is it irrational to hold that it is better that the beautiful world should exist, than the one which is ugly? Would it not be well, in any case, to do what we could to produce it rather than the other? Certainly I cannot help thinking that it would; and I hope that some may agree with me in this extreme instance. The instance is extreme. It is highly improbable, not to say, impossible, we should ever have such a choice before us. In any actual choice we should have to consider the possible effects of our action upon conscious beings, and among these possible effects there are always some, I think, which ought to be preferred to the existence of mere beauty. But this only means that in our present state, in which but a very small portion of the good is attainable, the pursuit of beauty for its own sake must always be postponed to the pursuit of some greater good, which is equally attainable. But it is enough for my purpose, if it be admitted that, *supposing* no greater good were at all attainable, then beauty must in itself be regarded as a greater good than ugliness; if it be admitted that, in that case, we should not be left without any reason for preferring one course of action to another, we should not be left without any duty whatever, but that it would then be our positive duty to make the world more beautiful, so far as we were able, since nothing better than beauty could then result from our efforts. If this be once admitted, if in any imaginable case you do admit that the existence of a more beautiful thing is better in itself than that of one more ugly, quite apart from its effects on any human feeling, then Prof. Sidgwick's principle has broken down. Then we shall have to include in our ultimate end something beyond the limits of human existence. I admit, of course, that our beautiful world would be better still, if there were human beings in it to contemplate and enjoy its beauty. But that admission makes nothing against my point. If it be once admitted that the beautiful world *in itself* is better than the ugly, then it follows, that however many beings may enjoy it, and however much better their enjoyment may be than it is itself, yet its mere existence adds *something* to the goodness of the whole: it is not only a means to our end, but also itself a part thereof.

51. In the second passage to which I referred above, Prof. Sidgwick returns from the discussion of Virtue and Pleasure, with which he has meanwhile been engaged, to consider what among the parts of Human Existence to which, as we saw, he has limited the ultimate end, can really be considered as such end. What I have just said, of course, appears to me to destroy the force of this part of his argument too. If, as I think, other things than any part of Human Existence can be ends-in-themselves, then Prof. Sidgwick cannot claim to have discovered the Summum Bonum, when he has merely determined what parts of Human Existence are in themselves desirable. But this error may be admitted to be utterly insignificant in comparison with that which we are now about to discuss.

"It may be said," says Prof. Sidgwick (III. xiv. §§4—5), "that we may...regard cognition of Truth, contemplation of Beauty, Free or Virtuous action, as in some measure preferable alternatives to Pleasure or Happiness—even though we admit that Happiness must be included as a part of Ultimate Good....I think, however, that this view ought not to commend itself to the sober judgment of reflective persons. In order to shew this, I must ask the reader to use the same twofold procedure that I before requested him to employ in considering the absolute and independent validity of common moral precepts. I appeal firstly to his intuitive judgment after due consideration of the question when fairly placed before it: and secondly to a comprehensive comparison of the ordinary judgments of mankind. As regards the first argument, to me at least it seems clear after reflection that these objective relations of the conscious

subject, when distinguished from the consciousness accompanying and resulting from them, are not ultimately and intrinsically
desirable; any more than material or other objects are, when
considered apart from any relation to conscious existence. Admitting that we have actual experience of such preferences
as have just been described, of which the ultimate object is
something that is not merely consciousness: it still seems to
me that when (to use Butler's phrase) we 'sit down in a cool
hour,' we can only justify to ourselves the importance that we
attach to any of these objects by considering its conduciveness,
in one way or another, to the happiness of sentient beings.

"The second argument, that refers to the common sense of
mankind, obviously cannot be made completely cogent; since,
as above stated, several cultivated persons do habitually judge
that knowledge, art, etc.,—not to speak of Virtue—are ends
independently of the pleasure derived from them. But we may
urge not only that all these elements of 'ideal good' are
productive of pleasure in various ways; but also that they seem
to obtain the commendation of Common Sense, roughly speaking,
in proportion to the degree of this productiveness. This seems
obviously true of Beauty; and will hardly be denied in respect
of any kind of social ideal: it is paradoxical to maintain that
any degree of Freedom, or any form of social order, would still
be commonly regarded as desirable even if we were certain that
it had no tendency to promote the general happiness. The
case of Knowledge is rather more complex; but certainly
Common Sense is most impressed with the value of knowledge,
when its 'fruitfulness' has been demonstrated. It is, however,
aware that experience has frequently shewn how knowledge,
long fruitless, may become unexpectedly fruitful, and how light
may be shed on one part of the field of knowledge from another
apparently remote: and even if any particular branch of scientific
pursuit could be shewn to be devoid of even this indirect utility,
it would still deserve some respect on utilitarian grounds; both
as furnishing to the inquirer the refined and innocent pleasures
of curiosity, and because the intellectual disposition which it
exhibits and sustains is likely on the whole to produce fruitful
knowledge. Still in cases approximating to this last, Common

Sense is somewhat disposed to complain of the mis-direction of valuable effort; so that the meed of honour commonly paid to Science seems to be graduated, though perhaps unconsciously, by a tolerably exact utilitarian scale. Certainly the moment the legitimacy of any branch of scientific inquiry is seriously disputed, as in the recent case of vivisection, the controversy on both sides is generally conducted on an avowedly utilitarian basis.

"The case of Virtue requires special consideration: since the encouragement in each other of virtuous impulses and dispositions is a main aim of men's ordinary moral discourse; so that even to raise the question whether this encouragement can go too far has a paradoxical air. Still, our experience includes rare and exceptional cases in which the concentration of effort on the cultivation of virtue has seemed to have effects adverse to general happiness, through being intensified to the point of moral fanaticism, and so involving a neglect of other conditions of happiness. If, then, we admit as actual or possible such 'infelicific' effects of the cultivation of Virtue, I think we shall also generally admit that, in the case supposed, conduciveness to general happiness should be the criterion for deciding how far the cultivation of Virtue should be carried."

There we have Prof. Sidgwick's argument completed. We ought not, he thinks, to aim at knowing the Truth, or at contemplating Beauty, except in so far as such knowledge or such contemplation contributes to increase the pleasure or to diminish the pain of sentient beings. Pleasure alone is good for its own sake: knowledge of the Truth is good only as a means to pleasure.

52. Let us consider what this means. What is pleasure? It is certainly something of which we may be conscious, and which, therefore, may be distinguished from our consciousness of it. What I wish first to ask is this: Can it really be said that we value pleasure, except in so far as we are conscious of it? Should we think that the attainment of pleasure, of which we never were and never could be conscious, was something to be aimed at for its own sake? It may be impossible that such pleasure should ever exist, that it should ever be thus

divorced from consciousness; although there is certainly much reason to believe that it is not only possible but very common. But, even supposing that it were impossible, that is quite irrelevant. Our question is: Is it the pleasure, as distinct from the consciousness of it, that we set value on? Do we think the pleasure valuable in itself, or must we insist that, if we are to think the pleasure good, we must have consciousness of it too?

This consideration is very well put by Socrates in Plato's dialogue *Philebus* (21 A).

'Would *you* accept, Protarchus,' says Socrates, 'to live your whole life in the enjoyment of the greatest pleasures?' 'Of course I would,' says Protarchus.

Socrates. Then would you think you needed anything else besides, if you possessed this one blessing in completeness?

Protarchus. Certainly not.

Socrates. Consider what you are saying. You would not need to be wise and intelligent and reasonable, nor anything like this? Would you not even care to keep your sight?

Protarchus. Why should I? I suppose I should have all I want, if I was pleased.

Socrates. Well, then, supposing you lived so, you would enjoy always throughout your life the greatest pleasure?

Protarchus. Of course.

Socrates. But, on the other hand, inasmuch as you would *not* possess intelligence and memory and knowledge and true opinion, you would, in the first place, necessarily be without the knowledge whether you were pleased or not. For you would be devoid of any kind of wisdom. You admit this?

Protarchus. I do. The consequence is absolutely necessary.

Socrates. Well, then, besides this, not having memory, you must also be unable to remember even that you ever were pleased; of the pleasure which falls upon you at the moment not the least vestige must afterwards remain. And again, not having true opinion, you cannot think that you are pleased when you are; and, being bereft of your reasoning faculties, you cannot even have the power to reckon that you will be pleased in future. You must live the life of an oyster, or of some other of those living creatures, whose home is the seas and whose souls are concealed in shelly bodies. Is all this so, or can we think otherwise than this?

Protarchus. How can we?

Socrates. Well, then, can we think such a life desirable?

Protarchus. Socrates, your reasoning has left me utterly dumb.'

Socrates, we see, persuades Protarchus that Hedonism is absurd. If we are really going to maintain that pleasure alone is good as an end, we must maintain that it is good, whether we are conscious of it or not. We must declare it reasonable to take as our ideal (an unattainable ideal it may be) that we should be as happy as possible, even on condition that we never know and never can know that we are happy. We must be willing to sell in exchange for the mere happiness every vestige of knowledge, both in ourselves and in others, both of happiness itself and of every other thing. Can we really still disagree? Can any one still declare it obvious that this is reasonable? That pleasure alone is good as an end?

The case, it is plain, is just like that of the colours[1], only, as yet, not nearly so strong. It is far more possible that we should some day be able to produce the intensest pleasure, without any consciousness that it is there, than that we should be able to produce mere colour, without its being any particular colour. Pleasure and consciousness can be far more easily distinguished from one another, than colour from the particular colours. And yet even if this were not so, we should be bound to distinguish them if we really wished to declare pleasure alone to be our ultimate end. Even if consciousness were an inseparable accompaniment of pleasure, a *sine quâ non* of its existence, yet, if pleasure is the only end, we are bound to call consciousness a mere *means* to it, in any intelligible sense that can be given to the word *means.* And if, on the other hand, as I hope is now plain, the pleasure would be comparatively valueless without the consciousness, then we are bound to say that pleasure is *not* the only end, that some consciousness at least must be included with it as a veritable part of the end.

[1] § 48 *sup.*

For our question now is solely what the end is: it is quite
another question how far that end may be attainable *by itself,*
or must involve the simultaneous attainment of other things.
It may well be that the *practical* conclusions at which Utilitarians do arrive, and even those at which they ought logically
to arrive, are not far from the truth. But in so far as their
reason for holding these conclusions to be true is that 'Pleasure
alone is good as an end,' they are *absolutely* wrong: and it is
with *reasons* that we are chiefly concerned in any scientific Ethics.

    53. It seems, then, clear that Hedonism is in error, so far
as it maintains that pleasure alone, and not the consciousness
of pleasure, is the sole good. And this error seems largely due
to the fallacy which I pointed out above in Mill—the fallacy
of confusing means and end. It is falsely supposed that, since
pleasure must always be accompanied by consciousness (which
is, itself, extremely doubtful), therefore it is indifferent whether
we say that pleasure or the consciousness of pleasure is the sole
good. *Practically,* of course, it would be indifferent at which
we aimed, if it were certain that we could not get the one without the other; but where the question is of what is good in
itself—where we ask: For the sake of what is it desirable to
get that which we aim at?—the distinction is by no means
unimportant. Here we are placed before an exclusive alternative. *Either* pleasure by itself (even though we can't get it)
would be all that is desirable, *or* a consciousness of it would be
more desirable still. Both these propositions cannot be true;
and I think it is plain that the latter is true; whence it follows
that pleasure is *not* the sole good.

    Still it may be said that, even if consciousness of pleasure,
and not pleasure alone, is the sole good, this conclusion is not
very damaging to Hedonism. It may be said that Hedonists
have always meant by pleasure the consciousness of pleasure,
though they have not been at pains to say so ; and this, I think
is, in the main, true. To correct their formula in this respect
could, therefore, only be a matter of practical importance, if
it is possible to produce pleasure without producing consciousness of it. But even this importance, which I think our
conclusion so far really has, is, I admit, comparatively slight.

What I wish to maintain is that even consciousness of pleasure is not the sole good: that, indeed, it is absurd so to regard it. And the chief importance of what has been said so far lies in the fact that the same method, which shews that consciousness of pleasure is more valuable than pleasure, seems also to shew that consciousness of pleasure is itself far less valuable than other things. The supposition that consciousness of pleasure is the sole good is due to a neglect of the same distinctions which have encouraged the careless assertion that pleasure is the sole good.

The method which I employed in order to shew that pleasure itself was not the sole good, was that of considering what value we should attach to it, if it existed in absolute isolation, stripped of all its usual accompaniments. And this is, in fact, the only method that can be safely used, when we wish to discover what degree of value a thing has in itself. The necessity of employing this method will be best exhibited by a discussion of the arguments used by Prof. Sidgwick in the passage last quoted, and by an exposure of the manner in which they are calculated to mislead.

54. With regard to the second of them, it only maintains that other things, which might be supposed to share with pleasure the attribute of goodness, ' seem to obtain the commendation of Common Sense, roughly speaking, in proportion to the degree' of their productiveness of pleasure. Whether even this rough proportion holds between the commendation of Common Sense and the felicific effects of that which it commends is a question extremely difficult to determine; and we need not enter into it here. For, even assuming it to be true, and assuming the judgments of Common Sense to be on the whole correct, what would it shew? It would shew, certainly, that pleasure was a good *criterion* of right action—that the same conduct which produced most pleasure would also produce most good on the whole. But this would by no means entitle us to the conclusion that the greatest pleasure *constituted* what was best on the whole: it would still leave open the alternative that the greatest quantity of pleasure was as a matter of fact, *under actual conditions,* generally accompanied by the greatest quantity of *other goods*, and that it therefore was *not* the sole good. It might indeed seem to be a strange coincidence that these two things should always, even in this world, be in proportion to one another. But the strangeness of this coincidence will certainly not entitle us to argue directly that it does not exist—that it is an illusion, due to the fact that pleasure is really the sole good. The coincidence may be susceptible of other explanations; and it would even be our duty to accept it unexplained, if direct intuition seemed to declare that pleasure was not the sole good. Moreover it must be remembered that the need for assuming such a coincidence rests in any case upon the extremely doubtful proposition that felicific effects *are* roughly in proportion to the approval of Common Sense. And it should be observed that, though Prof. Sidgwick maintains this to be the case, his detailed illustrations only tend to shew the very different proposition that a thing is not held to be good, unless it gives a balance of pleasure; not that the degree of commendation is in proportion to the quantity of pleasure.

55. The decision, then, must rest upon Prof. Sidgwick's first argument—'the appeal' to our 'intuitive judgment after due consideration of the question when fairly placed before it.' And here it seems to me plain that Prof. Sidgwick has failed, in two essential respects, to place the question fairly before either himself or his reader.

(1) What he has to shew is, as he says himself, not merely that 'Happiness must be included as a part of Ultimate Good.' This view, he says, 'ought not to commend itself to the sober judgment of reflective persons.' And why? Because 'these objective relations, when distinguished from the consciousness accompanying and resulting from them, are not ultimately and intrinsically desirable.' Now, this reason, which is offered as shewing that to consider Happiness as a mere part of Ultimate Good does not meet the facts of intuition, is, on the contrary, only sufficient to shew that it *is* a part of Ultimate Good. For from the fact that no value resides in one part of a whole, considered by itself, we cannot infer that all the value belonging to the whole does reside in the other part, considered by itself. Even if we admit that there is much value in the enjoyment of

Beauty, and none in the mere contemplation of it, which is
one of the constituents of that complex fact, it does not follow
that all the value belongs to the other constituent, namely
the pleasure which we take in contemplating it. It is quite
possible that this constituent also has no value in itself; that
the value belongs to the whole state, and to that only: so that
both the pleasure *and* the contemplation are mere parts of the
good, and both of them equally necessary parts. In short,
Prof. Sidgwick's argument here depends upon the neglect of
that principle, which I tried to explain in my first chapter and
which I said I should call the principle of 'organic relations[1].'
The argument is calculated to mislead, because it supposes
that, if we see a whole state to be valuable, and also see that
one element of that state has no value *by itself*, then the other
element, *by itself*, must have all the value which belongs to the
whole state. The fact is, on the contrary, that, since the whole
may be organic, the other element need have no value whatever,
and that even if it have some, the value of the whole may be
very much greater. For this reason, as well as to avoid confusion
between means and end, it is absolutely essential to consider
each distinguishable quality, *in isolation*, in order to decide what
value it possesses. Prof. Sidgwick, on the other hand, applies
this method of isolation only to *one* element in the wholes he is
considering. He does not ask the question: If consciousness
of pleasure existed absolutely by itself, would a sober judgment
be able to attribute much value to it? It is, in fact, always
misleading to take a whole, that is valuable (or the reverse), and
then to ask simply: To which of its constituents does this whole
owe its value or its vileness? It may well be that it owes it to
none; and, if one of them does appear to have some value in
itself, we shall be led into the grave error of supposing that all
the value of the whole belongs to it alone. It seems to me that
this error has commonly been committed with regard to pleasure.
Pleasure does seem to be a necessary constituent of most valuable
wholes; and, since the other constituents, into which we may
analyse them, may easily seem not to have any value, it is
natural to suppose that all the value belongs to pleasure. That

[1] pp. 27—30, 36.

this natural supposition does not follow from the premises is
certain; and that it is, on the contrary, ridiculously far from
the truth appears evident to my 'reflective judgment.' If we
apply either to pleasure or to consciousness of pleasure the only
safe method, that of isolation, and ask ourselves: Could we
accept, as a very good thing, that mere consciousness of pleasure,
and absolutely nothing else, should exist, even in the greatest
quantities? I think we can have no doubt about answering:
No. Far less can we accept this as the *sole* good. Even if we
accept Prof. Sidgwick's implication (which yet appears to me
extremely doubtful) that consciousness of pleasure has a greater
value by itself than Contemplation of Beauty, it seems to me
that a pleasurable Contemplation of Beauty has certainly an
immeasurably greater value than mere Consciousness of Pleasure.
In favour of this conclusion I can appeal with confidence to the
'sober judgment of reflective persons.'

56. (2) That the value of a pleasurable whole does not
belong solely to the pleasure which it contains, may, I think,
be made still plainer by consideration of another point in which
Prof. Sidgwick's argument is defective. Prof. Sidgwick maintains, as we saw, the doubtful proposition, that the *conduciveness*
to pleasure of a thing is in rough proportion to its commendation by Common Sense. But he does not maintain, what would
be undoubtedly false, that the pleasantness of every state is in
proportion to the commendation of that state. In other words,
it is only when you take into account *the whole consequences of
any state,* that he is able to maintain the coincidence of quantity
of pleasure with the objects approved by Common Sense. If
we consider each state by itself, and ask what is the judgment
of Common Sense as to its goodness *as an end,* quite apart from
its goodness as a means, there can be no doubt that Common
Sense holds many much less pleasant states to be better than
many far more pleasant: that it holds, with Mill, that there are
higher pleasures, which are more valuable, though less pleasant,
than those which are lower. Prof. Sidgwick might, of course,
maintain that in this Common Sense is merely confusing means
and ends: that what it holds to be better as an end, is in
reality only better as a means. But I think his argument is

defective in that he does not seem to see sufficiently plainly
that, as far as intuitions of goodness *as an end* are concerned,
he is running grossly counter to Common Sense ; that he does
not emphasise sufficiently the distinction between *immediate*
pleasantness and *conduciveness* to pleasure. In order to place
fairly before us the question what is good as an end we must
take states that are immediately pleasant and ask if the more
pleasant are always also the better; and whether, if some that
are less pleasant appear to be so, it is only because we think
they are likely to increase the number of the more pleasant.
That Common Sense would deny both these suppositions, and
rightly so, appears to me indubitable. It is commonly held
that certain of what would be called the lowest forms of sexual
enjoyment, for instance, are positively bad, although it is by
no means clear that they are not the most pleasant states we
ever experience. Common Sense would certainly not think it
a sufficient justification for the pursuit of what Prof. Sidgwick
calls the 'refined pleasures' here and now, that they are the
best means to the future attainment of a heaven, in which there
would be no more refined pleasures—no contemplation of beauty,
no personal affections—but in which the greatest possible
pleasure would be obtained by a perpetual indulgence in
bestiality. Yet Prof. Sidgwick would be bound to hold that,
if the greatest possible pleasure could be obtained in this way,
and if it were attainable, such a state of things would be a
heaven indeed, and that all human endeavours should be devoted
to its realisation. I venture to think that this view is as false
as it is paradoxical.

57. It seems to me, then, that if we place fairly before us
the question : Is consciousness of pleasure the sole good ? the
answer must be : No. And with this the last defence of
Hedonism has been broken down. In order to put the question
fairly we must isolate consciousness of pleasure. We must ask :
Suppose we were conscious of pleasure only, and of nothing else,
not even that we *were* conscious, would that state of things,
however great the quantity, be very desirable ? No one, I think,
can suppose it so. On the other hand, it seems quite plain,
that we do regard as very desirable, many complicated states

of mind in which the consciousness of pleasure is combined with consciousness of other things—states which we call 'enjoyment of' so and so. If this is correct, then it follows that consciousness of pleasure is not the sole good, and that many other states, in which it is included as a part, are much better than it. Once we recognise the principle of organic unities, any objection to this conclusion, founded on the supposed fact that the other elements of such states have no value in themselves, must disappear. And I do not know that I need say any more in refutation of Hedonism.

58. It only remains to say something of the two forms in which a hedonistic doctrine is commonly held—Egoism and Utilitarianism.

Egoism, as a form of Hedonism, is the doctrine which holds that we ought each of us to pursue our own greatest happiness as our ultimate end. The doctrine will, of course, admit that sometimes the best means to this end will be to give pleasure to others; we shall, for instance, by so doing, procure for ourselves the pleasures of sympathy, of freedom from interference, and of self-esteem ; and these pleasures, which we may procure by sometimes aiming directly at the happiness of other persons, may be greater than any we could otherwise get. Egoism in this sense must therefore be carefully distinguished from Egoism in another sense, the sense in which Altruism is its proper opposite. Egoism, as commonly opposed to Altruism, is apt to denote merely selfishness. In this sense, a man is an egoist, if all his actions are actually directed towards gaining pleasure for himself; whether he holds that he ought to act so, because he will thereby obtain for himself the greatest possible happiness on the whole, or not. Egoism may accordingly be used to denote the theory that we should always aim at getting pleasure for ourselves, because that is the best *means* to the ultimate end, whether the ultimate end be our own greatest pleasure or not. Altruism, on the other hand, may denote the theory that we ought always to aim at other people's happiness, on the ground that this is the best *means* of securing our own as well as theirs. Accordingly an Egoist, in the sense in which I am now going to talk of Egoism, an Egoist, who holds that his own greatest happiness is the ultimate end, may at the same time be an Altruist : he may hold that he ought to 'love his neighbour,' as the best means to being happy himself. And conversely an Egoist, in the other sense, may at the same time be a Utilitarian. He may hold that he ought always to direct his efforts towards getting pleasure for himself on the ground that he is thereby most likely to increase the general sum of happiness.

59. I shall say more later about this second kind of Egoism, this anti-altruistic Egoism, this Egoism as a doctrine of means. What I am now concerned with is that utterly distinct kind of Egoism, which holds that each man ought rationally to hold : My own greatest happiness is the only good thing there is : my actions can only be good as means, in so far as they help to win me this. This is a doctrine which is not much held by writers now-a-days. It is a doctrine that was largely held by English Hedonists in the 17th and 18th centuries : it is, for example, at the bottom of Hobbes' Ethics. But even the English school appear to have made one step forward in the present century : they are most of them now-a-days Utilitarians. They do recognise that if my own happiness is good, it would be strange that other people's happiness should not be good too.

In order fully to expose the absurdity of this kind of Egoism, it is necessary to examine certain confusions upon which its plausibility depends.

The chief of these is the confusion involved in the conception of ' my own good ' as distinguished from ' the good of others.' This is a conception which we all use every day ; it is one of the first to which the plain man is apt to appeal in discussing any question of Ethics : and Egoism is commonly advocated chiefly because its meaning is not clearly perceived. It is plain, indeed, that the name ' Egoism ' more properly applies to the theory that ' my own good ' is the sole good, than that my own pleasure is so. A man may quite well be an Egoist, even if he be not a Hedonist. The conception which is, perhaps, most closely associated with Egoism is that denoted by the words ' my own interest.' The Egoist is the man who holds that a tendency to promote his own interest is the sole possible, and sufficient, iustification of all his actions. But this conception of ' my own

interest' plainly includes, in general, very much more than my
own pleasure. It is, indeed, only because and in so far as 'my
own interest' has been thought to consist solely in my own
pleasure, that Egoists have been led to hold that my own
pleasure is the sole good. Their course of reasoning is as follows:
The only thing I ought to secure is my own interest; but my
own interest consists in my greatest possible pleasure; and
therefore the only thing I ought to pursue is my own pleasure.
That it is very natural, *on reflection*, thus to identify my own
pleasure with my own interest; and that it has been generally
done by modern *moralists*, may be admitted. But, when Prof.
Sidgwick points this out (III. xiv. § 5, Div. III.), he should have also
pointed out that this identification has by no means been made in
ordinary thought. When the plain man says 'my own interest,'
he does *not* mean 'my own pleasure'—he does not commonly
even include this—he means my own advancement, my own
reputation, the getting of a better income etc., etc. That Prof.
Sidgwick should not have noticed this, and that he should give
the reason he gives for the fact that the ancient *moralists* did
not identify 'my own interest' with my own pleasure, seems to
be due to his having failed to notice that very confusion in the
conception of 'my own good' which I am now to point out.
That confusion has, perhaps, been more clearly perceived by
Plato than by any other moralist, and to point it out suffices to
refute Prof. Sidgwick's own view that Egoism is rational.

What, then, is meant by 'my own good'? In what sense can
a thing be good *for me*? It is obvious, if we reflect, that the
only thing which can belong to me, which can be *mine*, is something which is good, and not the fact that it is good. When
therefore, I talk of anything I get as 'my own good,' I must
mean either that the thing I get is good, or that my possessing
it is good. In both cases it is only the thing or the possession
of it which is *mine*, and not *the goodness* of that thing or that
possession. There is no longer any meaning in attaching the
'my' to our predicate, and saying: The possession of this *by me*
is *my* good. Even if we interpret this by 'My possession of this
is what *I* think good,' the same still holds: for *what* I think is
that my possession of it is good *simply*; and, if I think rightly,

then the truth is that my possession of it *is* good simply—not, in any sense, *my* good; and, if I think wrongly, it is not good at all. In short, when I talk of a thing as 'my own good' all that I can mean is that something which will be exclusively mine, as my own pleasure is mine (whatever be the various senses of this relation denoted by 'possession'), is also *good absolutely*; or rather that my possession of it is *good absolutely*. The *good* of it can in no possible sense be 'private' or belong to me; any more than a thing can *exist* privately or *for* one person only. The only reason I can have for aiming at 'my own good,' is that it is *good absolutely* that what I so call should belong to me—*good absolutely* that I should *have* something, which, if I have it, others cannot have. But if it is *good absolutely* that I should have it, then everyone else has as much reason for aiming at *my* having it, as I have myself. If, therefore, it is true of *any* single man's 'interest' or 'happiness' that it ought to be his sole ultimate end, this can only mean that *that* man's 'interest' or 'happiness' is *the sole good, the* Universal Good, and the only thing that anybody ought to aim at. What Egoism holds, therefore, is that *each* man's happiness is the sole good—that a number of different things are *each* of them the only good thing there is—an absolute contradiction! No more complete and thorough refutation of any theory could be desired.

60. Yet Prof. Sidgwick holds that Egoism is rational; and it will be useful briefly to consider the reasons which he gives for this absurd conclusion. 'The Egoist,' he says (last Chap. § 1), 'may avoid the proof of Utilitarianism by declining to affirm,' either 'implicitly or explicitly, that his own greatest happiness is not merely the ultimate rational end for himself, but a part of Universal Good.' And in the passage to which he here refers us, as having there 'seen' this, he says · 'It cannot be proved that the difference between his own happiness and another's happiness is not *for him* all-important' (IV. ii. § 1). What does Prof. Sidgwick mean by these phrases 'the ultimate rational end for himself,' and '*for him* all-important'? He does not attempt to define them; and it is largely the use of such undefined phrases which causes absurdities to be committed in philosophy.

Is there any sense in which a thing can be an ultimate rational end for one person and not for another? By 'ultimate' must be meant at least that the end is good-in-itself—good in our undefinable sense; and by 'rational,' at least, that it is truly good. That a thing should be an ultimate rational end means, then, that it is truly good in itself; and that it is truly good in itself means that it is a part of Universal Good. Can we assign any meaning to that qualification 'for himself,' which will make it cease to be a part of Universal Good? The thing is impossible: for the Egoist's happiness must *either* be good in itself, and so a part of Universal Good, *or else* it cannot be good in itself at all: there is no escaping this dilemma. And if it is not good at all, what reason can he have for aiming at it? how can it be a rational end for him? That qualification 'for himself' has no meaning unless it implies '*not* for others'; and if it implies 'not for others,' then it cannot be a rational end for him, since it cannot be truly good in itself: the phrase 'an ultimate rational end for himself' is a contradiction in terms. By saying that a thing is an end for one particular person, or good for him, can only be meant one of four things. Either (1) it may be meant that the end in question is something which will belong exclusively to him; but in that case, if it is to be rational for him to aim at it, that he should exclusively possess it must be a part of Universal Good. Or (2) it may be meant that it is the only thing at which he ought to aim; but this can only be, because, by so doing, he will do the most he can towards realising Universal Good: and this, in our case, will only give Egoism as a doctrine of *means*. Or (3) it may be meant that the thing is what he desires or thinks good; and then, if he thinks wrongly, it is not a rational end at all, and, if he thinks rightly, it is a part of Universal Good. Or (4) it may be meant that it is peculiarly appropriate that a thing which will belong exclusively to him should also by him be approved or aimed at; but, in this case, both that it should belong to him and that he should aim at it must be parts of Universal Good: by saying that a certain relation between two things is fitting or appropriate, we can only mean that the existence of that relation is absolutely good

in itself (unless it be so as a means, which gives case (2)). By
no possible meaning, then, that can be given to the phrase that
his own happiness is the ultimate rational end for himself can
the Egoist escape the implication that his own happiness is
absolutely good; and by saying that it is *the* ultimate rational
end, he must mean that it is the only good thing—the whole
of Universal Good: and, if he further maintains, that each
man's happiness is the ultimate rational end for *him*, we
have the fundamental contradiction of Egoism—that an immense number of different things are, *each* of them, *the sole
good.*—And it is easy to see that the same considerations apply
to the phrase that 'the difference between his own happiness
and another's is *for him* all-important.' This can only mean
either (1) that his own happiness is the only end which will
affect him, or (2) that the only important thing for him
(as a means) is to look to his own happiness, or (3) that it
is only his own happiness which he cares about, or (4) that it is
good that each man's happiness should be the only concern
of that man. And none of these propositions, true as they may
be, have the smallest tendency to shew that if his own happiness
is desirable at all, it is not a part of Universal Good. Either
his own happiness is a good thing or it is not; and, in whatever
sense it may be all-important for him, it must be true that,
if it is not good, he is not justified in pursuing it, and that,
if it is good, everyone else has an equal reason to pursue it,
so far as they are able and so far as it does not exclude their
attainment of other more valuable parts of Universal Good.
In short it is plain that the addition of 'for him' 'for me'
to such words as 'ultimate rational end,' 'good,' 'important'
can introduce nothing but confusion. The only possible reason
that can justify any action is that by it the greatest possible
amount of what is good absolutely should be realised. And
if anyone says that the attainment of his own happiness
justifies his actions, he must mean that this is the greatest
possible amount of Universal Good which he can realise. And
this again can only be true either because *he* has no power
to realise more, in which case he only holds Egoism as a
doctrine of means; or else because his own happiness is the

greatest amount of Universal Good which can be realised at all, in which case we have Egoism proper, and the flagrant contradiction that every person's happiness is singly the greatest amount of Universal Good which can be realised at all.

61.   It should be observed that, since this is so, 'the relation of Rational Egoism to Rational Benevolence,' which Prof. Sidgwick regards 'as the profoundest problem of Ethics' (III. xiii. § 5, *n.* 1), appears in quite a different light to that in which he presents it. 'Even if a man,' he says, 'admits the self-evidence of the principle of Rational Benevolence, he may still hold that his own happiness is an end which it is irrational for him to sacrifice to any other; and that therefore a harmony between the maxim of Prudence and the maxim of Rational Benevolence must be somehow demonstrated, if morality is to be made completely rational. This latter view is that which I myself hold' (last Chap. § 1). Prof. Sidgwick then goes on to shew 'that the inseparable connection between Utilitarian Duty and the greatest happiness of the individual who conforms to it cannot be satisfactorily demonstrated on empirical grounds' (Ib. § 3). And the final paragraph of his book tells us that, since 'the reconciliation of duty and self-interest is to be regarded as a hypothesis logically necessary to avoid a fundamental *contradiction* in one chief department of our thought, it remains to ask how far this necessity constitutes a sufficient reason for accepting this hypothesis[1]' (Ib. § 5). To 'assume the existence of such a Being, as God, by the *consensus* of theologians, is conceived to be' would, he has already argued, ensure the required reconciliation; since the Divine Sanctions of such a God 'would, of course, suffice to make it always every one's interest to promote universal happiness to the best of his knowledge' (Ib. § 5).

Now what is this 'reconciliation of duty and self-interest,' which Divine Sanctions could ensure? It would consist in the mere fact that the same conduct which produced the greatest possible happiness of the greatest number would always also produce the greatest possible happiness of the agent. If this were the case (and our empirical knowledge shews that it is not

---

[1] The italics are mine.

the case in this world), 'morality' would, Prof. Sidgwick thinks, be 'completely rational': we should avoid 'an ultimate and fundamental contradiction in our apparent intuitions of what is Reasonable in conduct.' That is to say, we should avoid the necessity of thinking that it is as manifest an obligation to secure our own greatest Happiness (maxim of Prudence), as to secure the greatest Happiness on the whole (maxim of Benevolence). But it is perfectly obvious we should not. Prof. Sidgwick here commits the characteristic fallacy of Empiricism —the fallacy of thinking that an alteration in *facts* could make a contradiction cease to be a contradiction. That a single man's happiness should be *the sole good*, and that also everybody's happiness should be *the sole good*, is a contradiction which cannot be solved by the assumption that the same conduct will secure both : it would be equally contradictory, however certain we were that that assumption was justified. Prof. Sidgwick strains at a gnat and swallows a camel. He thinks the Divine Omnipotence must be called into play to secure that what gives other people pleasure should also give it to him—that only so can Ethics be made rational; while he overlooks the fact that even this exercise of Divine Omnipotence would leave in Ethics a contradiction, in comparison with which his difficulty is a trifle—a contradiction, which would reduce all Ethics to mere nonsense, and before which the Divine Omnipotence must be powerless to all eternity. That *each* man's happiness should be the *sole good*, which we have seen to be the principle of Egoism, is in itself a contradiction: and that it should also be true that the Happiness of all is the *sole good*, which is the principle of Universalistic Hedonism, would introduce another contradiction. And that these propositions should all be true might well be called 'the profoundest problem in Ethics': it would be a problem necessarily insoluble. But they *cannot* all be true, and there is no reason, but confusion, for the supposition that they are. Prof. Sidgwick confuses this contradiction with the mere fact (in which there is no contradiction) that our own greatest happiness and that of all do not seem always attainable by the same means. This fact, if Happiness were the sole good, would indeed be of some importance ; and, on any view, similar facts are of importance. But they are nothing but instances of the one important fact that in this world the quantity of good which is attainable is ridiculously small compared to that which is imaginable. That I cannot get the most possible pleasure for myself, if I produce the most possible pleasure on the whole, is no more *the* profoundest problem of Ethics, than that in any case I cannot get as much pleasure altogether as would be desirable. It only states that, if we get as much good as possible in one place, we may get less on the whole, because the quantity of attainable good is limited. To say that I have to choose between my own good and that of *all* is a false antithesis: the only rational question is how to choose between my own and that of *others*, and the principle on which this must be answered is exactly the same as that on which I must choose whether to give pleasure to this other person or to that.

62. It is plain, then, that the doctrine of Egoism is self-contradictory; and that one reason why this is not perceived, is a confusion with regard to the meaning of the phrase ' my own good.' And it may be observed that this confusion and the neglect of this contradiction are necessarily involved in the transition from Naturalistic Hedonism, as ordinarily held, to Utilitarianism. Mill, for instance, as we saw, declares: ' Each person, so far as he believes it to be attainable, desires his own happiness' (p. 53). And he offers this as a reason why the general happiness is desirable. We have seen that to regard it as such, involves, in the first place, the naturalistic fallacy. But moreover, even if that fallacy were not a fallacy, it could only be a reason for Egoism and not for Utilitarianism. Mill's argument is as follows: A man desires his own happiness; therefore his own happiness is desirable. Further: A man desires nothing but his own happiness; therefore his own happiness is alone desirable. We have next to remember, that everybody, according to Mill, so desires his own happiness: and then it will follow that everybody's happiness is alone desirable. And this is simply a contradiction in terms. Just consider what it means. Each man's happiness is the only thing desirable: several different things are *each* of them the *only* thing desirable. This is the fundamental contradiction of Egoism. In order to think that what his arguments tend to prove is not Egoism but Utilitarianism, Mill must think that he can infer from the proposition 'Each man's happiness is his own good,' the proposition 'The happiness of all is the good of all'; whereas in fact, if we understand what 'his own good' means, it is plain that the latter can only be inferred from 'The happiness of all is the good of each.' Naturalistic Hedonism, then, logically leads only to Egoism. Of course, a Naturalist might hold that what we aimed at was simply 'pleasure' not our own pleasure; and *that*, always assuming the naturalistic fallacy, would give an unobjectionable ground for Utilitarianism. But more commonly he will hold that it is his own pleasure he desires, or at least will confuse this with the other; and then he must logically be led to adopt Egoism and not Utilitarianism.

63. The second cause I have to give why Egoism should be thought reasonable, is simply its confusion with that other kind of Egoism—Egoism as a doctrine of means. This second Egoism has a right to say: You ought to pursue your own happiness, sometimes at all events; it may even say: Always. And when we find it saying this we are apt to forget its proviso: But only as a means to something else. The fact is we are in an imperfect state; we cannot get the ideal all at once. And hence it is often our bounden duty, we often *absolutely* '*ought*,' to do things which are good only or chiefly as means: we have to do the best we can, what is absolutely 'right,' but not what is absolutely good. Of this I shall say more hereafter. I only mention it here because I think it is much more plausible to say that we ought to pursue our own pleasure as a means than as an end, and that this doctrine, through confusion, lends some of its plausibility to the utterly different doctrine of Egoism proper: My own greatest pleasure is the only good thing.

64. So much for Egoism. Of Utilitarianism not much need be said; but two points may seem deserving of notice.

The first is that this name, like that of Egoism, does not naturally suggest that all our actions are to be judged according to the degree in which they are a means to *pleasure*. Its natural meaning is that the standard of right and wrong in conduct is its tendency to promote the *interest* of everybody. And by *interest* is commonly meant a variety of different goods, classed together only because they are what a man commonly desires for himself, so far as his desires have not that psychological quality which is meant by 'moral.' The 'useful' thus means, and was in ancient Ethics systematically used to mean, what is a means to the attainment of goods other than moral goods. It is quite an unjustifiable assumption that these goods are only good as means to pleasure or that they are commonly so regarded. The chief reason for adopting the name 'Utilitarianism' was, indeed, merely to emphasize the fact that right and wrong conduct must be judged by its results—as a means, in opposition to the strictly Intuitionistic view that certain ways of acting were right and others wrong, whatever their results might be. In thus insisting that what is right must mean what produces the best possible results Utilitarianism is fully justified. But with this correct contention there has been historically, and very naturally, associated a double error. (1) The best possible results were assumed to consist only in a limited class of goods, roughly coinciding with those which were popularly distinguished as the results of merely 'useful' or 'interested' actions; and these again were hastily assumed to be good only as means to pleasure. (2) The Utilitarians tend to regard everything as a mere means, neglecting the fact that some things which are good as means are also good as ends. Thus, for instance, assuming pleasure to be a good, there is a tendency to value present pleasure only as a means to future pleasure, and not, as is strictly necessary if pleasure is good as an end, also to *weigh it against* possible future pleasures. Much utilitarian argument involves the logical absurdity that what is here and now, never has any value in itself, but is only to be judged by its consequences; which again, of course, when they are realised, would have no value in themselves, but would be mere means to a still further future, and so on *ad infinitum*.

The second point deserving notice with regard to Utilitarianism is that, when the name is used for a form of Hedonism, it does not commonly, even in its description of its *end*, accurately distinguish between means and end. Its best-known formula is that the result by which actions are to be judged is 'the greatest happiness of the greatest number.' But it is plain that, if pleasure is the sole good, provided the quantity be equally great, an equally desirable result will have been obtained whether it be enjoyed by many or by few, or even if it be enjoyed by nobody. It is plain that, if we ought to aim at the greatest happiness of the greatest number, this can only, on the hedonistic principle, be because the existence of pleasure in a great number of persons seems to be the best *means* available for attaining the existence of the greatest quantity of pleasure. This may actually be the case; but it is fair to suspect that Utilitarians have been influenced, in their adoption of the hedonistic principle, by this failure to distinguish clearly between pleasure or consciousness of pleasure and its possession by a person. It is far easier to regard the possession of pleasure by a number of persons as the sole good, than so to regard the mere existence of an equally great quantity of pleasure. If, indeed, we were to take the Utilitarian principle strictly, and to assume them to mean that the possession of pleasure by many persons was good in itself, the principle is not hedonistic: it includes as a necessary part of the ultimate end, the existence of a number of persons, and this will include very much more than mere pleasure.

Utilitarianism, however, as commonly held, must be understood to maintain that either mere consciousness of pleasure, or consciousness of pleasure together with the minimum adjunct which may be meant by the existence of such consciousness in at least one *person*, is the *sole good*. This is its significance as an ethical doctrine; and as such it has already been refuted in my refutation of Hedonism. The most that can be said for it is that it does not seriously mislead in its practical conclusions, on the ground that, as an empirical fact, the method of acting which brings most good on the whole does also bring most pleasure. Utilitarians do indeed generally devote most of their arguments to shewing that the course of action which will bring most pleasure is in general such as common sense would approve. We have seen that Prof. Sidgwick appeals to this fact as tending to shew that pleasure is the sole good ; and we have also seen that it does not tend to shew this. We have seen how very flimsy the other arguments advanced for this proposition are; and that, if it be fairly considered by itself, it appears to be quite ridiculous. And, moreover, that the actions which produce most good on the whole do also produce most pleasure is extremely doubtful. The arguments tending to shew it are all more or less vitiated by the assumption that what appear to be necessary conditions for the attainment of most pleasure in the near future, will always continue so to be. And, even with this vicious assumption, they only succeed in making out a highly problematical case. How, therefore, this fact is to be explained, if it be a fact, need not concern us. It is sufficient to have shewn that many complex states of mind are much more valuable than the pleasure they contain. If this be so, *no form of Hedonism can be true.* And, since the practical guidance afforded by pleasure as a *criterion* is small in proportion as the calculation attempts to be accurate, we can well afford to await further investigation, before adopting a guide, whose utility is very doubtful and whose trustworthiness we have grave reason to suspect.

65. The most important points which I have endeavoured to establish in this chapter are as follows. (1) Hedonism must be strictly defined as the doctrine that ' Pleasure is the only thing which is good in itself': this view seems to owe its prevalence mainly to the naturalistic fallacy, and Mill's arguments may be taken as a type of those which are fallacious in this respect; Sidgwick alone has defended it without committing this fallacy, and its final refutation must therefore point out the errors in his arguments (36–38). (2) Mill's 'Utilitarianism' is criticised: it being shewn (*a*) that he commits the naturalistic fallacy in identifying 'desirable' with 'desired'; (*b*) that pleasure is not the only object of desire. The common arguments for Hedonism seem to rest on these two errors (39–44). (3) Hedonism is considered as an 'Intuition,' and it is pointed out (*a*) that Mill's allowance that some pleasures are inferior in quality to others implies both that it is an Intuition and that it is a false one (46–48); (*b*) that

Sidgwick fails to distinguish 'pleasure' from 'consciousness of pleasure,' and that it is absurd to regard the former, at all events, as the sole good (49–52); (c) that it seems equally absurd to regard 'consciousness of pleasure' as the sole good, since, if it were so, a world in which nothing else existed might be absolutely perfect: Sidgwick fails to put to himself this question, which is the only clear and decisive one (53–57). (4) What are commonly considered to be the two main types of Hedonism, namely, Egoism and Utilitarianism, are not only different from, but strictly contradictory of, one another; since the former asserts 'My own greatest pleasure is the *sole* good,' the latter 'The greatest pleasure of all is the *sole* good.' Egoism seems to owe its plausibility partly to the failure to observe this contradiction—a failure which is exemplified by Sidgwick; partly to a confusion of Egoism as doctrine of end, with the same as doctrine of means. If Hedonism is true, Egoism cannot be so; still less can it be so, if Hedonism is false. The end of Utilitarianism, on the other hand, would, if Hedonism were true, be, not indeed the best conceivable, but the best possible for us to promote; but it is refuted by the refutation of Hedonism (58–64).

CHAPTER IV.

66. In this chapter I propose to deal with a type of ethical theory which is exemplified in the ethical views of the Stoics, of Spinoza, of Kant, and especially of a number of modern writers, whose views in this respect are mainly due to the influence of Hegel. These ethical theories have this in common, that they use some *metaphysical* proposition as a ground for inferring some fundamental proposition of Ethics. They all imply, and many of them expressly hold, that ethical truths follow logically from metaphysical truths—that Ethics should be based on *Metaphysics*. And the result is that they all describe the Supreme Good in *metaphysical* terms.

What, then, is to be understood by 'metaphysical'? I use the term, as I explained in Chapter II., in opposition to 'natural.' I call those philosophers preeminently 'metaphysical' who have recognised most clearly that not everything which *is* is a 'natural object.' 'Metaphysicians' have, therefore, the great merit of insisting that our knowledge is not confined to the things which we can touch and see and feel. They have always been much occupied, not only with that other class of natural objects which consists in mental facts, but also with the class of objects or properties of objects, which certainly do not exist in time, are not therefore parts of Nature, and which, in fact, do not *exist* at all. To this class, as I have said, belongs what we mean by the adjective 'good.' It is not *goodness*, but only the things or qualities which are good, which can exist in time—can have duration, and begin and cease to exist—can be objects of *perception*. But the most prominent members of this class are perhaps numbers. It is quite certain that two natural objects may exist; but it is equally certain that *two* itself does not exist and never can. Two and two *are* four. But that does not mean that either two or four exists. Yet it certainly means *something*. Two *is* somehow, although it does not exist. And it is not only simple terms of propositions—the objects *about* which we know truths—that belong to this class. The truths which we know about them form, perhaps, a still more important subdivision. No truth does, in fact, *exist*; but this is peculiarly obvious with regard to truths like 'Two and two are four,' in which the objects, *about* which they are truths, do not exist either. It is with the recognition of such truths as these— truths which have been called 'universal'—and of their essential unlikeness to what we can touch and see and feel, that metaphysics proper begins. Such 'universal' truths have always played a large part in the reasonings of metaphysicians from Plato's time till now; and that they have directed attention to the difference between these truths and what I have called 'natural objects' is the chief contribution to knowledge which distinguishes them from that other class of philosophers— 'empirical' philosophers—to which most Englishmen have belonged.

But though, if we are to define 'metaphysics' by the contribution which it has actually made to knowledge, we should have to say that it has emphasized the importance of objects which do not exist at all, metaphysicians themselves have not recognised this. They have indeed recognised and insisted that there are, or may be, objects of knowledge which do not *exist in time*, or at least which we cannot perceive; and in recognising the *possibility* of these, as an object of investigation, they have, it may be admitted, done a service to mankind. But they have in general supposed that whatever does not exist in time, must at least *exist* elsewhere, if it is to *be* at all—that, whatever does not exist in Nature, must exist in some supersensible reality, whether timeless or not. Consequently they have held that the truths with which they have been occupied, over and above the objects of perception, were in some way truths about such supersensible reality. If, therefore, we are to define 'metaphysics' not by what it has attained, but by what it has attempted, we should say that it consists in the attempt to obtain knowledge, by processes of reasoning, of what exists but is *not* a part of Nature. Metaphysicians have actually held that they could give us such knowledge of non-natural existence. They have held that their science consists in giving us such knowledge as can be supported by reasons, of that supersensible reality of which religion professes to give us a fuller knowledge, without any reasons. When, therefore, I spoke above of 'metaphysical' propositions, I meant propositions about the existence of something supersensible—of something which is not an object of perception, and which cannot be inferred from what is an object of perception by the same rules of inference by which we infer the past and future of what we call 'Nature.' And when I spoke of 'metaphysical' terms, I meant terms which refer to qualities of such a supersensible reality, which do not belong to anything 'natural.' I admit that 'metaphysics' should investigate what reasons there may be for belief in such a supersensible reality; since I hold that its peculiar province is the truth about all objects which are not natural objects. And I think that the most prominent characteristic of metaphysics, in history, has been its profession to *prove* the truth about non-natural *existents*. I define 'metaphysical,' therefore, by a reference to supersensible *reality*; although I think that the only non-natural objects, about which it has *succeeded* in obtaining truth, are objects which do not exist at all.

So much, I hope, will suffice to explain what I mean by the term 'metaphysical,' and to shew that it refers to a clear and important distinction. It was not necessary for my purpose to make the definition exhaustive or to shew that it corresponds in essentials with established usage. The distinction between 'Nature' and a supersensible reality is very familiar and very important: and since the metaphysician endeavours to *prove* things with regard to a supersensible reality, and since he deals largely in truths which are *not* mere natural facts, it is plain that his arguments, and errors (if any), will be of a more subtle

kind than those which I have dealt with under the name of
'Naturalism.' For these two reasons it seemed convenient to
treat 'Metaphysical Ethics' by themselves.

67. I have said that those systems of Ethics, which I propose to call 'Metaphysical,' are characterised by the fact that
they describe the Supreme Good in 'metaphysical' terms; and
this has now been explained as meaning that they describe it
in terms of something which (they hold) does exist, but does
not exist in Nature—in terms of a supersensible reality. A
Metaphysical Ethics' is marked by the fact that it makes the
assertion : That which would be perfectly good is something
which exists, but is not natural ; that which has some characteristic possessed by a supersensible reality. Such an assertion
was made by the Stoics when they asserted that a life in accordance with Nature was perfect. For they did not mean by
'Nature,' what I have so defined, but something supersensible
which they inferred to exist, and which they held to be perfectly good. Such an assertion, again, is made by Spinoza
when he tells us that we are more or less perfect, in proportion
as we are more or less closely united with Absolute Substance
by the 'intellectual love' of God. Such an assertion is made
by Kant when he tells us that his 'Kingdom of Ends' is the
ideal. And such, finally, is made by modern writers who tell
us that the final and perfect end is to realise our *true* selves—a
self different both from the whole and from any part of that
which exists here and now in Nature.

Now it is plain that such ethical principles have a merit,
not possessed by Naturalism, in recognising that for perfect
goodness much more is required than any quantity of what
exists here and now or can be inferred as likely to exist in the
future. And moreover it is quite possible that their assertions
should be true, if we only understand them to assert that something which is real possesses all the characteristics necessary
for perfect goodness. But this is not all that they assert. They
also imply, as I said, that this ethical proposition *follows* from
some proposition which is metaphysical : that the question
'What is real ?' has some logical bearing upon the question
'What is good ?' It was for this reason that I described 'Meta-

physical Ethics' in Chapter II. as based upon the naturalistic fallacy. To hold that from any proposition asserting 'Reality is of this nature' we can infer, or obtain confirmation for, any proposition asserting 'This is good in itself' is to commit the naturalistic fallacy. And that a knowledge of what is real supplies reasons for holding certain things to be good in themselves is either implied or expressly asserted by all those who define the Supreme Good in metaphysical terms. This contention is part of what is meant by saying that Ethics should be 'based' on Metaphysics. It is meant that some knowledge of supersensible reality is necessary *as a premise* for correct conclusions as to what ought to exist. This view is, for instance, plainly expressed in the following statements: 'The truth is that the theory of Ethics which seems most satisfactory has a metaphysical basis......If we rest our view of Ethics on the idea of the development of the ideal self or of the rational universe, the significance of this cannot be made fully apparent without a metaphysical examination of the nature of self; *nor can its validity be established except by a discussion of the reality of the rational universe*[1].' The validity of an ethical conclusion about the nature of the ideal, it is here asserted, cannot be established except by considering the question whether that ideal is *real*. Such an assertion involves the naturalistic fallacy. It rests upon the failure to perceive that any truth which asserts 'This is good in itself' is quite unique in kind—that it cannot be reduced to any assertion about reality, and therefore must remain unaffected by any conclusions we may reach about the nature of reality. This confusion as to the unique nature of ethical truths is, I have said, involved in all those ethical theories which I have called metaphysical. It is plain that, but for some confusion of the sort, no-one would think it worth while even to describe the Supreme Good in metaphysical terms. If, for instance, we are told that the ideal consists in the realisation of the 'true self,' the very words suggest that the fact that the self in question is *true* is supposed to have some bearing on the fact that it is good. All the ethical truth

---

[1] Prof. J. S. Mackenzie, *A Manual of Ethics*, 4th ed., p. 431. The italics are mine.

which can possibly be conveyed by such an assertion would be just as well conveyed by saying that the ideal consisted in the realisation of a particular kind of self, which might be either real or purely imaginary. 'Metaphysical Ethics,' then, involve the supposition that Ethics can be *based* on Metaphysics; and our first concern with them is to make clear that this supposition must be false.

68. In what way can the nature of supersensible reality possibly have a bearing upon Ethics?

I have distinguished two kinds of ethical questions, which are far too commonly confused with one another. Ethics, as commonly understood, has to answer both the question 'What ought to be?' and the question 'What ought we to do?' The second of these questions can only be answered by considering what effects our actions will have. A complete answer to it would give us that department of Ethics which may be called the doctrine of *means* or practical Ethics. And upon this department of ethical enquiry it is plain that the nature of a supersensible reality may have a bearing. If, for instance, Metaphysics could tell us not only that we are immortal, but also, in any degree, what effects our actions in this life will have upon our condition in a future one, such information would have an undoubted bearing upon the question what we ought to do. The Christian doctrines of heaven and hell are in this way highly relevant to practical Ethics. But it is worthy of notice that the most characteristic doctrines of Metaphysics are such as either have no such bearing upon practical Ethics or have a purely negative bearing—involving the conclusion that there is nothing which we ought to do at all. They profess to tell us the nature not of a future reality, but of one that is eternal and which therefore no actions of ours can have power to alter. Such information *may* indeed have relevance to practical Ethics, but it must be of a purely negative kind. For, if it holds, not only that such an eternal reality exists, but also, as is commonly the case, that nothing else is real—that nothing either has been, is now, or will be real in time—then truly it will follow that nothing we can do will ever bring any good to pass. For it is certain that our actions can only affect the future; and if nothing can be real in the future, we can certainly not hope ever to make any good thing real. It would follow, then, that there can be nothing which we ought to do. We cannot possibly do any good ; for neither our efforts, nor any result which they may seem to effect, have any real existence. But this consequence, though it follows strictly from many metaphysical doctrines, is rarely drawn. Although a metaphysician may say that nothing is real but that which is eternal, he will generally allow that there is some reality also in the temporal: and his doctrine of an eternal reality need not interfere with practical Ethics, if he allows that, however good the eternal reality may be, yet some things will also exist in time, and that the existence of some will be better than that of others. It is, however, worth while to insist upon this point, because it is rarely fully realised.

If it is maintained that there is any validity at all in practical Ethics—that any proposition which asserts 'We ought to do so and so' can have any truth—this contention can only be consistent with the Metaphysics of an eternal reality, under two conditions. One of these is, (1) that the true eternal reality, which is to be our guide, cannot, as is implied by calling it true, be the *only* true reality. For a moral rule, bidding us realise a certain end, can only be justified, if it is possible that that end should, at least partially, be realised. Unless our efforts can effect the *real* existence of some good, however little, we certainly have no reason for making them. And if the eternal reality is the sole reality, then nothing good can possibly exist in time: we can only be told to try to bring into existence something which we know beforehand cannot possibly exist. If it is said that what exists in time can only be a manifestation of the true reality, it must at least be allowed that that manifestation is another true reality—a good which we really can cause to exist; for the production of something quite unreal, even if it were possible, cannot be a reasonable end of action. But if the manifestation of that which eternally exists *is* real, then that which eternally exists is not the sole reality.

And the second condition which follows from such a metaphysical principle of Ethics, is (2) that the eternal reality cannot be perfect—cannot be the sole good. For just as a reasonable rule of conduct requires that what we are told to realise should be capable of being truly real, so it requires that the realisation of this ideal shall be truly good. It is just that which *can* be realised by our efforts—the appearance of the eternal in time, or whatsoever else is allowed to be attainable—which must be truly good, if it is to be worth our efforts. That the eternal reality is good, will by no means justify us in aiming at its manifestation, unless that manifestation itself be also good. For the manifestation is different from the reality : its difference is allowed, when we are told that it can be made to exist, whereas the reality itself exists unalterably. And the existence of this manifestation is the only thing which we can hope to effect : that also is admitted. If, therefore, the moral maxim is to be justified, it is the existence of this manifestation, as distinguished from the existence of its corresponding reality, which must be truly good. The reality may be good too : but to justify the statement that we ought to produce anything, it must be maintained, that just that thing itself, and not something else which may be like it, is truly good. If it is not true that the existence of the manifestation will add something to the sum of good in the Universe, then we have no reason to aim at making it exist ; and if it is true that it will add something to the sum of good, then the existence of that which is eternal cannot be perfect by itself—it cannot include the whole of possible goods.

Metaphysics, then, will have a bearing upon practical Ethics—upon the question what we ought to do—if it can tell us anything about the future consequences of our actions beyond what can be established by ordinary inductive reasoning. But the most characteristic metaphysical doctrines, those which profess to tell us not about the future but about the nature of an eternal reality, can either have no bearing upon this practical question or else must have a purely destructive bearing. For it is plain that what exists eternally cannot be affected by our actions ; and only what is affected by our actions can have a bearing on their value as means. But the nature of an eternal reality either admits no inference as to the results of our actions, except in so far as it can *also* give us information about the future (and how it can do this is not plain), or else, if, as is usual, it is maintained to be the sole reality and the sole good, it shews that no results of our actions can have any value whatever.

69. But this bearing upon practical Ethics, such as it is, is not what is commonly meant when it is maintained that Ethics must be based on Metaphysics. It is not the assertion of this relation which I have taken to be characteristic of Metaphysical Ethics. What metaphysical writers commonly maintain is not merely that Metaphysics can help us to decide what the effects of our actions will be, but that it can tell us which among possible effects will be good and which will be bad. They profess that Metaphysics is a necessary basis for an answer to that other and primary ethical question: What ought to be? What is good in itself? That no truth about what is real can have any logical bearing upon the answer to this question has been proved in Chapter I. To suppose that it has, implies the naturalistic fallacy. All that remains for us to do is, therefore, to expose the main errors which seem to have lent plausibility to this fallacy in its metaphysical form. If we ask: What bearing can Metaphysics have upon the question, What is good? the only possible answer is: Obviously and absolutely none. We can only hope to enforce conviction that this answer is the only true one by answering the question: Why has it been supposed to have such a bearing? We shall find that metaphysical writers seem to have failed to distinguish this primary ethical question: What is good? from various other questions; and to point out these distinctions will serve to confirm the view that their profession to base Ethics on Metaphysics is solely due to confusion.

70. And, first of all, there is an ambiguity in the very question: What is good? to which it seems some influence must be attributed. The question may mean either: Which among existing things are good? or else: What *sort of* things are good, what are the things which, whether they *are* real or not, ought to be real? And of these two questions it is plain that to answer the first, we must know both the answer to the second and also the answer to the question: What is real? It asks us for a catalogue of all the good things in the Universe; and to answer it we must know both what things there are in the Universe and also which of them are good. Upon this question then our Metaphysics would have a bearing, if it can tell us what is real. It would help us to complete the list of things which are both real and good. But to make such a list is not the business of Ethics. So far as it enquires What is good? its business is finished when it has completed the list of things which ought to exist, whether they do exist or not. And if our Metaphysics is to have any bearing upon this part of the ethical problem, it must be because the fact that something is real gives a reason for thinking that it or something else is good, whether it be real or not. That any such fact can give any such reason is impossible; but it may be suspected that the contrary supposition has been encouraged by the failure to distinguish between the assertion 'This is good,' when it means '*This sort of thing* is good,' or 'This would be good, if it existed,' and the assertion 'This existing thing is good.' The latter proposition obviously cannot be true, unless the thing exists; and hence the proof of the thing's existence is a necessary step to its proof. Both propositions, however, in spite of this immense difference between them, are commonly expressed in the same terms. We use the same words, when we assert an ethical proposition about a subject that is actually real, and when we assert it about a subject considered as merely possible.

In this ambiguity of language we have, then, a possible source of error with regard to the bearing of truths that assert reality upon truths that assert goodness. And that this ambiguity is actually neglected by those metaphysical writers who profess that the Supreme Good consists in an eternal reality may be shewn in the following way. We have seen, in considering the possible bearing of Metaphysics upon Practical Ethics, that, since what exists eternally cannot possibly be affected by our actions, no practical maxim can possibly be true, if the sole reality is eternal. This fact, as I said, is commonly neglected by metaphysical writers: they assert both of the two contradictory propositions that the sole reality is eternal and that its realisation in the future is a good too. Prof. Mackenzie, we saw, asserts that we ought to aim at the realisation of 'the true self' or 'the rational universe': and yet Prof. Mackenzie holds, as the word 'true' plainly implies, that both 'the true self' and 'the rational universe' are eternally real. Here we have already a contradiction in the supposition that what is eternally real can be realised in the future; and it is comparatively unimportant whether or not we add to this the further contradiction involved in the supposition that the eternal is the sole reality. That such a contradiction should be supposed valid can only be explained by a neglect of the distinction between a real subject and the character which that real subject possesses. *What* is eternally real may, indeed, be realised in the future, if by this be only meant the *sort of thing* which is eternally real. But when we assert that a thing is good, what we mean is that its existence or reality is good; and the eternal existence of a thing cannot possibly be the same good as the existence in time of what, in a necessary sense, is nevertheless the *same* thing. When, therefore, we are told that the future realisation of the *true* self is good, this can at most only mean that the future realisation of a self *exactly like* the self, which is true and exists eternally, is good. If this fact were clearly stated, instead of consistently ignored, by those who advocate the view that the Supreme Good can be defined in these metaphysical terms, it seems probable that the view that a knowledge of reality is necessary to a knowledge of the Supreme Good would lose part of its plausibility. That that at which we ought to aim cannot possibly be that which is eternally real, even if it be exactly like it; and that the eternal reality cannot possibly be the sole good—these two propositions seem sensibly to diminish the probability that Ethics must be based on Metaphysics. It is not very plausible to maintain that because one thing is real, therefore something like it, which is not real, would be good. It seems, therefore, that some of the plausibility of Metaphysical Ethics may be reasonably attributed to the failure to observe that verbal ambiguity, whereby 'This is good' may mean either 'This real thing is good' or 'The existence of this thing (whether it exists or not) would be good.'

71. By exposing this ambiguity, then, we are enabled to see more clearly what must be meant by the question: Can Ethics be based on Metaphysics? and we are, therefore, more likely to find the correct answer. It is now plain that a metaphysical principle of Ethics which says 'This eternal reality is the Supreme Good' can only mean 'Something like this eternal reality would be the Supreme Good.' We are now to understand such principles as having the only meaning which they can consistently have, namely, as describing the kind of thing which ought to exist in the future, and which we ought to try to bring about. And, when this is clearly recognised, it seems more evident that the knowledge that such a kind of thing is also eternally real, cannot help us at all towards deciding the properly ethical question : Is the existence of that kind of good thing? If we can see that an eternal reality is good, we can see, equally easily, once the idea of such a thing has been suggested to us, that it *would* be good. The metaphysical construction of Reality would therefore be quite as useful, for the purposes of Ethics, if it were a mere construction of an imaginary Utopia : provided the kind of thing suggested is the same, fiction is as useful as truth, for giving us matter, upon which to exercise the judgment of value. Though, therefore, we admit that Metaphysics may serve an ethical purpose, in suggesting things, which would not otherwise have occurred to us, but which, when they are suggested, we see to be good ; yet, it is not as Metaphysics—as professing to tell us what is real—that it has this use. And, in fact, the pursuit of truth must limit the usefulness of Metaphysics in this respect. Wild and extravagant as are the assertions which metaphysicians have made about reality, it is not to be supposed but that they have been partially deterred from making them wilder still, by the idea that it was their business to tell nothing but the truth. But the wilder they are, and the less useful for Metaphysics, the more useful will they be for Ethics; since, in order to be sure that we have neglected nothing in the description of our ideal, we should have had before us as wide a field as possible of suggested goods. It is probable that this utility of Metaphysics, in suggesting possible ideals, may sometimes be what is meant by the assertion that Ethics should be based on Metaphysics. It is not uncommon to find that which suggests a truth confused with that on which it logically depends; and I have already pointed out that Metaphysical have, in general, this superiority over Naturalistic systems, that they conceive the Supreme Good as something differing more widely from what exists here and now. But, if it be recognised that, in this sense, Ethics should, far more emphatically, be *based on* fiction, metaphysicians will, I think, admit that a connection of this kind between Metaphysics and Ethics would by no means justify the importance which they attribute to the bearing of the one study on the other.

72. We may, then, attribute the obstinate prejudice that a knowledge of supersensible reality is a necessary step to a knowledge of what is good in itself, partly to a failure to perceive that the subject of the latter judgment is not anything *real* as such, and partly to a failure to distinguish the cause of our perception of a truth from the reason why it is true. But these two causes will carry us only a very little way in our explanation of why Metaphysics should have been supposed to have a bearing upon Ethics. The first explanation which I have given would only account for the supposition that a thing's reality is a *necessary condition* for its goodness. This supposition is, indeed, commonly made; we find it commonly presupposed that unless a thing can be shewn to be involved in the constitution of reality, it cannot be good. And it is, therefore, worth while to insist that this is not the case; that Metaphysics is not even necessary to furnish *part* of the basis of Ethics. But when metaphysicians talk of basing Ethics on Metaphysics they commonly mean much more than this. They commonly mean that Metaphysics is the *sole* basis of Ethics—that it furnishes not only one necessary condition but *all* the conditions necessary to prove that certain things are good. And this view may, at first sight, appear to be held in two different forms. It may be asserted that merely to prove a thing supersensibly real is sufficient to prove it good: that the truly real must, for that reason alone, be truly good. But more commonly it appears to be held that the real must be good because it possesses certain characters. And we may, I think, reduce the first kind of assertion to no more than this. When it is asserted that the real must be good, because it is real, it is commonly also held that this is only because, in order to be real, it must be of a certain kind. The reasoning by which it is thought that a metaphysical enquiry can give an ethical conclusion is of the following form. From a consideration of what it is to be real, we can infer that what is real must have certain supersensible properties : but to have these properties is identical with being good—it is the very meaning of the word : it follows therefore that what has these properties is good : and from a consideration of what it is to be real, we can again infer what it is that has these properties. It is plain that, if such reasoning were correct, any answer which could be given to the question 'What is good in itself?' could be arrived at by a purely metaphysical discussion and by that alone. Just as, when Mill supposed that ' to be good' *meant* ' to be desired,' the question ' What is good ? ' could be and must be answered solely by an empirical investigation of the question what was desired ; so here, if to be good means to have some supersensible property, the ethical question can and must be answered by a metaphysical enquiry into the question, What has this property ? What, then, remains to be done in order to destroy the plausibility of Metaphysical Ethics, is to expose the chief errors which seem to have led metaphysicians to suppose that to be good *means* to possess some supersensible property.

73. What, then, are the chief reasons which have made it seem plausible to maintain that to be good must *mean* to possess some supersensible property or to be related to some supersensible reality ?

We may, first of all, notice one, which seems to have had some influence in causing the view that good must be defined by *some* such property, although it does not suggest any *particular* property as the one required. This reason lies in the supposition that the proposition ' This is good ' or ' This would be good, if it existed ' must, in a certain respect, be of the same type as other propositions. The fact is that there is one type of proposition so familiar to everyone, and therefore having such a strong hold upon the imagination, that philosophers have always supposed that all other types must be reducible to it. This type is that of the objects of experience—of all those truths which occupy our minds for the immensely greater part of our waking lives: truths such as that somebody is in the room, that I am writing or eating or talking. All these truths, however much they may differ, have this in common that in them both the grammatical subject and the grammatical predicate stand for something which exists. Immensely the commonest type of truth, then, is one which asserts a relation between two existing things. Ethical truths are immediately felt not to conform to this type, and the naturalistic fallacy arises from the attempt to make out that, in some roundabout way, they do conform to it. It is immediately obvious that when we see a thing to be good, its goodness is not a property which we can take up in our hands, or separate from it even by the most delicate scientific instruments, and transfer to something else. It is not, in fact, like most of the predicates which we ascribe to things, a *part* of the thing to which we ascribe it. But philosophers suppose that the reason why we cannot take goodness up and move it about, is not that it is a different *kind* of object from any which can be moved about, but only that it *necessarily* exists together with anything with which it does exist. They explain the type of ethical truths by supposing it identical with the type of scientific laws. And it is only when they have done this that the naturalistic philosophers proper—those who are empiricists —and those whom I have called 'metaphysical' part company. These two classes of philosophers do, indeed, differ with regard to the nature of scientific laws. The former class tend to suppose that when they say 'This always accompanies that' they mean only 'This has accompanied, does now, and will accompany that in these particular instances': they reduce the scientific law quite simply and directly to the familiar type of proposition which I have pointed out. But this does not satisfy the metaphysicians. They see that when you say 'This would accompany that, *if* that existed,' you don't mean only that this and that have existed and will exist together so many times. But it is beyond even their powers to believe that what you do mean is merely what you say. They still think you must mean, somehow or other, that something does exist, since that is what you generally mean when you say anything. They are as unable as the empiricists to imagine that you can ever mean that $2 + 2 = 4$. The empiricists say this means that so many couples of couples of things have in each case been four things; and hence that 2 and 2 would not make 4, unless precisely those things had existed. The metaphysicians feel that this is wrong; but they themselves have no better account of its meaning to give than either, with Leibniz, that God's mind is in a certain state, or, with Kant, that your mind is in a certain state, or finally, with Mr Bradley, that something is in a certain state. Here, then, we have the root of the naturalistic fallacy. The metaphysicians have the merit of seeing that when you say 'This would be good, if it existed,' you can't mean merely 'This has existed and was desired,' however many times that may have been the case. They will admit that some good things have not existed in this world, and even that some may not have been desired. But what you can mean, except that *something* exists, they really cannot see. Precisely the same error which leads them to suppose that there must *exist* a supersensible Reality, leads them to commit the naturalistic fallacy with regard to the meaning of 'good.' Every truth, they think, must mean somehow that something exists; and since, unlike the empiricists, they recognise some truths which do not mean that anything exists here and now, these they think must mean that something exists *not* here and now. On the same principle, since 'good' is a predicate which neither does nor can exist, they are bound to suppose either that 'to be good' means to be related to some other particular thing which can exist and does exist 'in reality'; or else that it means merely 'to belong to the real world'—that goodness is transcended or absorbed in reality.

74. That such a reduction of *all* propositions to the type of those which assert either that something exists or that something which exists has a certain attribute (which means, that both exist in a certain relation to one another), is erroneous,

may easily be seen by reference to the particular class of ethical propositions. For whatever we may have proved to exist, and whatever two existents we may have proved to be necessarily connected with one another, it still remains a distinct and different question whether what thus exists is good; whether either or both of the two existents is so; and whether it is good that they should exist together. To assert the one is plainly and obviously *not* the same thing as to assert the other. We understand what we mean by asking: Is this, which exists, or necessarily exists, after all, good? and we perceive that we are asking a question which has *not* been answered. In face of this direct perception that the two questions are distinct, no proof that they *must* be identical can have the slightest value. That the proposition 'This is good' is thus distinct from every other proposition was proved in Chapter I.; and I may now illustrate this fact by pointing out how it is distinguished from two particular propositions with which it has commonly been identified. That so and so *ought to be done* is commonly called a moral *law*; and this phrase naturally suggests that this proposition is in some way analogous either to a natural law, or to a law in the legal sense, or to both. All three are, in fact, really analogous in one respect, and in one respect only: that they include a proposition which is *universal*. A moral law asserts 'This is good *in all cases*'; a natural law asserts 'This happens *in all cases*'; and a law, in the legal sense, 'It is commanded that this be done, or be left undone, *in all cases.*' But since it is very natural to suppose that the analogy extends further, and that the assertion 'This is good in all cases' is equivalent to the assertion 'This happens in all cases' or to the assertion 'It is commanded that this be done in all cases,' it may be useful briefly to point out that they are *not* equivalent.

75. The fallacy of supposing moral law to be analogous to natural law in respect of asserting that some action is one which is always necessarily done is contained in one of the most famous doctrines of Kant. Kant identifies what ought to be with the law according to which a Free or Pure Will *must* act —with the only kind of action which is possible for it. And by this identification he does not mean merely to assert that the Free

Will is *also* under the necessity of doing what it ought; he means that what it ought to do *means* nothing but its own law —the law according to which it must act. It differs from the human will just in that, what *we* ought to do, is what *it* necessarily does. It is 'autonomous'; and by this is meant (among other things) that there is no separate standard by which it can be judged: that the question 'Is the law by which this Will acts a good one?' is, in its case, meaningless. It follows that what is necessarily willed by this Pure Will is good, not *because* that Will is good, nor for any other reason; but merely because it is what is necessarily willed by a Pure Will.

Kant's assertion of the 'Autonomy of the Practical Reason' thus has the very opposite effect to that which he desired; it makes his Ethics ultimately and hopelessly 'heteronomous.' His Moral Law is 'independent' of Metaphysics only in the sense that according to him we can *know* it independently; he holds that we can only infer that there is Freedom, from the fact that the Moral Law is true. And so far as he keeps strictly to this view, he does avoid the error, into which most metaphysical writers fall, of allowing his opinions as to what is real to influence his judgments of what is good. But he fails to see that on his view the Moral Law is dependent upon Freedom in a far more important sense than that in which Freedom depends on the Moral Law. He admits that Freedom is the *ratio essendi* of the Moral Law, whereas the latter is only *ratio cognoscendi* of Freedom. And this means that, unless Reality be such as he says, no assertion that 'This is good' can possibly be true: it can indeed have no meaning. He has, therefore, furnished his opponents with a conclusive method of attacking the validity of the Moral Law. If they can only shew by some other means (which he denies to be possible but leaves theoretically open) that the nature of Reality is not such as he says, he cannot deny that they will have proved his ethical principle to be false. If that 'This ought to be done' *means* 'This is willed by a Free Will,' then, if it can be shewn that there is no Free Will which wills anything, it will follow that nothing ought to be done.

76. And Kant also commits the fallacy of supposing that

'This ought to be' means 'This is commanded.' He conceives the Moral Law to be an Imperative. And this is a very common mistake. 'This ought to be,' it is assumed, must mean 'This is commanded'; nothing, therefore, would be good unless it were commanded; and since commands in this world are liable to be erroneous, what ought to be in its ultimate sense means 'what is commanded by some real supersensible authority.' With regard to this authority it is, then, no longer possible to ask Is it righteous?' Its commands cannot fail to be right, because to be right means to be what it commands. Here, therefore, law, in the moral sense, is supposed analogous to law, in the legal sense, rather than, as in the last instance, to law in the natural sense. It is supposed that moral obligation is analogous to legal obligation, with this difference only that whereas the source of legal obligation is earthly, that of moral obligation is heavenly. Yet it is obvious that if by a source of obligation is meant only a power which binds you or compels you to do a thing, it is not because it does do this that you ought to obey it. It is only if it be itself so good, that it commands and enforces only what is good, that it can be a source of moral obligation. And in that case what it commands and enforces would be good, whether commanded and enforced or not. Just that which makes an obligation legal, namely the fact that it is commanded by a certain kind of authority, is entirely irrelevant to a moral obligation. However an authority be defined, its commands will be *morally* binding only if they are—morally binding; only if they tell us what ought to be or what is a means to that which ought to be.

77. In this last error, in the supposition that when I say 'You ought to do this' I must mean 'You are commanded to do this,' we have one of the reasons which has led to the supposition that the particular supersensible property by reference to which good must be defined is Will. And that ethical conclusions may be obtained by enquiring into the nature of a fundamentally real Will seems to be by far the commonest assumption of Metaphysical Ethics at the present day. But this assumption seems to owe its plausibility, not so much to the supposition that 'ought' expresses a 'command,' as to a far more fundamental error. This error consists in supposing that to ascribe certain predicates to a thing is the same thing as to say that that thing is the object of a certain kind of psychical state. It is supposed that to say that a thing is real or true is the same thing as to say that it is known in a certain way; and that the difference between the assertion that it is good and the assertion that it is real—between an ethical, therefore, and a metaphysical proposition—*consists* in the fact that whereas the latter asserts its relation to Cognition the former asserts its relation to Will.

Now that this is an error has been already shewn in Chapter I. That the assertion 'This is good' is *not* identical with the assertion 'This is willed,' either by a supersensible will, or otherwise, nor with any other proposition, has been proved; nor can I add anything to that proof. But in face of this proof it may be anticipated that two lines of defence may be taken up. (1) It may be maintained that, nevertheless, they really are identical, and facts may be pointed out which seem to prove that identity. Or else (2) it may be said that an *absolute* identity is not maintained: that it is only meant to assert that there is some special connection between will and goodness, such as makes an enquiry into the real nature of the former an essential step in the proof of ethical conclusions. In order to meet these two possible objections, I propose first to shew what possible connections there are or may be between goodness and will; and that none of these can justify us in asserting that 'This is good' is identical with 'This is willed.' On the other hand it will appear that some of them may be easily confused with this assertion of identity; and that therefore the confusion is likely to have been made. This part of my argument will, therefore, already go some way towards meeting the second objection. But what must be conclusive against this is to shew that any possible connection between will and goodness *except* the *absolute* identity in question, would not be sufficient to give an enquiry into Will the smallest relevance to the proof of any ethical conclusion.

78. It has been customary, since Kant's time, to assert that Cognition, Volition, and Feeling are three fundamentally distinct attitudes of the mind towards reality. They are three distinct ways of experiencing, and each of them informs us of a distinct aspect under which reality may be considered. The 'Epistemological' method of approaching Metaphysics rests on the assumption that by considering what is 'implied in' Cognition—what is its 'ideal'—we may discover what properties the world must have, if it is to be *true*. And similarly it is held that by considering what is 'implied in' the fact of Willing or Feeling—what is the 'ideal' which they presuppose—we may discover what properties the world must have, if it is to be good or beautiful. The orthodox Idealistic Epistemologist differs from the Sensationalist or Empiricist in holding that what we directly cognise is neither all true nor yet the whole truth : in order to reject the false and to discover further truths we must, he says, not take cognition merely as it presents itself, but discover what is *implied* in it. And similarly the orthodox Metaphysical Ethicist differs from the mere Naturalist, in holding that not everything which we actually will is good, nor, if good, completely good : what is really good is that which is implied in the essential nature of will. Others again think that Feeling, and not Will, is the fundamental *datum* for Ethics. But, in either case, it is agreed that Ethics has some relation to Will or Feeling which it has not to Cognition, and which other objects of study have to Cognition. Will or Feeling, on the one hand, and Cognition, on the other, are regarded as in some sense coordinate sources of philosophical knowledge—the one of Practical, the other of Theoretical philosophy.

What, that is true, can possibly be meant by this view ?

79. First of all, it may be meant that, just as, by reflection on our perceptual and sensory experience, we become aware of the distinction between truth and falsehood, so it is by reflection on our experiences of feeling and willing that we become aware of ethical distinctions. We should not know what was meant by thinking one thing better than another unless the attitude of our will or feeling towards one thing was different from its attitude towards another. All this may be admitted. But so far we have only the psychological fact that it is only *because* we will or feel things in a certain way, that we ever come to

think them good; just as it is only because we have certain
perceptual experiences, that we ever come to think things true.
Here, then, is a special connection between willing and goodness; but it is only a *causal* connection—that willing is a
necessary condition for the cognition of goodness.

But it may be said further that willing and feeling are not
only the origin of cognitions of goodness; but that to will a
thing, or to have a certain feeling towards a thing, is the *same
thing* as to think it good. And it may be admitted that even
this is *generally* true in a sense. It does seem to be true that
we hardly ever think a thing good, and never very decidedly,
without at the same time having a special attitude of feeling
or will towards it; though it is certainly not the case that this
is true universally. And the converse may possibly be true
universally: it may be the case that a perception of goodness
is included in the complex facts which we mean by willing and
by having certain kinds of feeling. Let us admit then, that
to think a thing good and to will it are *the same thing* in this
sense, that, wherever the latter occurs, the former also occurs
as a *part* of it; and even that they are *generally the same thing*
in the converse sense, that when the former occurs it is generally a part of the latter.

80. These facts may seem to give countenance to the
general assertion that to think a thing good is to prefer it or
approve it, in the sense in which preference and approval denote
certain kinds of will or feeling. It seems to be always true
that when we thus prefer or approve, there is included in that
fact the fact that we think good; and it is certainly true, in
an immense majority of instances, that when we think good,
we also prefer or approve. It is natural enough, then, to say
that to think good is to prefer. And what more natural than to
add : When I say a thing is good, I *mean* that I prefer it ?
And yet this natural addition involves a gross confusion. Even
if it be true that to think good is the same thing as to prefer
(which, as we have seen, is *never* true in the sense that they
are absolutely identical; and not *always* true, even in the sense
that they occur together), yet it is not true that *what* you
think, when you think a thing good, is *that* you prefer it.

Even if your thinking the thing good is the same thing as your preference of it, yet the goodness of the thing—that *of* which you think—is, for that very reason, obviously *not* the same thing as your preference of it. Whether you have a certain thought or not is one question; and whether what you think is true is quite a different one, upon which the answer to the first has not the least bearing. The fact that you prefer a thing does not tend to shew that the thing is good; even if it does shew that you think it so.

It seems to be owing to this confusion, that the question 'What is good?' is thought to be identical with the question 'What is preferred?' It is said, with sufficient truth, that you would never know a thing was good unless you preferred it, just as you would never know a thing existed unless you perceived it. But it is added, and this is false, that you would never know a thing was good unless you *knew* that you preferred it, or that it existed unless you *knew* that you perceived it. And it is finally added, and this is utterly false, that you cannot distinguish the fact that a thing is good from the fact that you prefer it, or the fact that it exists from the fact that you perceive it. It is often pointed out that I cannot at any given moment distinguish what is true from what I think so: and this is true. But though I cannot distinguish *what* is true from *what* I think so, I always can distinguish what I mean by saying *that* it is true from what I mean by saying *that* I think so. For I understand the meaning of the supposition that what I think true may nevertheless be false. When, therefore, I assert that it is true I mean to assert something different from the fact that I think so. *What* I think, namely *that* something is true, is always quite distinct from the fact that I think it. The assertion that it is true does not even *include* the assertion that I think it so; although, of course, whenever I do think a thing true, it is, as a matter of fact, also true that I do think it. This tautologous proposition that for a thing to be thought true it is necessary that it should be thought, is, however, commonly identified with the proposition that for a thing to *be* true it is necessary that it should be thought. A very little reflection should suffice to convince anyone that this identification is erroneous; and a very little more will shew that, if so, we must mean by 'true' something which includes no reference to thinking or to any other psychical fact. It may be difficult to discover precisely *what* we mean—to hold the object in question before us, so as to compare it with other objects: but that we do mean something distinct and unique can no longer be matter of doubt. That 'to be true' *means* to be thought in a certain way is, therefore, certainly false. Yet this assertion plays the most essential part in Kant's 'Copernican revolution' of philosophy, and renders worthless the whole mass of modern literature, to which that revolution has given rise, and which is called Epistemology. Kant held that what was unified in a certain manner by the synthetic activity of thought was *ipso facto* true : that this was the very meaning of the word. Whereas it is plain that the only connection which can possibly hold between being true and being thought in a certain way, is that the latter should be a *criterion* or test of the former. In order, however, to establish that it is so, it would be necessary to establish by the methods of induction that what was true was always thought in a certain way. Modern Epistemology dispenses with this long and difficult investigation at the cost of the self-contradictory assumption that 'truth' and the criterion of truth are one and the same thing.

81. It is, then, a very natural, though an utterly false supposition that for a thing to *be* true is the same thing as for it to be perceived or thought of in a certain way. And since, for the reasons given above, the fact of preference seems roughly to stand in the same relation to thinking things good, in which the fact of perception stands to thinking that they are true or exist, it is very natural that for a thing to *be* good should be supposed identical with its being preferred in a certain way. But once this coordination of Volition and Cognition has been accepted, it is again very natural that every fact which seems to support the conclusion that being true is identical with being cognised should confirm the corresponding conclusion that being good is identical with being willed. It will, therefore, be in place to point out another confusion, which

6   M

seems to have had great influence in causing acceptance of the view that to be true is the same thing as to be cognised.

This confusion is due to a failure to observe that when we say we have a *sensation* or *perception* or that we *know* a thing, we mean to assert not only that our mind is cognitive, but *also* that that which it cognises is true. It is not observed that the usage of these words is such that, if a thing be untrue, that fact alone is sufficient to justify us in saying that the person who says he perceives or knows it, does not *perceive* or *know* it, without our either enquiring whether, or assuming that, his state of mind differs in any respect from what it would have been had he perceived or known. By this denial we do not accuse him of an error in introspection, even if there was such an error: we do not deny that he was aware of a certain object, nor even that his state of mind was exactly such as he took it to be: we merely deny that the object, of which he was aware, had a certain property. It is, however, commonly supposed that when we assert a thing to be perceived or known, we are asserting one fact only; and since of the two facts which we really assert, the existence of a physical state is by far the easier to distinguish, it is supposed that this is the only one which we do assert. Thus perception and sensation have come to be regarded as if they denoted certain states of mind and nothing more; a mistake which was the easier to make since the commonest state of mind, to which we give a name which does not imply that its object is true, namely imagination, may, with some plausibility, be supposed to differ from sensation and perception not only in the property possessed by its object, but also in its character as a state of mind. It has thus come to be supposed that the only difference between perception and imagination, by which they can be defined, must be a merely psychical difference: and, if this were the case, it would follow at once that to *be* true was identical with being cognised in a certain way; since the assertion that a thing is perceived does certainly *include* the assertion that it is true, and if, nevertheless, that it is perceived means *only* that the mind has a certain attitude towards it, then its truth must be identical with the fact that it is regarded in this way. We may, then, attribute the view that to be true *means* to be cognised in a certain way partly to the failure to perceive that certain words, which are commonly supposed to stand for nothing more than a certain kind of cognitive state, do, in fact, *also* include a reference to the truth of the object of such states.

82. I will now sum up my account of the apparent connections between will and ethical propositions, which seem to support the vague conviction that 'This is good' is somehow identical with 'This is willed in a certain way.' (1) It may be maintained, with sufficient show of truth, that it is only because certain things were originally willed, that we ever came to have ethical convictions at all. And it has been too commonly assumed that to shew what was the cause of a thing is the same thing as to shew what the thing itself is. It is, however, hardly necessary to point out that this is not the case. (2) It may be further maintained, with some plausibility, that to think a thing good and to will it in a certain way are *now* as a matter of fact identical. We must, however, distinguish certain possible meanings of this assertion. It may be admitted that when we think a thing good, we *generally* have a special attitude of will or feeling towards it; and that, perhaps, when we will it in a certain way, we do always think it good. But the very fact that we can thus distinguish the question whether, though the one is always accompanied by the other, yet this other may not always be accompanied by the first, shews that the two things are not, in the strict sense, identical. The fact is that, whatever we mean by will, or by any form of will, the fact we mean by it certainly always includes something else *beside* the thinking a thing good: and hence that, when willing and thinking good are asserted to be identical, the most that can be meant is that this other element in will always both accompanies and is accompanied by the thinking good; and this, as has been said, is of very doubtful truth. Even, however, if it were strictly true, the fact that the two things can be distinguished is fatal to the assumed coordination between will and cognition, in one of the senses in which that assumption is commonly made. For it is only in respect of the *other* element in will, that volition differs from cognition; whereas it is only in respect of the fact that volition, or some form of volition, *includes* a *cognition* of goodness, that will can have the same relation to ethical, which cognition has to metaphysical, propositions. Accordingly the fact of volition, *as a whole*, that is, if we include in it the element which makes it volition and distinguishes it from cognition, has *not* the same relation to ethical propositions which cognition has to those which are metaphysical. Volition and cognition are *not* coordinate ways of experiencing, since it is only in so far as volition denotes a *complex* fact, which includes in it the one identical simple fact, which is meant by *cognition*, that volition is a way of experiencing at all.

But, (3) if we allow the terms 'volition' or 'will' to stand for 'thinking good,' although they certainly do not commonly stand for this, there still remains the question: What connection would this fact establish between volition and Ethics? Could the enquiry into what was willed be identical with the ethical enquiry into what was good? It is plain enough that they could not be identical; though it is also plain why they should be thought so. The question 'What is good?' is confused with the question 'What is thought good?' and the question 'What is true?' with the question 'What is thought true?' for two main reasons. (1) One of these is the general difficulty that is found in distinguishing what is cognised from the cognition of it. It is observed that I certainly cannot cognise anything that is true without cognising it. Since, therefore, whenever I know a thing that is true, the thing is certainly cognised, it is assumed that for a thing to *be* true at all is the same thing as for it to be cognised. And (2) it is not observed that certain words, which are supposed to denote only peculiar species of cognition, do as a matter of fact *also* denote that the object cognised is true. Thus if 'perception' be taken to denote only a certain kind of mental fact, then, since the object of it is always true, it becomes easy to suppose that to be true means only to be object to a mental state of that kind. And similarly it is easy to suppose that to be truly good differs from being falsely thought so, solely in respect of the fact that to be the former is to be the object of a volition differing from that of which an apparent good is the object, in the same way in which a perception (on this supposition) differs from an illusion.

83. Being good, then, is not identical with being willed or felt in any kind of way, any more than being true is identical with being thought in any kind of way. But let us suppose this to be admitted : Is it still possible that an enquiry into the nature of will or feeling should be a necessary step to the proof of ethical conclusions ? If being good and being willed are *not* identical, then the most that can be maintained with regard to the connection of goodness with will is that what is good is always *also* willed in a certain way, and that what is willed in a certain way is always *also* good. And it may be said that this is all that is meant by those metaphysical writers who profess to base Ethics upon the Metaphysics of Will. What would follow from this supposition ?

It is plain that if what is willed in a certain way were always *also* good, then the fact that a thing was so willed would be a *criterion* of its goodness. But in order to establish that will is a criterion of goodness, we must be able to shew first and separately that in a great number of the instances in which we find a certain kind of will we also find that the objects of that will are good. We might, then, perhaps, be entitled to infer that in a few instances, where it was not obvious whether a thing was good or not but was obvious that it was willed in the way required, the thing was really good, since it had the property which in all other instances we had found to be accompanied by goodness. A reference to will might thus, just conceivably, become of use towards the end of our ethical investigations, when we had already been able to shew, independently, of a vast number of different objects that they were really good and in what degree they were so. And against even this conceivable utility it may be urged (1) That it is impossible to see why it should not be as easy (and it would certainly be the more secure way) to prove that the thing in question was good, by the same methods which we had used in proving that other things were good, as by reference to our criterion ; and (2) That, if we set ourselves seriously to find out what things are good, we shall see reason to think (as will appear in Chapter VI.) that they have *no* other property, both common and peculiar to them, beside their goodness—that, in fact, there is no criterion of goodness.

84. But to consider whether any form of will is or is not a criterion of goodness is quite unnecessary for our purpose here; since none of those writers who profess to base their Ethics on an investigation of will have ever recognised the need of proving directly and independently that all the things which are willed in a certain way are good. They make no attempt to shew that will is a *criterion* of goodness; and no stronger evidence could be given that they do not recognise that this, at most, is all it can be. As has been just pointed out, if we are to maintain that whatever is willed in a certain way is also good, we must in the first place be able to shew that certain things have one property 'goodness,' and that the same things *also* have the other property that they are willed in a certain way. And secondly we must be able to shew this in a very large number of instances, if we are to be entitled to claim any assent for the proposition that these two properties *always* accompany one another: even when this was shewn it would still be doubtful whether the inference from 'generally' to 'always' would be valid, and almost certain that this doubtful principle would be useless. But the very question which it is the business of Ethics to answer is this question what things are good; and, so long as Hedonism retains its present popularity, it must be admitted that it is a question upon which there is scarcely any agreement and which therefore requires the most careful examination. The greatest and most difficult part of the business of Ethics would therefore require to have been already accomplished before we could be entitled to claim that anything was a *criterion* of goodness. If, on the other hand, to be willed in a certain way was *identical* with being good, then indeed we should be entitled to start our ethical investigations by enquiring what was willed in the way required. That this is the way in which metaphysical writers start their investigations seems to shew conclusively that they are influenced by the idea that 'goodness' is *identical* with 'being willed.' They do not recognise that the question 'What is good?' is a *different* one from the question 'What is willed in a certain way?' Thus we find Green explicitly stating that '*the* common characteristic of the good is that it satisfies some desire[1].' If we are to take this statement strictly, it obviously asserts that good things have no characteristic in common, except that they satisfy some desire—not even, therefore, that they are good. And this can be only the case, if being good is *identical* with satisfying desire: if 'good' is merely another name for 'desire-satisfying.' There could be no plainer instance of the naturalistic fallacy. And we cannot take the statement as a mere verbal slip, which does not affect the validity of Green's main argument. For he nowhere either gives or pretends to give any reason for believing anything to be good in any sense, except that it is what would satisfy a particular kind of desire —the kind of desire which he tries to shew to be that of a moral agent. An unhappy alternative is before us. Such reasoning would give valid reasons for his conclusions, if, and only if, being good and being desired in a particular way were identical: and in this case, as we have seen in Chapter I., his conclusions would not be ethical. On the other hand, if the two are not identical, his conclusions may be ethical and may even be right, but he has not given us a single reason for believing them. The thing which a scientific Ethics is required to shew, namely that certain things are really good, he has assumed to begin with, in assuming that things which are willed in a certain way are always good. We may, therefore, have as much respect for Green's conclusions as for those of any other man who details to us his ethical convictions: but that any of his arguments are such as to give us any reason for holding that Green's convictions are more likely to be true than those of any other man, must be clearly denied. The *Prolegomena to Ethics* is quite as far as Mr Spencer's *Data of Ethics*, from making the smallest contribution to the solution of ethical problems.

85. The main object of this chapter has been to shew that Metaphysics, understood as the investigation of a supposed supersensible reality, can have no logical bearing whatever upon

[1] *Prolegomena to Ethics*, p. 178.

the answer to the fundamental ethical question 'What is good in itself?' That this is so, follows at once from the conclusion of Chapter I., that 'good' denotes an ultimate, unanalysable predicate; but this truth has been so systematically ignored, that it seemed worth while to discuss and distinguish, in detail, the principal relations, which do hold, or have been supposed to hold, between Metaphysics and Ethics. With this view I pointed out:—(1) That Metaphysics may have a bearing on *practical* Ethics—on the question 'What ought we to do?'— so far as it may be able to tell us what the future effects of our action will be: what it can *not* tell us is whether those effects are good or bad in themselves. One particular type of metaphysical doctrine, which is very frequently held, undoubtedly has such a bearing on *practical* Ethics: for, if it is true that the sole reality is an eternal, immutable Absolute, then it follows that no actions of ours can have any real effect, and hence that no *practical* proposition can be true. The same conclusion follows from the ethical proposition, commonly combined with this metaphysical one—namely that this eternal Reality is also the sole good (68). (2) That metaphysical writers, as where they fail to notice the contradiction just noticed between any *practical* proposition and the assertion that an eternal reality is the sole good, seem frequently to confuse the proposition that one particular existing thing is good, with the proposition that the existence of that kind of thing *would* be good, wherever it might occur. To the proof of the former proposition Metaphysics might be relevant, by shewing that the thing existed; to the proof of the latter it is wholly irrelevant: it can only serve the *psychological* function of suggesting things which may be valuable—a function which would be still better performed by pure fiction (69—71).

But the most important source of the supposition that Metaphysics is relevant to Ethics, seems to be the assumption that 'good' *must* denote some *real* property of things—an assumption which is mainly due to two erroneous doctrines, the first *logical*, the second *epistemological*. Hence (3) I discussed the *logical* doctrine that all propositions assert a relation

between existents; and pointed out that the assimilation of
ethical propositions either to natural laws or to commands
are instances of this *logical* fallacy (72—76). And finally
(4) I discussed the *epistemological* doctrine that to be good is
equivalent to being willed or felt in some particular way; a
doctrine which derives support from the analogous error, which
Kant regarded as the cardinal point of his system and which
has received immensely wide acceptance—the erroneous view
that to be 'true' or 'real' is equivalent to being thought in
a particular way. In this discussion the main points to which
I desire to direct attention are these: (*a*) That Volition and
Feeling are *not* analogous to Cognition in the manner assumed;
since in so far as these words denote an attitude of the mind
towards an object, they are themselves merely instances of
Cognition: they differ only in respect of the kind of object
of which they take cognisance, and in respect of the other
mental accompaniments of such cognitions: (*b*) That universally
the *object* of a cognition must be distinguished from the cognition of which it is the object; and hence that in no case
can the question whether the object is *true* be identical with
the question how it is cognised or whether it is cognised at all :
it follows that even if the proposition 'This is good' were
always the object of certain kinds of will or feeling, the *truth*
of that proposition could in no case be established by proving
that it was their object; far less can that proposition itself be
identical with the proposition that its subject is the object of a
volition or a feeling (77—84).

CHAPTER V.

86. IN the present chapter we have again to take a great step in ethical method. My discussion hitherto has fallen under two main heads. Under the first, I tried to shew what 'good'—the adjective 'good'—*means*. This appeared to be the first point to be settled in any treatment of Ethics, that should aim at being systematic. It is necessary we should know this, should know what good means, before we can go on to consider what is good—what things or qualities are good. It is necessary we should know it for two reasons. The first reason is that 'good' is the notion upon which all Ethics depends. We cannot hope to understand what we mean, when we say that this is good or that is good, until we understand quite clearly, not only what 'this' is or 'that' is (which the natural sciences and philosophy can tell us) but also what is meant by calling them good, a matter which is reserved for Ethics only. Unless we are quite clear on this point, our ethical reasoning will be always apt to be fallacious. We shall think that we are proving that a thing is 'good,' when we are really only proving that it is something else; since unless we know what 'good' means, unless we know what is meant by that notion in itself, as distinct from what is meant by any other notion, we shall not be able to tell when we are dealing with it and when we are dealing with something else, which is perhaps like it, but yet not the same. And the second reason why we should settle first of all this question 'What good means?' is a reason of method. It is this, that we can never

know on what *evidence* an ethical proposition rests, until we
know the nature of the notion which makes the proposition
ethical. We cannot tell what is possible, by way of proof,
in favour of one judgment that 'This or that is good,' or against
another judgment 'That this or that is bad,' until we have
recognised what the nature of such propositions must always
be. In fact, it follows from the meaning of good and bad, that
such propositions are all of them, in Kant's phrase, 'synthetic':
they all must rest in the end upon some proposition which
must be simply accepted or rejected, which cannot be logically
deduced from any other proposition. This result, which follows
from our first investigation, may be otherwise expressed by
saying that the fundamental principles of Ethics must be self-
evident. But I am anxious that this expression should not be
misunderstood. The expression 'self-evident' means properly
that the proposition so called is evident or true, *by itself* alone;
that it is not an inference from some proposition other than
itself. The expression does *not* mean that the proposition is
true, because it is evident to you or me or all mankind, because
in other words it appears to us to be true. That a proposition
appears to be true can never be a valid argument that true it
really is. By saying that a proposition is self-evident, we mean
emphatically that its appearing so to us, is *not* the reason why
it is true: for we mean that it has absolutely no reason. It
would not be a self-evident proposition, if we could say of it:
I cannot think otherwise and therefore it is true. For then its
evidence or proof would not lie in itself, but in something else,
namely our conviction of it. That it appears true to us may
indeed be the *cause* of our asserting it, or the reason why we
think and say that it is true: but a reason in this sense is
something utterly different from a logical reason, or reason why
something is true. Moreover, it is obviously not a reason of
the same thing. The *evidence* of a proposition to us is only
a reason for *our holding it* to be true: whereas a logical reason,
or reason in the sense in which self-evident propositions have
no reason, is a reason why *the proposition itself* must be true,
not why we hold it so to be. Again that a proposition is
evident to us may not only be the reason why we do think or

affirm it, it may even be a *reason* why we ought to think it or affirm it. But a reason, in this sense too, is not a logical reason for the truth of the proposition, though it is a logical reason for the rightness of holding the proposition. In our common language, however, these three meanings of 'reason' are constantly confused, whenever we say 'I have a reason for thinking that true.' But it is absolutely essential, if we are to get clear notions about Ethics or, indeed, about any other, especially any philosophical, study, that we should distinguish them. When, therefore, I talk of Intuitionistic Hedonism, I must not be understood to imply that my denial that 'Pleasure is the only good' is *based* on my Intuition of its falsehood. My Intuition of its falsehood is indeed *my* reason for *holding* and declaring it untrue; it is indeed the only valid reason for so doing. But that is just because there is *no* logical reason for it; because there is no proper evidence or reason of its falsehood except itself alone. It is untrue, because it is untrue, and there is no other reason: but I *declare* it untrue, because its untruth is evident to me, and I hold that that is a sufficient reason for my assertion. We must not therefore look on Intuition, as if it were an alternative to reasoning. Nothing whatever can take the place of *reasons* for the truth of any proposition: intuition can only furnish a reason for *holding* any proposition to be true: this however it must do when any proposition is self-evident, when, in fact, there are no reasons which prove its truth.

87. So much, then, for the first step in our ethical method, the step which established that good is good and nothing else whatever, and that Naturalism was a fallacy. A second step was taken when we began to consider proposed self-evident principles of Ethics. In this second division, resting on our result that good means good, we began the discussion of propositions asserting that such and such a thing or quality or concept was good. Of such a kind was the principle of Intuitionistic or Ethical Hedonism—the principle that 'Pleasure alone is good.' Following the method established by our first discussion, I claimed that the untruth of this proposition was self-evident. I could do nothing to *prove* that it was untrue;

I could only point out as clearly as possible what it means, and how it contradicts other propositions which appear to be equally true. My only object in all this was, necessarily, to convince. But even if I did convince, that does not prove that we are right. It justifies us in *holding* that we are so; but nevertheless we may be wrong. On one thing, however, we may justly pride ourselves. It is that we have had a better chance of answering our question rightly, than Bentham or Mill or Sidgwick or others who have contradicted us. For we have *proved* that these have never even asked themselves the question which they professed to answer. They have confused it with another question: small wonder, therefore, if their answer is different from ours. We must be quite sure that the same question has been put, before we trouble ourselves at the different answers that are given to it. For all we know, the whole world would agree with us, if they could once clearly understand the question upon which we want their votes. Certain it is, that in all those cases where we found a difference of opinion, we found also that the question had *not* been clearly understood. Though, therefore, we cannot prove that we are right, yet we have reason to believe that everybody, unless he is mistaken as to what he thinks, will think the same as we. It is as with a sum in mathematics. If we find a gross and palpable error in the calculations, we are not surprised or troubled that the person who made this mistake has reached a different result from ours. We think he will admit that his result is wrong, if his mistake is pointed out to him. For instance if a man has to add up $5 + 7 + 9$, we should not wonder that he made the result to be 34, if he started by making $5 + 7 = 25$. And so in Ethics, if we find, as we did, that 'desirable' is confused with 'desired,' or that 'end' is confused with 'means,' we need not be disconcerted that those who have committed these mistakes do not agree with us. The only difference is that in Ethics, owing to the intricacy of its subject-matter, it is far more difficult to persuade anyone either that he has made a mistake or that that mistake affects his result.

In this second division of my subject—the division which is occupied with the question, 'What is good in itself?'—I have hitherto only tried to establish one definite result, and that a negative one: namely that pleasure is *not* the sole good. This result, if true, refutes half, or more than half, of the ethical theories which have ever been held, and is, therefore, not without importance. It will, however, be necessary presently to deal positively with the question: What things are good and in what degrees?

88. But before proceeding to this discussion I propose, first, to deal with the *third* kind of ethical question—the question: What ought we to do?

The answering of this question constitutes the third great division of ethical enquiry; and its nature was briefly explained in Chap. I. (§§ 15—17). It introduces into Ethics, as was there pointed out, an entirely new question—the question what things are related as *causes* to that which is good in itself; and this question can only be answered by an entirely new method— the method of empirical investigation; by means of which causes are discovered in the other sciences. To ask what kind of actions we ought to perform, or what kind of conduct is right, is to ask what kind of effects such action and conduct will produce. Not a single question in practical Ethics can be answered except by a causal generalisation. All such questions do, indeed, *also* involve an ethical judgment proper—the judgment that certain effects are better, in themselves, than others. But they *do* assert that these better things are effects—are causally connected with the actions in question. Every judgment in practical Ethics may be reduced to the form: This is a cause of that good thing.

89. That this is the case, that the questions, What is right? what is my duty? what ought I to do? belong exclusively to this third branch of ethical enquiry, is the first point to which I wish to call attention. All moral laws, I wish to shew, are merely statements that certain kinds of actions will have good effects. The very opposite of this view has been generally prevalent in Ethics. 'The right' and 'the useful' have been supposed to be at least *capable* of conflicting with one another, and, at all events, to be essentially distinct. It has been characteristic of a certain school of moralists, as of moral common sense, to declare that the end will never justify the means. What I wish first to point out is that 'right' does and can mean nothing but 'cause of a good result,' and is thus identical with 'useful'; whence it follows that the end always will justify the means, and that no action which is not justified by its results can be right. That there may be a true proposition, meant to be conveyed by the assertion 'The end will not justify the means,' I fully admit: but that, in another sense, and a sense far more fundamental for ethical theory, it is utterly false, must first be shewn.

That the assertion 'I am morally bound to perform this action' is identical with the assertion 'This action will produce the greatest possible amount of good in the Universe' has already been briefly shewn in Chap I. (§ 17); but it is important to insist that this fundamental point is demonstrably certain. This may, perhaps, be best made evident in the following way. It is plain that when we assert that a certain action is our absolute duty, we are asserting that the performance of that action at that time is unique in respect of value. But no dutiful action can possibly have unique value in the sense that it is the sole thing of value in the world; since, in that case, *every* such action would be the *sole* good thing, which is a manifest contradiction. And for the same reason its value cannot be unique in the sense that it has more intrinsic value than anything else in the world; since *every* act of duty would then be the *best* thing in the world, which is also a contradiction. It can, therefore, be unique only in the sense that the whole world will be better, if it be performed, than if any possible alternative were taken. And the question whether this is so cannot possibly depend solely on the question of its own intrinsic value. For any action will also have effects different from those of any other action; and if any of these have intrinsic value, their value is exactly as relevant to the total goodness of the Universe as that of their cause. It is, in fact, evident that, however valuable an action may be in itself, yet, owing to its existence, the sum of good in the Universe may conceivably be made less than if some other action, less valuable in itself, had been performed. But to say that this is the case is to say that it would have been better that the action should not have been done; and this again is obviously equivalent to the statement that it ought not to have been done—that it was not what duty required. 'Fiat iustitia, ruat caelum' can only be justified on the ground that by the doing of justice the Universe gains more than it loses by the falling of the heavens. It is, of course, possible that this is the case: but, at all events, to assert that justice *is* a duty, in spite of such consequences, is to assert that it is the case.

Our 'duty,' therefore, can only be defined as that action, which will cause more good to exist in the Universe than any possible alternative. And what is 'right' or 'morally permissible' only differs from this, as what will *not* cause *less* good than any possible alternative. When, therefore, Ethics presumes to assert that certain ways of acting are 'duties' it presumes to assert that to act in those ways will always produce the greatest possible sum of good. If we are told that to 'do no murder' is a duty, we are told that the action, whatever it may be, which is called murder, will under no circumstances cause so much good to exist in the Universe as its avoidance.

90.   But, if this be recognised, several most important consequences follow, with regard to the relation of Ethics to conduct.

(1)   It is plain that no moral law is self-evident, as has commonly been held by the Intuitional school of moralists. The Intuitional view of Ethics consists in the supposition that certain rules, stating that certain actions are always to be done or to be omitted, may be taken as self-evident premises. I have shewn with regard to judgments of what is *good in itself,* that this is the case; no reason can be given for them. But it is the essence of Intuitionism to suppose that rules of action—statements not of what ought to *be,* but of what we ought to do— are in the same sense intuitively certain. Plausibility has been lent to this view by the fact that we do undoubtedly make immediate judgments that certain actions are obligatory or wrong: we are thus often intuitively certain of our duty, *in a psychological sense.* But, nevertheless, these judgments are not self-evident and cannot be taken as ethical premises, since, as has now been shewn, they are capable of being

confirmed or refuted by an investigation of causes and effects. It is, indeed, possible that some of our immediate intuitions are true; but since *what* we intuit, *what* conscience tells us, is that certain actions will always produce the greatest sum of good possible under the circumstances, it is plain that reasons can be given, which will shew the deliverances of conscience to be true or false.

91. (2) In order to shew that any action is a duty, it is necessary to know both what are the other conditions, which will, conjointly with it, determine its effects; to know exactly what will be the effects of these conditions; and to know all the events which will be in any way affected by our action throughout an infinite future. We must have all this causal knowledge, and further we must know accurately the degree of value both of the action itself and of all these effects; and must be able to determine how, in conjunction with the other things in the Universe, they will affect its value as an organic whole. And not only this: we must also possess all this knowledge with regard to the effects of every possible alternative; and must then be able to see by comparison that the total value due to the existence of the action in question will be greater than that which would be produced by any of these alternatives. But it is obvious that our causal knowledge alone is far too incomplete for us ever to assure ourselves of this result. Accordingly it follows that we never have any reason to suppose that an action is our duty: we can never be sure that any action will produce the greatest value possible.

Ethics, therefore, is quite unable to give us a list of duties: but there still remains a humbler task which may be possible for Practical Ethics. Although we cannot hope to discover which, in a given situation, is the best of all possible alternative actions, there may be some possibility of shewing which among the alternatives, *likely to occur to any one,* will produce the greatest sum of good. This second task is certainly all that Ethics can ever have accomplished: and it is certainly all that it has ever collected materials for proving; since no one has ever attempted to exhaust the possible alternative actions in any particular case. Ethical philosophers have in fact confined their

attention to a very limited class of actions, which have been
selected because they are those which most commonly occur to
mankind as possible alternatives. With regard to these they
may possibly have shewn that one alternative is better, *i.e.*
produces a greater total of value, than others. But it seems
desirable to insist, that though they have represented this result
as a determination of *duties*, it can never really have been so.
For the term duty is certainly so used that, if we are subsequently persuaded that any possible action would have produced more good than the one we adopted, we admit that we
failed to do our duty. It will, however, be a useful task if
Ethics can determine which among alternatives *likely to occur*
will produce the greatest total value. For, though this alternative cannot be proved to be the best possible, yet it may
be better than any course of action which we should otherwise
adopt.

92. A difficulty in distinguishing this task, which Ethics
may perhaps undertake with some hope of success, from the
hopeless task of finding duties, arises from an ambiguity in the
use of the term ' possible.' An action may, in one perfectly
legitimate sense, be said to be ' impossible ' solely because the
idea of doing it does not occur to us. In this sense, then, the
alternatives which do actually occur to a man would be the
only *possible* alternatives ; and the best of these would be the
best possible action under the circumstances, and hence would
conform to our definition of ' duty.' But when we talk of the
best *possible* action as our duty, we mean by the term any
action which no *other* known circumstance would prevent,
provided the idea of it occurred to us. And this use of the
term is in accordance with popular usage. For we admit that.
a man may fail to do his duty, through neglecting to think
of what he *might* have done. Since, therefore, we say that
he *might* have done, what nevertheless did not occur to him,
it is plain that we do not limit his *possible* actions to those of
which he thinks. It might be urged, with more plausibility,
that we mean by a man's duty only the best of those actions
of which he *might* have thought. And it is true that we do
not blame any man very severely for omitting an action of

which, as we say, 'he could not be expected to think.' But
even here it is plain that we recognise a distinction between
what he might have done and what he might have thought of
doing: we regard it as a pity that he did not do otherwise.
And 'duty' is certainly used in such a sense, that it would be
a contradiction in terms to say it was a pity that a man did his
duty.

We must, therefore, distinguish a possible action from an
action of which it is possible to think. By the former we mean
an action which no known cause would prevent, *provided* the
idea of it occurred to us: and that one among such actions,
which will produce the greatest total good, is what we mean by
duty. Ethics certainly cannot hope to discover what kind of
action is always our duty in this sense. It may, however, hope
to decide which among one or two such possible actions is the
best: and those which it has chosen to consider are, as a matter
of fact, the most important of those with regard to which men
deliberate whether they shall or shall not do them. A decision
with regard to these may therefore be easily confounded with
a decision with regard to which is the best possible action.
But it is to be noted that even though we limit ourselves to
considering which is the better among alternatives likely to be
thought of, the fact that these alternatives might be thought
of is not included is what we mean by calling them possible
alternatives. Even if in any particular case it was impossible
that the idea of them should have occurred to a man, the
question we are concerned with is, which, if it had occurred,
would have been the best alternative? If we say that murder
is always a worse alternative, we mean to assert that it is so,
even where it was impossible for the murderer to think of
doing anything else.

The utmost, then, that Practical Ethics can hope to discover
is which, among a few alternatives possible under certain
circumstances, will, on the whole, produce the best result.
It may tell us which is the best, in this sense, of certain
alternatives about which we are likely to deliberate; and since
we may also know that, even if we choose none of these, what
we shall, in that case, do is unlikely to be as good as one of

them, it may thus tell us which of the alternatives, among which we *can* choose, it is best to choose. If it could do this it would be sufficient for practical guidance.

93. But (3) it is plain that even this is a task of immense difficulty. It is difficult to see how we can establish even a probability that by doing one thing we shall obtain a better total result than by doing another. I shall merely endeavour to point out how much is assumed, when we assume that there is such a probability, and on what lines it seems possible that this assumption may be justified. It will be apparent that it has never yet been justified—that no sufficient reason has ever yet been found for considering one action more right or more wrong than another.

(*a*) The first difficulty in the way of establishing a probability that one course of action will give a better total result than another, lies in the fact that we have to take account of the effects of both throughout an infinite future. We have no certainty but that, if we do one action now, the Universe will, throughout all time, differ in some way from what it would have been, if we had done another; and, if there is such a permanent difference, it is certainly relevant to our calculation. But it is quite certain that our causal knowledge is utterly insufficient to tell us what different effects will probably result from two different actions, except within a comparatively short space of time; we can certainly only pretend to calculate the effects of actions within what may be called an 'immediate' future. No one, when he proceeds upon what he considers a rational consideration of effects, would guide his choice by any forecast that went beyond a few centuries at most; and, in general, we consider that we have acted rationally, if we think we have secured a balance of good within a few years or months or days. Yet, if a choice guided by such considerations is to be rational, we must certainly have some reason to believe that no consequences of our action in a further future will generally be such as to reverse the balance of good that is probable in the future which we can foresee. This large postulate must be made, if we are ever to assert that the results of one action will be even probably better than those of another. Our utter ignorance of the far future gives us no justification for saying that it is even probably right to choose the greater good within the region over which a probable forecast may extend. We do, then, assume that it is improbable that effects, after a certain time, will, in general, be such as to reverse the comparative value of the alternative results within that time. And that this assumption is justified must be shewn before we can claim to have given any reason whatever for acting in one way rather than in another. It may, perhaps, be justified by some such considerations as the following. As we proceed further and further from the time at which alternative actions are open to us, the events of which either action would be part cause become increasingly dependent on those other circumstances, which are the same, whichever action we adopt. The effects of any individual action seem, after a sufficient space of time, to be found only in trifling modifications spread over a very wide area, whereas its immediate effects consist in some prominent modification of a comparatively narrow area. Since, however, most of the things which have any great importance for good or evil are things of this prominent kind, there may be a probability that after a certain time all the effects of any particular action become so nearly indifferent, that any difference between their value and that of the effects of another action, is very unlikely to outweigh an obvious difference in the value of the immediate effects. It does in fact appear to be the case that, in most cases, whatever action we now adopt, 'it will be all the same a hundred years hence,' so far as the existence at that time of anything greatly good or bad is concerned : and this might, perhaps, be *shewn* to be true, by an investigation of the manner in which the effects of any particular event become neutralised by lapse of time. Failing such a proof, we can certainly have no rational ground for asserting that one of two alternatives is even probably right and another wrong. If any of our judgments of right and wrong are to pretend to probability, we must have reason to think that the effects of our actions in the far future will not have value sufficient to outweigh any superiority of one set of effects over another in the immediate future.

94. (*b*) We must assume, then, that if the effects of one action are generally better than those of another, so far forward in the future as we are able to foresee any probable difference in their effects at all, then the total effect upon the Universe of the former action is also generally better. We certainly cannot hope directly to compare their effects except within a limited future; and all the arguments, which have ever been used in Ethics, and upon which we commonly act in common life, directed to shewing that one course is superior to another, are (apart from theological dogmas) confined to pointing out such probable immediate advantages. The question remains then; Can we lay down any general rules to the effect that one among a few alternative actions will generally produce a greater total of good in the immediate future?

It is important to insist that this question, limited as it is, is the utmost, to which, with any knowledge we have at present or are likely to have for a long time to come, Practical Ethics can hope to give an answer. I have already pointed out that we cannot hope to discover which is the *best* possible alternative in any given circumstances, but only which, among a few, is better than the others. And I have also pointed out that there is certainly no more than a probability, even if we are entitled to assert so much, that what is better in regard to its immediate effects will also be better on the whole. It now remains to insist that, even with regard to these immediate effects, we can only hope to discover which, among a few alternatives, will *generally* produce the greatest balance of good in the immediate future. We can secure no title to assert that obedience to such commands as 'Thou shalt not lie,' or even 'Thou shalt do no murder,' is *universally* better than the alternatives of lying and murder. Reasons why no more than a *general* knowledge is possible have been already given in Chap. I. (§ 16); but they may be recapitulated here. In the first place, of the effects, which principally concern us in ethical discussions, as having intrinsic value, we know the causes so little, that we can scarcely claim, with regard to any single one, to have obtained even a *hypothetical* universal law, such as has been obtained in the exact sciences. We cannot even say: If this action is performed, under exactly these circumstances, and if no others interfere, this important effect, at least, will always be produced. But, in the second place, an ethical law is not merely hypothetical. If we are to know that it will *always* be better to act in a certain way, under certain circumstances, we must know not merely what effects such actions will produce, *provided* no other circumstances interfere, but also that no other circumstances will interfere. And this it is obviously impossible to know with more than probability. An ethical law has the nature not of a scientific law but of a scientific *prediction*: and the latter is always merely probable, although the probability may be very great. An engineer is entitled to assert that, if a bridge be built in a certain way, it will probably bear certain loads for a certain time; but he can never be absolutely certain that it has been built in the way required, nor that, even if it has, some accident will not intervene to falsify his prediction. With any ethical law, the same must be the case; it can be no more than a generalisation: and here, owing to the comparative absence of accurate hypothetical knowledge, on which the prediction should be based, the probability is comparatively small. But finally, for an ethical generalisation, we require to know not only what effects will be produced, but also what are the comparative values of those effects; and on this question too, it must be admitted, considering what a prevalent opinion Hedonism has been, that we are very liable to be mistaken. It is plain, then, that we are not soon likely to know more than that one kind of action will *generally* produce better effects than another; and that more than this has certainly never been proved. In no two cases will *all* the effects of any kind of action be precisely the same, because in each case some of the circumstances will differ; and although the effects, that are important for good or evil, may be generally the same, it is extremely unlikely that they will always be so.

95. (*c*) If, now, we confine ourselves to a search for actions which are *generally* better as means than any probable alternative, it seems possible to establish as much as this in defence of most of the rules most universally recognised by Common Sense. I do not propose to enter upon this defence in detail, but merely to point out what seem to be the chief distinct principles by the use of which it can be made.

In the first place, then, we can only shew that one action is generally better than another as a means, provided that certain other circumstances are given. We do, as a matter of fact, only observe its good effects under certain circumstances; and it may be easily seen that a sufficient change in these would render doubtful what seem the most universally certain of general rules. Thus, the general disutility of murder can only be proved, provided the majority of the human race will certainly persist in existing. In order to prove that murder, if it were so universally adopted as to cause the speedy extermination of the race, would not be good as a means, we should have to disprove the main contention of pessimism— namely that the existence of human life is on the whole an evil. And the view of pessimism, however strongly we may be convinced of its truth or falsehood, is one which never has been either proved or refuted conclusively. That universal murder would not be a good thing at this moment can therefore not be proved. But, as a matter of fact, we can and do assume with certainty that, even if a few people are willing to murder, most people will not be willing. When, therefore, we say that murder is in general to be avoided, we only mean that it is so, so long as the majority of mankind will certainly not agree to it, but will persist in living. And that, under these circumstances, it is generally wrong for any single person to commit murder seems capable of proof. For, since there is in any case no hope of exterminating the race, the only effects which we have to consider are those which the action will have upon the increase of the goods and the diminution of the evils of human life. Where the best is not attainable (assuming extermination to be the best) one alternative may still be better than another. And, apart from the immediate evils which murder generally produces, the fact that, if it were a common practice, the feeling of insecurity, thus caused, would absorb much time, which might be spent to better purpose, is perhaps conclusive against it. So long as men desire to live as strongly as they do, and so long as it is certain that they will continue to do so, anything which hinders them from devoting their energy to the attainment of positive goods, seems plainly bad as a means. And the general practice of murder, falling so far short of universality as it certainly must in all known conditions of society, seems certainly to be a hindrance of this kind.

A similar defence seems possible for most of the rules, most universally enforced by legal sanctions, such as respect of property; and for some of those most commonly recognised by Common Sense, such as industry, temperance and the keeping of promises. In any state of society in which men have that intense desire for property of some sort, which seems to be universal, the common legal rules for the protection of property must serve greatly to facilitate the best possible expenditure of energy. And similarly: Industry is a means to the attainment of those necessaries, without which the further attainment of any great positive goods is impossible; temperance merely enjoins the avoidance of those excesses, which, by injuring health, would prevent a man from contributing as much as possible to the acquirement of these necessaries; and the keeping of promises greatly facilitates cooperation in such acquirement.

Now all these rules seem to have two characteristics to which it is desirable to call attention. (1) They seem all to be such that, in any known state of society, a *general* observance of them *would* be good as a means. The conditions upon which their utility depends, namely the tendency to preserve and propagate life and the desire of property, seem to be so universal and so strong, that it would be impossible to remove them; and, this being so, we can say that, under any conditions which could actually be given, the general observance of these rules would be good as a means. For, while there seems no reason to think that their observance ever makes a society worse than one in which they are not observed, it is certainly necessary as a means for any state of things in which the greatest

possible goods can be attained. And (2) these rules, since they
can be recommended as a means to that which is itself only
a necessary condition for the existence of any great good, can
be defended independently of correct views upon the primary
ethical question of what is good in itself. On any view commonly
taken, it seems certain that the preservation of civilised society,
which these rules are necessary to effect, is necessary for the
existence, in any great degree, of anything which may be held
to be good in itself.

96. But not by any means all the rules commonly recognised combine these two characteristics. The arguments offered
in defence of Common Sense morality very often presuppose
the existence of conditions, which cannot be fairly assumed to
be so universally necessary as the tendency to continue life and
to desire property. Such arguments, accordingly, only prove
the utility of the rule, so long as certain conditions, which may
alter, remain the same: it cannot be claimed of the rules thus
defended, that they would be generally good as means in every
state of society: in order to establish this *universal* general
utility, it would be necessary to arrive at a correct view of what
is good or evil in itself. This, for instance, seems to be the case
with most of the rules comprehended under the name of Chastity.
These rules are commonly defended, by Utilitarian writers or
writers who assume as their end the conservation of society,
with arguments which presuppose the necessary existence of
such sentiments as conjugal jealousy and paternal affection.
These sentiments are no doubt sufficiently strong and general
to make the defence valid for many conditions of society.
But it is not difficult to imagine a civilised society existing
without them; and, in such a case, if chastity were still to be
defended, it would be necessary to establish that its violation
produced evil effects, other than those due to the assumed
tendency of such violation to disintegrate society. Such a defence may, no doubt, be made; but it would require an examination into the primary ethical question of what is good and
bad in itself, far more thorough than any ethical writer has
ever offered to us. Whether this be so in this particular case
or not, it is certain that a distinction, not commonly recognised,

should be made between those rules, of which the social utility
depends upon the existence of circumstances, more or less likely
to alter, and those of which the utility seems certain under all
possible conditions.

97. It is obvious that all the rules, which were enumerated
above as likely to be useful in *almost any* state of society, can
also be defended owing to results which they produce under
conditions which exist only in particular states of society. And
it should be noticed that we are entitled to reckon among these
conditions the sanctions of legal penalties, of social disapproval,
and of private remorse, where these exist. These sanctions are,
indeed, commonly treated by Ethics only as motives for the
doing of actions of which the utility can be proved independently of the existence of these sanctions. And it may
be admitted that sanctions *ought* not to be attached to actions
which would not be right independently. Nevertheless it is
plain that, where they do exist, they are not only motives but
also justifications for the actions in question. One of the chief
reasons why an action should not be done in any particular
state of society is that it will be punished; since the punishment is in general itself a greater evil than would have been
caused by the omission of the action punished. Thus the
existence of a punishment may be an adequate reason for regarding an action as generally wrong, even though it has no
other bad effects but even slightly good ones. The fact that
an action will be punished is a condition of exactly the same
kind as others of more or less permanence, which must be taken
into account in discussing the general utility or disutility of
an action in a particular state of society.

98. It is plain, then, that the rules commonly recognised
by Common Sense, in the society in which we live, and commonly
advocated as if they were all equally and universally right and
good, are of very different orders. Even those which seem to
be most universally good as means, can only be shewn to be
so, because of the existence of conditions, which, though perhaps
evils, may be taken to be necessary; and even these owe their
more obvious utilities to the existence of other conditions, which
cannot be taken to be necessary except over longer or shorter

periods of history, and many of which are evils. Others seem
to be justifiable *solely* by the existence of such more or less
temporary conditions, unless we abandon the attempt to shew
that they are means to that preservation of society, which is
itself a mere means, and are able to establish that they are
directly means to things good or evil in themselves, but which
are not commonly recognised to be such.

If, then, we ask what rules are or would be useful to be
observed in the society in which we live, it seems possible to
prove a definite utility in most of those which are in general
both recognised and practised. But a great part of ordinary
moral exhortation and social discussion consists in the advocat-
ing of rules, which are *not* generally practised; and with regard
to these it seems very doubtful whether a case for their general
utility can ever be conclusively made out. Such proposed rules
commonly suffer from three main defects. In the first place,
(1) the actions which they advocate are very commonly such
as it is impossible for most individuals to perform by any
volition. It is far too usual to find classed together with
actions, which can be performed, if only they be willed, others,
of which the possibility depends upon the possession of a peculiar
disposition, which is given to few and cannot even be acquired.
It may, no doubt, be useful to point out that those who have
the necessary disposition should obey these rules ; and it would,
in many cases, be desirable that everybody should have this
disposition. But it should be recognised that, when we regard
a thing as a moral rule or law, we mean that it is one which
almost everybody can observe by an effort of volition, in that
state of society to which the rule is supposed to apply. (2) Actions are often advocated, of which, though they themselves are
possible, yet the proposed good effects are not possible, because
the conditions necessary for their existence are not sufficiently
general. A rule, of which the observance would produce good
effects, if human nature were in other respects different from
what it is, is advocated as if its general observance would produce the same effects now and at once. In fact, however, by
the time that the conditions necessary to make its observance
useful have arisen, it is quite as likely that other conditions,

rendering its observance unnecessary or positively harmful, may also have arisen; and yet this state of things may be a better one than that in which the rule in question would have been useful. (3) There also occurs the case in which the usefulness of a rule depends upon conditions likely to change, or of which the change would be as easy and more desirable than the observance of the proposed rule. It may even happen that the general observance of the proposed rule would itself destroy the conditions upon which its utility depends.

One or other of these objections seems generally to apply to proposed changes in social custom, advocated as being better rules to follow than those now actually followed; and, for this reason, it seems doubtful whether Ethics can establish the utility of any rules other than those generally practised. But its inability to do so is fortunately of little practical moment. The question whether the general observance of a rule not generally observed, would or would not be desirable, cannot much affect the question how any individual ought to act; since, on the one hand, there is a large probability that he will not, by any means, be able to bring about its general observance, and, on the other hand, the fact that its general observance would be useful could, in any case, give him no reason to conclude that he himself ought to observe it in the absence of such general observance.

With regard, then, to the actions commonly classed in Ethics, as duties, crimes, or sins, the following points seem deserving of notice. (1) By so classing them we mean that they are actions which it is possible for an individual to perform or avoid, if he only *wills* to do so; and that they are actions which *everybody* ought to perform or avoid, when occasion arises. (2) We can certainly not prove of any such action that it ought to be done or avoided under *all* circumstances; we can only prove that its performance or avoidance will *generally* produce better results than the alternative. (3) If further we ask of what actions as much as this can be proved, it seems only possible to prove it with regard to those which are actually generally practised among us. And of these some only are such that their general performance would be useful in any state of society that seems possible; of others the utility depends upon conditions which exist now, but which seem to be more or less alterable.

99. (*d*) So much, then, for moral rules or laws, in the ordinary sense—rules which assert that it is generally useful, under more or less common circumstances, for *everybody* to perform or omit some definite kind of action. It remains to say something with regard to the principles by which *the individual* should decide what he ought to do, (*a*) with regard to those actions as to which some general rule is certainly true, and (*β*) with regard to those where such a certain rule is wanting.

(*a*) Since, as I have tried to shew, it is impossible to establish that any kind of action will produce a better total result than its alternative *in all cases*, it follows that in some cases the neglect of an established rule will probably be the best course of action possible. The question then arises: Can the individual ever be justified in assuming that his is one of these exceptional cases? And it seems that this question may be definitely answered in the negative. For, if it is certain that in a large majority of cases the observance of a certain rule is useful, it follows that there is a large probability that it would be wrong to break the rule in any particular case; and the uncertainty of our knowledge both of effects and of their value, in particular cases, is so great, that it seems doubtful whether the individual's judgment that the effects will probably be good in his case can ever be set against the general probability that that kind of action is wrong. Added to this general ignorance is the fact that, if the question arises at all, our judgment will generally be biassed by the fact that we strongly desire one of the results which we hope to obtain by breaking the rule. It seems, then, that with regard to any rule which is *generally* useful, we may assert that it ought *always* to be observed, not on the ground that in *every* particular case it will be useful, but on the ground that in *any* particular case the probability of its being so is greater than that of our being likely to decide rightly that we have before us an instance of its disutility. In short, though we may be sure that there are cases where the rule should be broken, we can never know which those cases are,

and ought, therefore, never to break it. It is this fact which
seems to justify the stringency with which moral rules are
usually enforced and sanctioned, and to give a sense in which
we may accept as true the maxims that 'The end never justifies
the means' and 'That we should never do evil that good may
come.' The 'means' and the 'evil,' intended by these maxims,
are, in fact, the breaking of moral rules generally recognised
and practised, and which, therefore, we may assume to be generally useful. Thus understood, these maxims merely point out
that, in any particular case, although we cannot clearly perceive
any balance of good produced by keeping the rule and do seem
to see one that would follow from breaking it, nevertheless the
rule should be observed. It is hardly necessary to point out
that this is so only because it is certain that, in general, the
end does justify the means in question, and that therefore there
is a *probability* that in this case it will do so also, although we
cannot see that it will.

But moreover the universal observance of a rule which is
generally useful has, in many cases, a special utility, which
seems deserving of notice. This arises from the fact that, even
if we can clearly discern that our case is one where to break the
rule is advantageous, yet, so far as our example has any effect
at all in encouraging similar action, it will certainly tend to
encourage breaches of the rule which are not advantageous.
We may confidently assume that what will impress the imagination of others will not be the circumstances in which our case
differs from ordinary cases and which justify our exceptional
action, but the points in which it resembles other actions that
are really criminal. In cases, then, where example has any
influence at all, the effect of an exceptional right action will
generally be to encourage wrong ones. And this effect will
probably be exercised not only on other persons but on the
agent himself. For it is impossible for any one to keep his
intellect and sentiments so clear, but that, if he has once
approved of a generally wrong action, he will be more likely
to approve of it also under other circumstances than those
which justified it in the first instance. This inability to discriminate exceptional cases offers, of course, a still stronger

reason for the universal enforcement, by legal or social sanctions, of actions generally useful. It is undoubtedly well to punish a man, who has done an action, right in his case but generally wrong, even if his example would not be likely to have a dangerous effect. For sanctions have, in general, much more influence upon conduct than example; so that the effect of relaxing them in an exceptional case will almost certainly be an encouragement of similar action in cases which are not exceptional.

The individual can therefore be confidently recommended *always* to conform to rules which are both generally useful and generally practised. In the case of rules of which the general observance *would* be useful but does not exist, or of rules which are generally practised but which are not useful, no such universal recommendations can be made. In many cases the sanctions attached may be decisive in favour of conformity to the existing custom. But it seems worth pointing out that, even apart from these, the general utility of an action most commonly depends upon the fact that it is generally practised: in a society where certain kinds of theft are the common rule, the utility of abstinence from such theft on the part of a single individual becomes exceedingly doubtful, even though the common rule is a bad one. There is, therefore, a strong probability in favour of adherence to an existing custom, even if it be a bad one. But we cannot, in this case, assert with any confidence that this probability is always greater than that of the individual's power to judge that an exception will be useful; since we are here supposing certain one relevant fact—namely, that the rule, which he proposes to follow, *would* be better than that which he proposes to break, *if* it were generally observed. Consequently the effect of his example, so far as it tends to break down the existing custom, will here be for the good. The cases, where another rule would certainly be better than that generally observed, are, however, according to what was said above, very rare; and cases of doubt, which are those which arise most frequently, carry us into the next division of our subject.

100. (β) This next division consists in the discussion of the method by which an individual should decide what to do with regard to possible actions of which the general utility

cannot be proved. And it should be observed, that, according
to our previous conclusions, this discussion will cover almost all
actions, except those which, in our present state of society, are
generally practised. For it has been urged that a proof of
general utility is so difficult, that it can hardly be conclusive
except in a very few cases. It is certainly not possible with
regard to all actions which *are* generally practised; though
here, if the sanctions are sufficiently strong, they are sufficient
by themselves to prove the general utility of the individual's
conformity to custom. And if it is possible to prove a general
utility in the case of some actions, *not* generally practised, it
is certainly not possible to do so by the ordinary method,
which tries to shew in them a tendency to that preservation
of society, which is itself a mere means, but only by the
method, by which in any case, as will be urged, the individual
ought to guide his judgment—namely, by shewing their direct
tendency to produce what is good in itself or to prevent what
is bad.

The extreme improbability that any general rule with
regard to the utility of an action will be correct seems, in
fact, to be the chief principle which should be taken into
account in discussing how the individual should guide his
choice. If we except those rules which are both generally
practised and strongly sanctioned among us, there seem to
be hardly any of such a kind that equally good arguments
cannot be found both for and against them. The most that
can be said for the contradictory principles which are urged
by moralists of different schools as universal duties, is, in
general, that they point out actions which, for persons of a
particular character and in particular circumstances, would and
do lead to a balance of good. It is, no doubt, possible that
the particular dispositions and circumstances which generally
render certain kinds of action advisable, might to some degree
be formulated. But it is certain that this has never yet been
done; and it is important to notice that, even if it were done,
it would not give us, what moral laws are usually supposed
to be—rules which it would be desirable for every one, or
even for most people, to follow. Moralists commonly assume

7   M

that, in the matter of actions or habits of action, usually
recognised as duties or virtues, it is desirable that every one
should be alike. Whereas it is certain that, under actual
circumstances, and possible that, even in a much more ideal
condition of things, the principle of division of labour, according
to special capacity, which is recognised in respect of employ-
ments, would also give a better result in respect of virtues.

It seems, therefore, that, in cases of doubt, instead of
following rules, of which he is unable to see the good effects
in his particular case, the individual should rather guide his
choice by a direct consideration of the intrinsic value or
vileness of the effects which his action may produce. Judgments of intrinsic value have this superiority over judgments
of means that, if once true, they are always true; whereas
what is a means to a good effect in one case, will not be so
in another. For this reason the department of Ethics, which
it would be most useful to elaborate for practical guidance,
is that which discusses what things have intrinsic value and
in what degrees; and this is precisely that department which
has been most uniformly neglected, in favour of attempts to
formulate rules of conduct.

We have, however, not only to consider the relative goodness
of different effects, but also the relative probability of their
being attained. A less good, that is more likely to be attained,
is to be preferred to a greater, that is less probable, if the
difference in probability is great enough to outweigh the
difference in goodness. And this fact seems to entitle us to
assert the general truth of three principles, which ordinary
moral rules are apt to neglect. (1) That a lesser good, for
which any individual has a strong preference (if only it be a
good, and not an evil), is more likely to be a proper object for
him to aim at, than a greater one, which he is unable to
appreciate. For natural inclination renders it immensely more
easy to attain that for which such inclination is felt. (2) Since
almost every one has a much stronger preference for things
which closely concern himself, it will in general be right for
a man to aim rather at goods affecting himself and those in
whom he has a strong personal interest, than to attempt a

more extended beneficence. Egoism is undoubtedly superior to Altruism as a doctrine of means: in the immense majority of cases the best thing we can do is to aim at securing some good in which we are concerned, since for that very reason we are far more likely to secure it. (3) Goods, which can be secured in a future so near as to be called 'the present,' are in general to be preferred to those which, being in a further future, are, for that reason, far less certain of attainment. If we regard all that we do from the point of view of its rightness, that is to say as a mere means to good, we are apt to neglect one fact, at least, which is certain; namely, that a thing that is really good in itself, if it exist now, has precisely the same value as a thing of the same kind which may be caused to exist in the future. Moreover moral rules, as has been said, are, in general, not directly means to positive goods but to what is necessary for the existence of positive goods; and so much of our labour must in any case be devoted to securing the continuance of what is thus a mere means—the claims of industry and attention to health determine the employment of so large a part of our time, that, in cases where choice is open, the certain attainment of a present good will in general have the strongest claims upon us. If it were not so, the whole of life would be spent in merely assuring its continuance; and, so far as the same rule were continued in the future, that for the sake of which it is worth having, would never exist at all.

101. (4) A fourth conclusion, which follows from the fact that what is 'right' or what is our 'duty' must in any case be defined as what is a means to good, is, as was pointed out above (§ 89), that the common distinction between these and the 'expedient' or 'useful,' disappears. Our 'duty' is merely that which will be a means to the best possible, and the expedient, if it is really expedient, must be just the same. We cannot distinguish them by saying that the former is something which we ought to do, whereas of the latter we cannot say we '*ought*.' In short the two concepts are not, as is commonly assumed by all except Utilitarian moralists, simple concepts ultimately distinct. There is no such distinction in

Ethics. The only fundamental distinction is between what is good in itself and what is good as a means, the latter of which implies the former. But it has been shewn that the distinction between 'duty' and 'expediency' does not correspond to this: both must be defined as means to good, though both *may also* be ends in themselves. The question remains, then: What is the distinction between duty and expediency?

One distinction to which these distinct words refer is plain enough. Certain classes of action commonly excite the specifically moral sentiments, whereas other classes do not. And the word 'duty' is commonly applied only to the class of actions which excite moral approval, or of which the omission excites moral disapproval—especially to the latter. Why this moral sentiment should have become attached to some kinds of actions and not to others is a question which can certainly not yet be answered; but it may be observed that we have no reason to think that the actions to which it was attached were or are, in all cases, such as aided or aid the survival of a race: it was probably originally attached to many religious rites and ceremonies which had not the smallest utility in this respect. It appears, however, that, among us, the classes of action to which it is attached also have two other characteristics in enough cases to have influenced the meaning of the words 'duty' and 'expediency.' One of these is that 'duties' are, in general, actions which a considerable number of individuals are strongly tempted to omit. The second is that the omission of a 'duty' generally entails consequences markedly disagreeable to *some one else*. The first of these is a more universal characteristic than the second: since the disagreeable effects on other people of the 'self-regarding duties,' prudence and temperance, are not so marked as those on the future of the agent himself; whereas the temptations to imprudence and intemperance are very strong. Still, on the whole, the class of actions called duties exhibit both characteristics: they are not only actions, against the performance of which there are strong natural inclinations, but also actions of which the most obvious effects, commonly considered goods, are effects on other people. Expedient actions, on the other hand, are actions to which strong natural inclinations prompt us almost universally, and of which all the most obvious effects, commonly considered good, are effects upon the agent. We may then roughly distinguish 'duties' from expedient actions, as actions with regard to which there is a moral sentiment, which we are often tempted to omit, and of which the most obvious effects are effects upon others than the agent.

But it is to be noticed that none of these characteristics, by which a 'duty' is distinguished from an expedient action, gives us any reason to infer that the former class of actions are more useful than the latter—that they tend to produce a greater balance of good. Nor, when we ask the question, 'Is this my duty?' do we mean to ask whether the action in question has these characteristics: we are asking simply whether it will produce the best possible result on the whole. And if we asked this question with regard to expedient actions, we should quite as often have to answer it in the affirmative as when we ask it with regard to actions which have the three characteristics of 'duties.' It is true that when we ask the question, 'Is this expedient?' we are asking a different question—namely, whether it will have certain kinds of effect, with regard to which we do not enquire whether they are good or not. Nevertheless, if it should be doubted in any particular case whether these effects were good, this doubt is understood as throwing doubt upon the action's expediency: if we are required to *prove* an action's expediency, we can only do so by asking precisely the same question by which we should prove it a duty—namely, 'Has it the best possible effects on the whole?'

Accordingly the question whether an action is a duty or merely expedient, is one which has no bearing on the ethical question whether we ought to do it. In the sense in which either duty or expediency are taken as ultimate *reasons* for doing an action, they are taken in exactly the same sense: if I ask whether an action is *really* my duty or *really* expedient, the predicate of which I question the applicability to the action in question is precisely the same. In both cases I am asking, 'Is this event the best on the whole that I can effect?'; and whether the event in question be some effect upon what is *mine* (as it usually is, where we talk of expediency) or some other event (as is usual, where we talk of duty), this distinction has no more relevance to my answer than the distinction between two different effects on me or two different effects on others. The true distinction between duties and expedient actions is not that the former are actions which it is in any sense more useful or obligatory or better to perform, but that they are actions which it is more useful to praise and to enforce by sanctions, since they are actions which there is a temptation to omit.

102.   With regard to 'interested' actions, the case is somewhat different. When we ask the question, 'Is this really to my interest?' we appear to be asking exclusively whether its *effects upon me* are the best possible; and it may well happen that what will effect me in the manner, which is really the best possible, will not produce the best possible results on the whole. Accordingly *my true interest* may be different from the course which is really expedient and dutiful. To assert that an action is 'to my interest,' is, indeed, as was pointed out in Chap. III. (§§ 59—61), to assert that its effects are really good. 'My own good' only denotes some event affecting me, which is good absolutely and objectively; it is the thing, and not its goodness, which is *mine*; everything must be either 'a part of universal good' or else not good at all; there is no third alternative conception 'good for me.'   But 'my interest,' though it must be something truly good, is only one among possible good effects; and hence, by effecting it, though we shall be doing *some* good, we may be doing less good on the whole, than if we had acted otherwise. Self-sacrifice may be a real duty; just as the sacrifice of any single good, whether affecting ourselves or others, may be necessary in order to obtain a better total result. Hence the fact that an action is really to my interest, can never be a sufficient reason for doing it: by shewing that it is not a means to the best possible, we do not shew that it is not to my interest, as we do shew that it is not expedient.   Nevertheless there is no necessary conflict between duty and interest: what is to my interest may also be a means to the best possible.

And the chief distinction conveyed by the distinct words 'duty' and 'interest' seems to be not this source of possible conflict, but the same which is conveyed by the contrast between 'duty' and 'expediency.' By 'interested' actions are *mainly* meant those which, whether a means to the best possible or not, are such as have their most obvious effects on the agent; which he generally has no temptation to omit; and with regard to which we feel no moral sentiment. That is to say, the distinction is not primarily ethical. Here too 'duties' are not, in general, more useful or obligatory than interested actions; they are only actions which it is more useful to praise.

103. (5) A fifth conclusion, of some importance, in relation to Practical Ethics concerns the manner in which 'virtues' are to be judged. What is meant by calling a thing a 'virtue'?

There can be no doubt that Aristotle's definition is right, in the main, so far as he says that it is an 'habitual disposition' to perform certain actions: this is one of the marks by which we should distinguish a virtue from other things. But 'virtue' and 'vice' are also ethical terms: that is to say, when we use them seriously, we mean to convey praise by the one and dispraise by the other. And to praise a thing is to assert either that it is good in itself or else that it is a means to good. Are we then to include in our definition of virtue that it must be a thing good in itself?

Now it is certain that virtues are commonly regarded as good in themselves. The feeling of moral approbation with which we generally regard them partly consists in an attribution to them of intrinsic value. Even a Hedonist, when he feels a moral sentiment towards them, is regarding them as good-in-themselves; and Virtue has been the chief competitor with Pleasure for the position of *sole* good. Nevertheless I do not think we can regard it as part of the definition of virtue that it should be good in itself. For the name has so far an independent meaning, that if in any particular case a disposition commonly considered virtuous were proved not to be good in itself, we should not think that a sufficient reason for saying that it *was* not a virtue but was only *thought* to be so. The test for the ethical connotation of virtue is the same as that for duty:

What should we require to be proved about a particular instance, in order to say that the name was wrongly applied to it? And the test which is thus applied both to virtues and duties, and considered to be final, is the question: Is it a means to good? If it could be shewn of any particular disposition, commonly considered virtuous, that it was generally harmful, we should at once say: Then it is not really virtuous. Accordingly a virtue may be defined as an habitual disposition to perform certain actions, which generally produce the best possible results. Nor is there any doubt as to the kind of actions which it is 'virtuous' habitually to perform. They are, in general, those which are duties, with this modification that we also include those which *would* be duties, if only it were possible for people in general to perform them. Accordingly with regard to virtues, the same conclusion holds as with regard to duties. If they are really virtues they must be generally good as means; nor do I wish to dispute that most virtues, commonly considered as such, as well as most duties, really are means to good. But it does not follow that they are a bit more useful than those dispositions and inclinations which lead us to perform interested actions. As duties from expedient actions, so virtues are distinguished from other useful dispositions, not by any superior utility, but by the fact that they are dispositions, which it is particularly useful to praise and to sanction, because there are strong and common temptations to neglect the actions to which they lead.

Virtues, therefore, are habitual dispositions to perform actions which are duties, or which would be duties if a volition were sufficient on the part of most men to ensure their performance. And duties are a particular class of those actions, of which the performance has, at least generally, better total results than the omission. They are, that is to say, actions generally good as means: but not all such actions are duties; the name is confined to that particular class which it is often difficult to perform, because there are strong temptations to the contrary. It follows that in order to decide whether any particular disposition or action is a virtue or a duty, we must face all the difficulties enumerated in section (3) of this chapter.

We shall not be entitled to assert that any disposition or action is a virtue or duty except as a result of an investigation, such as was there described. We must be able to prove that the disposition or action in question is generally better as a means than any alternatives possible and likely to occur; and this we shall only be able to prove for particular states of society: what is a virtue or a duty in one state of society may not be so in another.

104. But there is another question with regard to virtues and duties which must be settled by intuition alone—by the properly guarded method which was explained in discussing Hedonism. This is the question whether the dispositions and actions, commonly regarded (rightly or not) as virtues or duties, are good in themselves; whether they have intrinsic value. Virtue or the exercise of virtue has very commonly been asserted by moralists to be either the sole good, or, at least, the best of goods. Indeed, so far as moralists have discussed the question what is good in itself at all, they have generally assumed that it must be either virtue or pleasure. It would hardly have been possible that such a gross difference of opinion should exist, or that it should have been assumed the discussion *must* be limited to two such alternatives, if the meaning of the question had been clearly apprehended. And we have already seen that the meaning of the question has hardly ever been clearly apprehended. Almost all ethical writers have committed the naturalistic fallacy—they have failed to perceive that the notion of intrinsic value is simple and unique; and almost all have failed, in consequence, to distinguish clearly between means and end—they have discussed, as if it were simple and unambiguous, the question, 'What ought we to do?' or 'What ought to exist now?' without distinguishing whether the reason why a thing ought to be done or to exist now, is that it is itself possessed of intrinsic value, or that it is a means to what has intrinsic value. We shall, therefore, be prepared to find that virtue has as little claim to be considered the sole or chief good as pleasure; more especially after seeing that, so far as definition goes, to call a thing a virtue is merely to declare that it is a means to good. The advocates of virtue have, we shall see, this superiority over the Hedonists, that inasmuch as virtues are very complex mental facts, there are included in them many things which are good in themselves and good in a much higher degree than pleasure. The advocates of Hedonism, on the other hand, have the superiority that their method emphasizes the distinction between means and ends; although they have not apprehended the distinction clearly enough to perceive that the special ethical predicate, which they assign to pleasure as *not* being a mere means, must also apply to many other things.

105. With regard, then, to the intrinsic value of virtue, it may be stated broadly: (1) that the majority of dispositions, which we call by that name, and which really do conform to the definition, so far as that they are dispositions generally valuable as means, at least in our society, have no intrinsic value whatever; and (2) that no one element which is contained in the minority, nor even all the different elements put together, can without gross absurdity be regarded as the sole good. As to the second point it may be observed that even those who hold the view that the sole good is to be found in virtue, almost invariably hold other views contradictory of this, owing chiefly to a failure to analyse the meaning of ethical concepts. The most marked instance of this inconsistency is to be found in the common Christian conception that virtue, though the sole good, can yet be rewarded by something other than virtue. Heaven is commonly considered as the reward of virtue; and yet it is also commonly considered, that, in order to be such a reward, it must contain some element, called happiness, which is certainly not completely identical with the mere exercise of those virtues which it rewards. But if so, then something which is not virtue must be either good in itself or an element in what has most intrinsic value. It is not commonly observed that if a thing is really to be a reward, it must be something good in itself: it is absurd to talk of rewarding a person by giving him something, which is less valuable than what he already has or which has no value at all. Thus Kant's view that virtue renders us *worthy* of happiness is in flagrant contradiction with the view, which he implies and which is associated with his name, that a Good Will is the only thing having intrinsic value. It does not, indeed, entitle us to make the charge sometimes made, that Kant is, inconsistently, an Eudaemonist or Hedonist: for it does not imply that happiness is the sole good. But it does imply that the Good Will is *not* the sole good: that a state of things in which we are both virtuous and happy is better in itself than one in which the happiness is absent.

106. In order, however, justly to consider the claims of virtue to intrinsic value, it is necessary to distinguish several very different mental states, all of which fall under the general definition that they are habitual dispositions to perform duties. We may thus distinguish three very different states, all of which are liable to be confused with one another, upon each of which different moral systems have laid great stress, and for each of which the claim has been made that it alone constitutes virtue, and, by implication, that it is the sole good. We may first of all distinguish between (*a*) that permanent characteristic of mind, which consists in the fact that the performance of duty has become in the strict sense a habit, like many of the operations performed in the putting on of clothes, and (*b*) that permanent characteristic, which consists in the fact that what may be called good motives habitually help to cause the performance of duties. And in the second division we may distinguish between the habitual tendency to be actuated by one motive, namely, the desire to do duty for duty's sake, and all other motives, such as love, benevolence, etc. We thus get the three kinds of virtue, of which we are now to consider the intrinsic value.

(*a*) There is no doubt that a man's character may be such that he habitually performs certain duties, without the thought ever occurring to him, when he wills them, either that they are duties or that any good will result from them. Of such a man we cannot and do not refuse to say that he possesses the virtue consisting in the disposition to perform those duties. I, for instance, am honest in the sense that I habitually abstain from any of the actions legally qualified as thieving, even where some other persons would be strongly tempted to commit them. It would be grossly contrary to common usage to deny that, for this reason, I really have the virtue of honesty: it is quite certain that I have an habitual disposition to perform a duty.

And that as many people as possible should have a like disposition is, no doubt, of great utility : it is good as a means. Yet I may safely assert that neither my various performances of this duty, nor my disposition to perform them, have the smallest intrinsic value. It is because the majority of instances of virtue seem to be of this nature, that we may venture to assert that virtues have, in general, no intrinsic value whatsoever. And there seems good reason to think that the more generally they are of this nature the more useful they are; since a great economy of labour is effected when a useful action becomes habitual or instinctive. But to maintain that a virtue, which includes no more than this, is good in itself is a gross absurdity. And of this gross absurdity, it may be observed, the Ethics of Aristotle is guilty. For his definition of virtue does not exclude a disposition to perform actions in this way, whereas his descriptions of the particular virtues plainly *include* such actions: that an action, in order to exhibit virtue, must be done τοῦ καλοῦ ἕνεκα is a qualification which he allows often to drop out of sight. And, on the other hand, he seems certainly to regard the exercise of *all* virtues as an end in itself. His treatment of Ethics is indeed, in the most important points, highly unsystematic and confused, owing to his attempt to base it on the naturalistic fallacy; for strictly we should be obliged by his words to regard θεωρία as the *only* thing good in itself, in which case the goodness which he attributes to the practical virtues cannot be intrinsic value; while on the other hand he does not seem to regard it merely as utility, since he makes no attempt to shew that they are means to θεωρία. But there seems no doubt that on the whole he regards the exercise of the practical virtues as a good of the same kind as (*i.e.* having intrinsic value), only in a less degree than, θεωρία; so that he cannot avoid the charge that he recommends as having intrinsic value, such instances of the exercise of virtue as we are at present discussing—instances of a disposition to perform actions which, in the modern phrase, have merely an 'external rightness.' That he is right in applying the word 'virtue' to such a disposition cannot be doubted. But the protest against the view that 'external rightness' is sufficient to constitute either 'duty' or 'virtue'—a protest which is

commonly, and with some justice, attributed as a merit to
Christian morals—seems, in the main, to be a mistaken way of
pointing out an important truth: namely, that where there is
only 'external rightness' there is certainly no intrinsic value.
It is commonly assumed (though wrongly) that to call a thing
a virtue means that it has intrinsic value: and on this
assumption the view that virtue does not consist in a mere
disposition to do externally right actions does really constitute
an advance in ethical truth beyond the Ethics of Aristotle.
The inference that, if virtue includes in its meaning 'good in
itself,' then Aristotle's definition of virtue is not adequate and
expresses a false ethical judgment, is perfectly correct: only the
premiss that virtue does include this in its meaning is mistaken.

107. (b) A man's character may be such that, when he
habitually performs a particular duty, there is, in each case of
his performance, present in his mind, a love of some intrinsically
good consequence which he expects to produce by his action or
a hatred of some intrinsically evil consequence which he hopes to
prevent by it. In such a case this love or hatred will generally
be part cause of his action, and we may then call it one of his
motives. Where such a feeling as this is present habitually in
the performance of duties, it cannot be denied that the state of
the man's mind, in performing it, contains something intrinsically good. Nor can it be denied that, where a disposition to
perform duties consists in the disposition to be moved to them
by such feelings, we call that disposition a virtue. Here, therefore, we have instances of virtue, the exercise of which really
contains something that is good in itself. And, in general, we
may say that wherever a virtue does consist in a disposition to
have certain motives, the exercise of that virtue *may* be intrinsically good; although the degree of its goodness may vary
indefinitely according to the precise nature of the motives and
their objects. In so far, then, as Christianity tends to emphasize
the importance of motives, of the 'inward' disposition with
which a right action is done, we may say that it has done a
service to Ethics. But it should be noticed that, when Christian
Ethics, as represented by the New Testament, are praised for

this, two distinctions of the utmost importance, which they entirely neglect, are very commonly overlooked. In the first place the New Testament is largely occupied with continuing the tradition of the Hebrew prophets, by recommending such virtues as 'justice' and 'mercy' as against mere ritual observances; and, in so far as it does this, it is recommending virtues which may be *merely* good as means, exactly like the Aristotelian virtues. This characteristic of its teaching must therefore be rigorously distinguished from that which consists in its enforcement of such a view as that to be angry without a cause is as bad as actually to commit murder. And, in the second place, though the New Testament does praise some things which are only good as means, and others which are good in themselves, it entirely fails to recognise this distinction. Though the state of the man who is angry may be really as bad in itself as that of the murderer, and so far Christ may be right, His language would lead us to suppose that it is *also* as bad in every way, that it *also causes* as much evil: and this is utterly false. In short, when Christian Ethics approves, it does not distinguish whether its approval asserts 'This is a means to good' or 'This is good in itself'; and hence it both praises things merely good as means, as if they were good in themselves, and things merely good in themselves as if they were also good as means. Moreover it should be noticed, that if Christian Ethics does draw attention to those elements in virtues which are good in themselves, it is by no means alone in this. The Ethics of Plato are distinguished by upholding, far more clearly and consistently than any other system, the view that intrinsic value belongs exclusively to those states of mind which consist in love of what is good or hatred of what is evil.

108. But (c) the Ethics of Christianity are distinguished from those of Plato by emphasizing the value of one particular motive—that which consists in the emotion excited by the idea, not of any intrinsically good consequences of the action in question, nor even of the action itself, but by that of its rightness. This idea of abstract 'rightness' and the various degrees of the specific emotion excited by it are what constitute the specifically 'moral sentiment' or 'conscience.' An action seems to be most properly termed 'internally right[1],' solely in virtue of the fact that the agent has previously regarded it as right: the idea of 'rightness' must have been present to his mind, but need not necessarily have been among his motives. And we mean by a 'conscientious' man, one who, when he deliberates, always has this idea in his mind, and does not act until he believes that his action is right.

The presence of this idea and its action as a motive certainly seem to have become more common objects of notice and commendation owing to the influence of Christianity; but it is important to observe that there is no ground for the view, which Kant implies, that it is the *only* motive which the New Testament regards as intrinsically valuable. There seems little doubt that when Christ tells us to 'Love our neighbours as ourselves,' He did not mean merely what Kant calls 'practical love'—beneficence of which the *sole* motive is the idea of its rightness, or the emotion caused by that idea. Among the 'inward dispositions' of which the New Testament inculcates the value, there are certainly included what Kant terms mere 'natural inclinations,' such as pity etc.

But what are we to say of virtue, when it consists in a disposition to be moved to the performance of duties by this idea? It seems difficult to deny that the emotion excited by rightness as such has some intrinsic value; and still more difficult to deny that its presence may heighten the value of some wholes into which it enters. But, on the other hand, it certainly has not more value than many of the motives treated in our last section—emotions of love towards things really good in themselves. And as for Kant's implication that it is the sole good[2], this is inconsistent with other of his own views. For he certainly regards it as *better* to perform the actions, to which he maintains that it prompts us—namely, 'material' duties—than to omit them. But, if better at all, then, these actions must be

---

[1] This sense of the term must be carefully distinguished from that in which the agent's intention may be said to be ' right,' if only the results he intended would have been the best possible.

[2] Kant, so far as I know, never expressly states this view, but it is implied *e.g.* in his argument against Heteronomy.

better either in themselves or as a means. The former hypothesis would directly contradict the statement that this motive
was *sole* good, and the latter is excluded by Kant himself since
he maintains that no actions can *cause* the existence of this
motive. And it may also be observed that the other claim
which he makes for it, namely, that it is *always* good as
a means, can also not be maintained. It is as certain as
anything can be that very harmful actions may be done from
conscientious motives; and that Conscience does not always
tell us the truth about what actions are right. Nor can it be
maintained even that it is *more* useful than many other motives.
All that can be admitted is that it is one of the things which
are generally useful.

What more I have to say with regard to those elements in
some virtues which are good in themselves, and with regard to
their relative degrees of excellence, as well as the proof that
all of them together cannot be the sole good, may be deferred
to the next chapter.

109. The main points in this chapter, to which I desire to
direct attention, may be summarised as follows:—(1) I first
pointed out how the subject-matter with which it deals, namely,
ethical judgments on conduct, involves a question, utterly
different in kind from the two previously discussed, namely:
(*a*) What is the nature of the predicate peculiar to Ethics?
and (*b*) What kinds of things themselves possess this predicate?
Practical Ethics asks, not 'What ought to be?' but 'What ought
we to do?'; it asks what actions are *duties*, what actions are
right, and what *wrong*: and all these questions can only be
answered by shewing the relation of the actions in question, as
causes or *necessary conditions*, to what is good in itself. The
enquiries of Practical Ethics thus fall entirely under the *third*
division of ethical questions—questions which ask, 'What is
good as a means?' which is equivalent to 'What is a means
to good—what is cause or necessary condition of things good
in themselves?' (86—88). But (2) it asks this question, almost
exclusively, with regard to actions which it is possible for most
men to perform, if only they *will* them; and with regard to
these, it does not ask merely, which among them will have *some*

good or bad result, but which, among all the actions possible to
volition at any moment, will produce the best *total* result. To
assert that an action is a duty, is to assert that it is such
a possible action, which will *always*, in certain known circumstances, produce better results than any other. It follows
that universal propositions of which duty is predicate, so far
from being self-evident, always require a proof, which it is
beyond our present means of knowledge ever to give (89—92).
But (3) all that Ethics has attempted or can attempt, is to
shew that certain actions, possible by volition, *generally* produce
better or worse total results than any probable alternative :
and it must obviously be very difficult to shew this with regard
to the total results even in a comparatively near future;
whereas that what has the best results in such a near future,
also has the best on the whole, is a point requiring an
investigation which it has not received. If it is true, and if,
accordingly, we give the name of 'duty' to actions which
generally produce better total results in the near future than
any possible alternative, it may be possible to prove that a few
of the commonest rules of duty are true, but *only* in certain
conditions of society, which may be more or less universally
presented in history ; and such a proof is only possible *in some
cases* without a correct judgment of what things are good
or bad in themselves—a judgment which has never yet been
offered by ethical writers. With regard to actions of which the
general utility is thus proved, the individual should *always*
perform them ; but in other cases, where rules are commonly
offered, he should rather judge of the probable results in
his particular case, guided by a correct conception of what
things are intrinsically good or bad (93—100). (4) In order
that any action may be shewn to be a duty, it must be
shewn to fulfil the above conditions ; but the actions commonly
called 'duties' do not fulfil them to any greater extent
than 'expedient' or 'interested' actions: by calling them
'duties' we only mean that they have, *in addition*, certain
non-ethical predicates. Similarly by 'virtue' is mainly meant
a permanent disposition to perform 'duties' in this restricted

sense: and accordingly a virtue, if it is really a virtue, must be good *as a means*, in the sense that it fulfils the above conditions; but it is not *better* as a means than non-virtuous dispositions; it generally has no value in itself; and, where it has, it is far from being the sole good or the best of goods. Accordingly 'virtue' is not, as is commonly implied, an unique *ethical* predicate (101—109).

CHAPTER VI.

THE IDEAL.

110. THE title of this chapter is ambiguous. When we call a state of things 'ideal' we may mean three distinct things, which have only this in common: that we always do mean to assert, of the state of things in question, not only that it is good in itself, but that it is good in itself in a much higher degree than many other things. The first of these meanings of 'ideal' is (1) that to which the phrase '*The* Ideal' is most properly confined. By this is meant the *best* state of things *conceivable*, the Summum Bonum or Absolute Good. It is in this sense that a right conception of Heaven would be a right conception of the Ideal: we mean by the Ideal a state of things which would be absolutely perfect. But this conception may be quite clearly distinguished from a second, namely, (2) that of the best *possible* state of things in this world. This second conception may be identified with that which has frequently figured in philosophy as the 'Human Good,' or the *ultimate* end towards which our action should be directed. It is in this sense that Utopias are said to be Ideals. The constructor of an Utopia may suppose many things to be possible, which are in fact impossible; but he always assumes that some things, at least, are rendered impossible by natural laws, and hence his construction differs essentially from one which may disregard *all* natural laws, however certainly established. At all events the question 'What is the best state of things which we could *possibly* bring about?' is quite distinct from the question 'What would be the best state of things conceivable?' But, thirdly, we may mean

by calling a state of things 'ideal' merely (3) that it is good
in itself in a high degree. And it is obvious that the question
what things are 'ideal' in this sense is one which must be
answered before we can pretend to settle what is the Absolute
or the Human Good. It is with the Ideal, in this third sense,
that this chapter will be principally concerned. Its main
object is to arrive at some positive answer to the fundamental
question of Ethics—the question: 'What things are goods or
ends in themselves?' To this question we have hitherto
obtained only a negative answer: the answer that pleasure
is certainly not the *sole* good.

111.   I have just said that it is upon a correct answer
to this question that correct answers to the two other questions,
What is the Absolute Good? and What is the Human Good?
must depend; and, before proceeding to discuss it, it may
be well to point out the relation which it has to these two
questions.

(1) It is just possible that the Absolute Good may be
entirely composed of qualities which we cannot even imagine.
This is possible, because, though we certainly do know a great
many things that are good-in-themselves, and good in a high
degree, yet what is best does not necessarily contain all the
good things there are. That this is so follows from the
principle explained in Chap. I. (§§ 18—22), to which it was there
proposed that the name 'principle of organic unities' should be
confined. This principle is that the intrinsic value of a whole
is neither identical with nor proportional to the sum of the
values of its parts. It follows from this that, though in order
to obtain the greatest possible sum of values in its parts,
the Ideal would necessarily contain all the things which have
intrinsic value in any degree, yet the whole which contained
all these parts might not be so valuable as some other whole,
from which certain positive goods were omitted. But if a
whole, which does not contain all positive goods, may yet
be better than a whole which does, it follows that the best
whole *may* be one, which contains *none* of the positive goods
with which we are acquainted.

It is, therefore, *possible* that we cannot discover what

the Ideal is. But it is plain that, though this possibility
cannot be denied, no one can have any right to assert that
it is realised—that the Ideal *is* something unimaginable. We
cannot judge of the comparative values of things, unless
the things we judge are before our minds. We cannot, therefore, be entitled to assert that anything, which we cannot
imagine, would be better than some of the things which we
can; although we are also not entitled to deny the possibility
that this may be the case. Consequently our search for the
Ideal must be limited to a search for that one, among all
the wholes composed of elements known to us, which seems to
be better than all the rest. We shall never be entitled to
assert that this whole is Perfection, but we shall be entitled
to assert that it is *better* than any other which may be presented
as a rival.

But, since anything which we can have any *reason* to think
ideal must be composed of things that are known to us, it
is plain that a comparative valuation of these must be our chief
instrument for deciding what is ideal. The best ideal we can
construct will be that state of things which contains the
greatest number of things having positive value, and which
contains nothing evil or indifferent—*provided* that the presence
of none of these goods, or the absence of things evil or
indifferent, seems to diminish the value of the whole. And,
in fact, the chief defect of such attempts as have been made by
philosophers to construct an Ideal—to describe the Kingdom
of Heaven—seems to consist in the fact that they omit many
things of very great positive value, although it is plain that
this omission does *not* enhance the value of the whole. Where
this is the case, it may be confidently asserted that the ideal
proposed is not ideal. And the review of positive goods, which
I am about to undertake, will, I hope, shew that no ideals yet
proposed are satisfactory. Great positive goods, it will appear,
are so numerous, that any whole, which shall contain them all,
must be of vast complexity. And though this fact renders
it difficult, or, humanly speaking, impossible, to decide what
is The Ideal, what is the absolutely best state of things
imaginable, it is sufficient to condemn those Ideals, which

are formed by omission, without any visible gain in consequence of such omission. Philosophers seem usually to have sought only for the *best* of single things; neglecting the fact that a whole composed of two great goods, even though one of these be obviously inferior to the other, may yet be often seen to be decidedly superior to either by itself.

(2) On the other hand, Utopias—attempted descriptions of a Heaven upon Earth—commonly suffer not only from this, but also from the opposite defect. They are commonly constructed on the principle of merely omitting the great positive evils, which exist at present, with utterly inadequate regard to the goodness of what they retain: the so-called goods, to which they have regard, are, for the most part, things which are, at best, mere means to good—things, such as freedom, *without* which, possibly, nothing very good can exist in this world, but which are of no value in themselves and are by no means certain even to produce anything of value. It is, of course, necessary to the purpose of their authors, whose object is merely to construct the best that may be possible in this world, that they should include, in the state of things which they describe, many things, which are themselves indifferent, but which, according to natural laws, seem to be absolutely necessary for the existence of anything which is good. But, in fact, they are apt to include many things, of which the necessity is by no means apparent, under the mistaken idea that these things are goods-in-themselves, and not merely, here and now, a means to good: while, on the other hand, they also omit from their description great positive goods, of which the attainment seems to be quite as possible as many of the changes which they recommend. That is to say, conceptions of the Human Good commonly err, not only, like those of the Absolute Good, in omitting some great goods, but also by including things indifferent; and they both omit and include in cases where the limitations of natural necessity, by the consideration of which they are legitimately differentiated from conceptions of the Absolute Good, will not justify the omission and inclusion. It is, in fact, obvious that in order to decide correctly at what state of things we ought to aim, we must not

only consider what results it is possible for us to obtain, but
also which, among equally possible results, will have the
greatest value. And upon this second enquiry the comparative
valuation of known goods has a no less important bearing than
upon the investigation of the Absolute Good.

112. The method which must be employed in order to
decide the question 'What things have intrinsic value, and
in what degrees?' has already been explained in Chap. III.
(§§ 55, 57). In order to arrive at a correct decision on the first
part of this question, it is necessary to consider what things are
such that, if they existed *by themselves*, in absolute isolation,
we should yet judge their existence to be good; and, in order
to decide upon the relative *degrees* of value of different things,
we must similarly consider what comparative value seems to
attach to the isolated existence of each. By employing this
method, we shall guard against two errors, which seem to have
been the chief causes which have vitiated previous conclusions
on the subject. The first of these is (1) that which consists in
supposing that what seems absolutely necessary here and now,
for the existence of anything good—what we cannot do without—is therefore good in itself. If we isolate such things,
which are mere means to good, and suppose a world in which
they alone, and nothing but they, existed, their intrinsic
worthlessness becomes apparent. And, secondly, there is the
more subtle error (2) which consists in neglecting the principle
of organic unities. This error is committed, when it is
supposed, that, if one part of a whole has no intrinsic value, the
value of the whole must reside entirely in the other parts.
It has, in this way, been commonly supposed, that, if all
valuable wholes could be seen to have one and only one common
property, the wholes must be valuable solely *because* they
possess this property; and the illusion is greatly strengthened,
if the common property in question seems, considered by itself,
to have more value than the other parts of such wholes,
considered by themselves. But, if we consider the property
in question, *in isolation*, and then compare it with the whole,
of which it forms a part, it may become easily apparent that,
existing by itself, the property in question has not nearly

so much value, as has the whole to which it belongs. Thus, if we compare the value of a certain amount of pleasure, *existing absolutely by itself,* with the value of certain 'enjoyments,' containing an equal amount of pleasure, it may become apparent that the 'enjoyment' is much better than the pleasure, and also, in some cases, much worse. In such a case it is plain that the 'enjoyment' does *not* owe its value *solely* to the pleasure it contains, although it might easily have appeared to do so, when we only considered the other constituents of the enjoyment, and seemed to see that, without the pleasure, they would have had no value. It is now apparent, on the contrary, that the whole 'enjoyment' owes its value quite equally to the presence of the other constituents, *even though* it may be true that the pleasure is the only constituent having any value by itself. And similarly, if we are told that all things owe their value solely to the fact that they are 'realisations of the true self,' we may easily refute this statement, by asking whether the predicate that is meant by 'realising the true self,' supposing that it could exist alone, would have any value whatsoever. Either the *thing,* which does 'realise the true self,' has intrinsic value or it has not ; and if it has, then it certainly does not owe its value solely to the fact that it realises the true self.

113. If, now, we use this method of absolute isolation, and guard against these errors, it appears that the question we have to answer is far less difficult than the controversies of Ethics might have led us to expect. Indeed, once the meaning of the question is clearly understood, the answer to it, in its main outlines, appears to be so obvious, that it runs the risk of seeming to be a platitude. By far the most valuable things, which we know or can imagine, are certain states of consciousness, which may be roughly described as the pleasures of human intercourse and the enjoyment of beautiful objects. No one, probably, who has asked himself the question, has ever doubted that personal affection and the appreciation of what is beautiful in Art or Nature, are good in themselves ; nor, if we consider strictly what things are worth having *purely for their own sakes,* does it appear probable that any one will think that

anything else has *nearly* so great a value as the things which
are included under these two heads. I have myself urged in
Chap. III. (§ 50) that the mere existence of what is beautiful
does appear to have *some* intrinsic value; but I regard it as
indubitable that Prof. Sidgwick was so far right, in the view
there discussed, that such mere existence of what is beautiful
has value, so small as to be negligible, in comparison with that
which attaches to the *consciousness* of beauty. This simple
truth may, indeed, be said to be universally recognised. What
has *not* been recognised is that it is the ultimate and fundamental truth of Moral Philosophy. That it is only for the sake
of these things—in order that as much of them as possible may
at some time exist—that any one can be justified in performing
any public or private duty; that they are the *raison d'être*
of virtue; that it is they—these complex wholes *themselves*,
and not any constituent or characteristic of them—that form
the rational ultimate end of human action and the sole criterion
of social progress: these appear to be truths which have been
generally overlooked.

That they are truths—that personal affections and aesthetic
enjoyments include *all* the greatest, and *by far* the greatest,
goods we can imagine, will, I hope, appear more plainly in the
course of that analysis of them, to which I shall now proceed.
All the things, which I have meant to include under the above
descriptions, are highly complex *organic unities*; and in discussing the consequences, which follow from this fact, and the
elements of which they are composed, I may hope at the same
time both to confirm and to define my position.

114. I. I propose to begin by examining what I have
called aesthetic enjoyments, since the case of personal affections
presents some additional complications. It is, I think, universally admitted that the proper appreciation of a beautiful
object is a good thing in itself; and my question is: What are
the main elements included in such an appreciation?

(1) It is plain that in those instances of aesthetic appreciation, which we think most valuable, there is included, not
merely a bare cognition of what is beautiful in the object, but
also some kind of feeling or emotion. It is not sufficient that

a man should merely see the beautiful qualities in a picture
and know that they are beautiful, in order that we may give
his state of mind the highest praise. We require that he
should also *appreciate* the beauty of that which he sees and
which he knows to be beautiful—that he should feel and see
its beauty. And by these expressions we certainly mean that
he should have an appropriate emotion towards the beautiful
qualities which he cognises. It is perhaps the case that all
aesthetic emotions have some common quality; but it is certain
that differences in the emotion seem to be appropriate to differences in the kind of beauty perceived: and by saying that
different emotions are *appropriate* to different kinds of beauty,
we mean that the whole which is formed by the consciousness
of that kind of beauty *together with* the emotion appropriate to
it, is better than if any other emotion had been felt in contemplating that particular beautiful object. Accordingly we have
a large variety of different emotions, each of which is a necessary
constituent in some state of consciousness which we judge to
be good. All of these emotions are essential elements in great
positive goods; they are *parts* of organic wholes, which have
great intrinsic value. But it is important to observe that these
wholes are organic, and that, hence, it does not follow that the
emotion, *by itself*, would have any value whatsoever, nor yet
that, if it were directed to a different object, the whole thus
formed might not be positively bad. And, in fact, it seems to
be the case that if we distinguish the emotional element, in
any aesthetic appreciation, from the cognitive element, which
accompanies it and is, in fact, commonly thought of as a part
of the emotion; and if we consider what value this emotional
element would have, *existing by itself*, we can hardly think that
it has any great value, even if it has any at all. Whereas,
if the same emotion be directed to a different object, if, for
instance, it is felt towards an object that is positively ugly, the
whole state of consciousness is certainly often positively bad in
a high degree.

115.   (2) In the last paragraph I have pointed out the two
facts, that the presence of some emotion is necessary to give
any very high value to a state of aesthetic appreciation, and

that, on the other hand, this same emotion, in itself, may have little or no value: it follows that these emotions give to the wholes of which they form a part a value far greater than that which they themselves possess. The same is obviously true of the cognitive element which must be combined with these emotions in order to form these highly valuable wholes; and the present paragraph will attempt to define what is meant by this cognitive element, so far as to guard against a possible misunderstanding. When we talk of seeing a beautiful object, or, more generally, of the cognition or consciousness of a beautiful object, we may mean by these expressions something which forms no part of any valuable whole. There is an ambiguity in the use of the term 'object,' which has probably been responsible for as many enormous errors in philosophy and psychology as any other single cause. This ambiguity may easily be detected by considering the proposition, which, though a contradiction in terms, is obviously true: That when a man sees a beautiful picture, he may see nothing beautiful whatever. The ambiguity consists in the fact that, by the 'object' of vision (or cognition), may be meant *either* the qualities actually seen *or* all the qualities possessed by the thing seen. Thus in our case: when it is said that the picture is beautiful, it is meant that it contains qualities which are beautiful; when it is said that the man sees the picture, it is meant that he sees a great number of the qualities contained in the picture; and when it is said that, nevertheless, he sees nothing beautiful, it is meant that he does *not* see those qualities of the picture which are beautiful. When, therefore, I speak of the cognition of a beautiful object, as an essential element in a valuable aesthetic appreciation, I must be understood to mean only the cognition of *the beautiful qualities* possessed by that object, and *not* the cognition of other qualities of the object possessing them. And this distinction must itself be carefully distinguished from the other distinction expressed above by the distinct terms 'seeing the beauty of a thing' and 'seeing its beautiful qualities.' By 'seeing the beauty of a thing' we commonly mean the having an emotion towards its beautiful qualities; whereas in the 'seeing of its beautiful qualities' we do not include any emotion.

By the cognitive element, which is equally necessary with emotion to the existence of a valuable appreciation, I mean merely the actual cognition or consciousness of any or all of an object's *beautiful qualities*—that is to say any or all of those elements in the object which possess any positive beauty. That such a cognitive element is essential to a valuable whole may be easily seen, by asking: What value should we attribute to the proper emotion excited by hearing Beethoven's Fifth Symphony, if that emotion were entirely unaccompanied by any consciousness, either of the notes, or of the melodic and harmonic relations between them ? And that the mere *hearing* of the Symphony, even accompanied by the appropriate emotion, is not sufficient, may be easily seen, if we consider what would be the state of a man, who should hear all the notes, but should *not* be aware of any of those melodic and harmonic relations, which are necessary to constitute the smallest beautiful elements in the Symphony.

116. (3) Connected with the distinction just made between 'object' in the sense of the qualities actually before the mind, and 'object' in the sense of the whole thing which possesses the qualities actually before the mind, is another distinction of the utmost importance for a correct analysis of the constituents necessary to a valuable whole. It is commonly and rightly thought that to see beauty in a thing which has no beauty is in some way inferior to seeing beauty in that which really has it. But under this single description of 'seeing beauty in that which has no beauty,' two very different facts, and facts of very different value, may be included. We may mean *either* the attribution to an object of really beautiful qualities which it does not possess *or* the feeling towards qualities, which the object does possess but which are in reality not beautiful, an emotion which is appropriate only to qualities really beautiful. Both these facts are of very frequent occurrence ; and in most instances of emotion both no doubt occur together : but they are obviously quite distinct, and the distinction is of the utmost importance for a correct estimate of values. The former may be called an error of judgment, and the latter an error of taste ; but it is important to observe that the 'error of taste' commonly involves a false judgment *of value*; whereas the 'error of judgment' is merely a false judgment *of fact*.

Now the case which I have called an error of taste, namely, where the actual qualities we admire (whether possessed by the 'object' or not) are ugly, can in any case have no value, except such as may belong to the emotion *by itself*; and in most, if not in all, cases it is a considerable positive evil. In this sense, then, it is undoubtedly right to think that seeing beauty in a thing which has no beauty is inferior in value to seeing beauty where beauty really is. But the other case is much more difficult. In this case there is present all that I have hitherto mentioned as necessary to constitute a great positive good: there is a cognition of qualities really beautiful, together with an appropriate emotion towards these qualities. There can, therefore, be no doubt that we have here a great positive good. But there is present also something else; namely, a belief that these beautiful qualities exist, and that they exist in a certain relation to other things—namely, to some properties of the object to which we attribute these qualities: and further the object of this belief is false. And we may ask, with regard to the whole thus constituted, whether the presence of the belief, and the fact that what is believed is false, make any difference to its value? We thus get three different cases of which it is very important to determine the relative values. Where both the cognition of beautiful qualities and the appropriate emotion are present we may *also* have either, (1) a belief in the existence of these qualities, of which the object, *i.e.* that they exist, is true: or (2) a mere cognition, without belief, when it is (*a*) true, (*b*) false, that the object of the cognition, *i.e.* the beautiful qualities, exists: or (3) a belief in the existence of the beautiful qualities, when they do not exist. The importance of these cases arises from the fact that the second defines the pleasures of imagination, including a great part of the appreciation of those works of art which are *representative*; whereas the first contrasts with these the appreciation of what is beautiful in Nature, and the human affections. The third, on the other hand, is contrasted with both, in that it is chiefly exemplified in what is called misdirected affection; and it is possible also that the love of God, in the case of a believer, should fall under this head.

117. Now all these three cases, as I have said, have something in common, namely, that, in them all, we have a cognition of really beautiful qualities together with an appropriate emotion towards those qualities. I think, therefore, it cannot be doubted (nor is it commonly doubted) that all three include great positive goods; they are all things of which we feel convinced that they are worth having for their own sakes. And I think that the value of the second, in either of its two subdivisions, is precisely the same as the value of the element common to all three. In other words, in the case of purely imaginative appreciations we have merely the cognition of really beautiful qualities together with the appropriate emotion; and the question, whether the object cognised exists or not, seems here, where there is no belief either in its existence or in its non-existence, to make absolutely no difference to the value of the total state. But it seems to me that the two other cases do differ in intrinsic value both from this one and from one another, even though the object cognised and the appropriate emotion should be identical in all three cases. I think that the additional presence of a belief in the reality of the object makes the total state much better, if the belief is true; and worse, if the belief is false. In short, where there is belief, in the sense in which we *do* believe in the existence of Nature and horses, and do *not* believe in the existence of an ideal landscape and unicorns, the *truth* of what is believed does make a great difference to the value of the organic whole. If this be the case, we shall have vindicated the belief that *knowledge*, in the ordinary sense, as distinguished on the one hand from belief in what is false and on the other from the mere awareness of what is true, does contribute towards intrinsic value—that, at least in some cases, its presence as a part makes a whole more valuable than it could have been without.

Now I think there can be no doubt that we do judge that

there is a difference of value, such as I have indicated, between the three cases in question. We do think that the emotional contemplation of a natural scene, supposing its qualities equally beautiful, is in some way a better state of things than that of a painted landscape : we think that the world would be improved if we could substitute for the best works of representative art *real* objects equally beautiful. And similarly we regard a misdirected affection or admiration, even where the error involved is a mere error of judgment and not an error of taste, as in some way unfortunate. And further, those, at least, who have a strong respect for truth, are inclined to think that a merely poetical contemplation of the Kingdom of Heaven *would* be superior to that of the religious believer, *if* it were the case that the Kingdom of Heaven does not and will not really exist. Most persons, on a sober, reflective judgment, would feel some hesitation even in preferring the felicity of a madman, convinced that the world was ideal, to the condition either of a poet imagining an ideal world, or of themselves enjoying and appreciating the lesser goods which do and will exist. But, in order to assure ourselves that these judgments are really judgments of intrinsic value upon the question before us, and to satisfy ourselves that they are correct, it is necessary clearly to distinguish our question from two others which have a very important bearing upon our total judgment of the cases in question.

118. In the first place (*a*) it is plain that, where we believe, the question whether what we believe is true or false, will generally have a most important bearing upon the value of our belief *as a means*. Where we believe, we are apt to act upon our belief, in a way in which we do not act upon our cognition of the events in a novel. The truth of what we believe is, therefore, very important as preventing the pains of disappointment and still more serious consequences. And it might be thought that a misdirected attachment was unfortunate solely for this reason : that it leads us to count upon results, which the real nature of its object is not of a kind to ensure. So too the Love of God, where, as usual, it includes the belief that he will annex to certain actions consequences, either in this life or the next, which the course of nature gives no reason to expect, may lead the believer to perform actions of which the actual consequences, supposing no such God to exist, may be much worse than he might otherwise have effected: and it might be thought that this was the sole reason (as it is a sufficient one) why we should hesitate to encourage the Love of God, in the absence of any proof that he exists. And similarly it may be thought that the only reason why beauty in Nature should be held superior to an equally beautiful landscape or imagination, is that its existence would ensure greater permanence and frequency in our emotional contemplation of that beauty. It is, indeed, certain that the chief importance of most *knowledge*—of the truth of most of the things which we believe—does, in this world, consist in its extrinsic advantages: it is immensely valuable *as a means.*

And secondly, (*b*) it may be the case that the existence of that which we contemplate is itself a great positive good, so that, for this reason alone, the state of things described by saying, that the object of our emotion really exists, would be intrinsically superior to that in which it did not. This reason for superiority is undoubtedly of great importance in the case of human affections, where the object of our admiration is the mental qualities of an admirable person; for that *two* such admirable persons should exist is greatly better than that there should be only one: and it would also discriminate the admiration of inanimate nature from that of its representations in art, in so far as we may allow a small intrinsic value to the existence of a beautiful object, apart from any contemplation of it. But it is to be noticed that this reason would not account for any difference in value between the cases where the truth was believed and that in which it was merely cognised, without either belief or disbelief. In other words, so far as this reason goes, the difference between the two subdivisions of our second class (that of imaginative contemplation) would be as great as between our first class and the second subdivision of our second. The superiority of the mere *cognition* of a beautiful object, when that object also happened to exist, over the same cognition when the object did not exist, would,

on this count, be as great as that of the *knowledge* of a beautiful
object over the mere imagination of it.

119. These two reasons for discriminating between the
value of the three cases we are considering, must, I say, be
carefully distinguished from that, of which I am now questioning
the validity, if we are to obtain a correct answer concerning this
latter. The question I am putting is this: Whether the *whole*
constituted by the fact that there is an emotional contemplation
of a beautiful object, which both is believed to be and is *real*,
does not derive some of its value from the fact that the object
is real? I am asking whether the value of this whole, *as a whole*,
is not greater than that of those which differ from it, *either* by
the absence of belief, with or without truth, *or*, belief being
present, by the mere absence of truth? I am not asking *either*
whether it is not superior to them as a means (which it certainly
is), *nor* whether it may not contain a more valuable *part*, namely,
the existence of the object in question. My question is solely
whether the existence of its object does not constitute an
addition to the value of the whole, quite distinct from the
addition constituted by the fact that this whole does contain a
valuable part.

If, now, we put this question, I cannot avoid thinking that
it should receive an affirmative answer. We can put it clearly
by the method of isolation; and the sole decision must rest with
our reflective judgment upon it, as thus clearly put. We can
guard against the bias produced by a consideration of value
as a means by supposing the case of an illusion as complete
and permanent as illusions in this world never can be. We can
imagine the case of a single person, enjoying throughout eternity
the contemplation of scenery as beautiful, and intercourse with
persons as admirable, as can be imagined; while yet the whole
of the objects of his cognition are absolutely unreal. I think we
should definitely pronounce the existence of a universe, which
consisted solely of such a person, to be *greatly* inferior in value
to one in which the objects, in the existence of which he believes,
did really exist just as he believes them to do; and that it would
be thus inferior *not only* because it would lack the goods which
consist in the existence of the objects in question, but *also*

merely because his belief would be false. That it would be inferior *for this reason alone* follows if we admit, what also appears to me certain, that the case of a person, merely imagining, without believing, the beautiful objects in question, would, *although these objects really existed,* be yet inferior to that of the person who also believed in their existence. For here all the additional good, which consists in the existence of the objects, is present, and yet there still seems to be a great difference in value between this case and that in which their existence is believed. But I think that my conclusion may perhaps be exhibited in a more convincing light by the following considerations. (1) It does not seem to me that the small degree of value which we may allow to the existence of beautiful inanimate objects is nearly equal in amount to the difference which I feel that there is between the appreciation (accompanied by belief) of such objects, when they really exist, and the purely imaginative appreciation of them when they do not exist. This inequality is more difficult to verify where the object is an admirable person, since a *great* value must be allowed to his existence. But yet I think it is not paradoxical to maintain that the superiority of reciprocal affection, where both objects are worthy and both exist, over an unreciprocated affection, where both are worthy but one does not exist, does not lie solely in the fact that, in the former case, we have two good things instead of one, but also in the fact that each is such as the other believes him to be. (2) It seems to me that the important contribution to value made by true belief may be very plainly seen in the following case. Suppose that a worthy object of affection does really exist and is believed to do so, but that there enters into the case this error of fact, that the qualities loved, though exactly like, are yet not the *same* which really do exist. This state of things is easily imagined, and I think we cannot avoid pronouncing that, *although* both persons here exist, it is yet not so satisfactory as where the very person loved and believed to exist is also the one which actually does exist.

120. If all this be so, we have, in this third section, added to our two former results the third result that a true belief in the reality of an object greatly increases the value of many

valuable wholes. Just as in sections (1) and (2) it was maintained that aesthetic and affectionate emotions had little or no
value apart from the cognition of appropriate objects, and that
the cognition of these objects had little or no value apart from
the appropriate emotion, so that the whole, in which both were
combined, had a value greatly in excess of the sum of the
values of its parts; so, according to this section, if there be
added to these wholes a true belief in the reality of the object,
the new whole thus formed has a value greatly in excess of the
sum obtained by adding the value of the true belief, considered
in itself, to that of our original wholes. This new case only
differs from the former in this, that, whereas the true belief, by
itself, has quite as little value as either of the two other
constituents taken singly, yet they, taken together, seem to form
a whole of very great value, whereas this is not the case with
the two wholes which might be formed by adding the true
belief to either of the others.

The importance of the result of this section seems to lie
mainly in two of its consequences. (1) That it affords some
justification for the immense intrinsic value, which seems to be
commonly attributed to the mere *knowledge* of some truths,
and which was expressly attributed to some kinds of knowledge
by Plato and Aristotle. Perfect knowledge has indeed competed
with perfect love for the position of Ideal. If the results of this
section are correct, it appears that knowledge, though having
little or no value by itself, is an absolutely essential constituent
in the highest goods, and contributes immensely to their value.
And it appears that this function may be performed not only
by that case of knowledge, which we have chiefly considered,
namely, knowledge of the reality of the beautiful object cognised,
but also by knowledge of the numerical identity of this object
with that which really exists, and by the knowledge that the
existence of that object is truly good. Indeed all knowledge,
which is directly concerned with the nature of the constituents
of a beautiful object, would seem capable of adding greatly to
the value of the contemplation of that object, although, by
itself, such knowledge would have no value at all.—And (2) The
second important consequence, which follows from this section,

is that the presence of true belief may, in spite of a great
inferiority in the value of the emotion and the beauty of its
object, constitute with them a whole equal or superior in value
to wholes, in which the emotion and beauty are superior, but
in which a true belief is wanting or a false belief present. In
this way we may justify the attribution of equal or superior
value to an appreciation of an inferior real object, as compared
with the appreciation of a greatly superior object which is a
mere creature of the imagination. Thus a just appreciation of
nature and of real persons may maintain its equality with an
equally just appreciation of the products of artistic imagination,
in spite of much greater beauty in the latter. And similarly
though God may be admitted to be a more perfect object than
any actual human being, the love of God may yet be inferior to
human love, *if* God does not exist.

121. (4) In order to complete the discussion of this first
class of goods—goods which have an essential reference to
beautiful objects—it would be necessary to attempt a classi-
fication and comparative valuation of all the different forms of
beauty, a task which properly belongs to the study called
Aesthetics. I do not, however, propose to attempt any part
of this task. It must only be understood that I intend to
include among the essential constituents of the goods I have
been discussing, every form and variety of beautiful object, if
only it be truly beautiful; and, *if* this be understood, I think
it may be seen that the consensus of opinion with regard to
what is positively beautiful and what is positively ugly, and
even with regard to great differences in degree of beauty, is
quite sufficient to allow us a hope that we need not greatly err
in our judgments of good and evil. In anything which is
thought beautiful by any considerable number of persons, there
is probably *some* beautiful quality; and differences of opinion
seem to be far more often due to exclusive attention, on the
part of different persons, to different qualities in the same
object, than to the positive error of supposing a quality that
is ugly to be really beautiful. When an object, which some
think beautiful, is denied to be so by others, the truth is
usually that it lacks some beautiful quality or is deformed by

some ugly one, which engage the exclusive attention of the critics.

I may, however, state two general principles, closely connected with the results of this chapter, the recognition of which would seem to be of great importance for the investigation of what things are truly beautiful. The first of these is (1) a definition of beauty, of what is meant by saying that a thing is truly beautiful. The naturalistic fallacy has been quite as commonly committed with regard to beauty as with regard to good: its use has introduced as many errors into Aesthetics as into Ethics. It has been even more commonly supposed that the beautiful may be *defined* as that which produces certain effects upon our feelings; and the conclusion which follows from this—namely, that judgments of taste are merely *subjective*—that precisely the same thing may, according to circumstances, be *both* beautiful *and* not beautiful—has very frequently been drawn. The conclusions of this chapter suggest a definition of beauty, which may partially explain and entirely remove the difficulties which have led to this error. It appears probable that the beautiful should be *defined* as that of which the admiring contemplation is good in itself. That is to say: To assert that a thing is beautiful is to assert that the cognition of it is an essential element in one of the intrinsically valuable wholes we have been discussing; so that the question, whether it is *truly* beautiful or not, depends upon the *objective* question whether the whole in question is or is not truly good, and does not depend upon the question whether it would or would not excite particular feelings in particular persons. This definition has the double recommendation that it accounts both for the apparent connection between goodness and beauty and for the no less apparent difference between these two conceptions. It appears, at first sight, to be a strange coincidence, that there should be two *different* objective predicates of value, 'good' and 'beautiful,' which are nevertheless so related to one another that whatever is beautiful is also good. But, if our definition be correct, the strangeness disappears; since it leaves only one *unanalysable* predicate of value, namely 'good,' while 'beautiful,' though not identical with, is to be defined by reference to this,

8   M

being thus, at the same time, different from and necessarily connected with it. In short, on this view, to say that a thing is beautiful is to say, not indeed that it is *itself* good, but that it is a necessary element in something which is : to prove that a thing is truly beautiful is to prove that a whole, to which it bears a particular relation as a part, is truly good. And in this way we should explain the immense predominance, among objects commonly considered beautiful, of *material* objects— objects of the external senses; since these objects, though themselves having, as has been said, little or no intrinsic value, are yet essential constituents in the largest group of wholes which have intrinsic value. These wholes themselves may be, and are, also beautiful; but the comparative rarity, with which we regard them as themselves *objects* of contemplation, seems sufficient to explain the association of beauty with external objects.

And secondly (2) it is to be observed that beautiful objects are themselves, for the most part, organic unities, in this sense, that they are wholes of great complexity, such that the contemplation of any part, by itself, may have no value, and yet that, unless the contemplation of the whole includes the contemplation of that part, it will lose in value. From this it follows that there can be no single criterion of beauty. It will never be true to say : This object owes its beauty *solely* to the presence of this characteristic ; nor yet that : Wherever this characteristic is present, the object must be beautiful. All that can be true is that certain objects are beautiful, *because* they have certain characteristics, in the sense that they would not be beautiful *unless* they had them. And it may be possible to find that certain characteristics are more or less universally present in all beautiful objects, and are, in this sense, more or less important conditions of beauty. But it is important to observe that the very qualities, which differentiate one beautiful object from all others, are, if the object be truly beautiful, as *essential* to its beauty, as those which it has in common with ever so many others. The object would no more have the beauty it has, without its specific qualities, than without those that are generic; and the generic qualities, *by themselves*, would fail, as completely, to give beauty, as those which are specific.

122. II. It will be remembered that I began this survey of great unmixed goods, by dividing all the greatest goods we know into the two classes of aesthetic enjoyments, on the one hand, and the pleasures of human intercourse or of personal affection, on the other. I postponed the consideration of the latter on the ground that they presented additional complications In what this additional complication consists, will now be evident; and I have already been obliged to take account of it, in discussing the contribution to value made by true belief. It consists in the fact that in the case of personal affection, the object itself is not *merely* beautiful, while possessed of little or no intrinsic value, but is itself, in part at least, of great intrinsic value. All the constituents which we have found to be necessary to the most valuable aesthetic enjoyments, namely, appropriate emotion, cognition of truly beautiful qualities, and true belief, are equally necessary here; but here we have the additional fact that the object must be not only truly beautiful, but also truly good in a high degree.

It is evident that this additional complication only occurs in so far as there is included in the object of personal affection some of the *mental* qualities of the person towards whom the affection is felt. And I think it may be admitted that, wherever the affection is most valuable, the appreciation of mental qualities must form a large part of it, and that the presence of this part makes the whole far more valuable than it could have been without it. But it seems very doubtful whether this appreciation, by itself, can possess as much value as the whole in which it is combined with an appreciation of the appropriate *corporeal* expression of the mental qualities in question. It is certain that in all actual cases of valuable affection, the bodily expressions of character, whether by looks, by words, or by actions, do form a part of the object towards which the affection is felt, and that the fact of their inclusion appears to heighten the value of the whole state. It is, indeed, very difficult to imagine what the cognition of mental qualities *alone*, unaccompanied by *any* corporeal expression, would be like; and, in so far as we succeed in making this abstraction, the whole considered certainly appears to have less value. I

8-2

therefore conclude that the importance of an admiration of admirable mental qualities lies chiefly in the immense superiority of a whole, in which it forms a part, to one in which it is absent, and not in any high degree of intrinsic value which it possesses by itself. It even appears to be doubtful, whether, in itself, it possesses so much value as the appreciation of mere corporeal beauty undoubtedly does possess; that is to say, whether the appreciation of what has great intrinsic value is so valuable as the appreciation of what is merely beautiful.

But further if we consider the nature of admirable mental qualities, by themselves, it appears that a proper appreciation of them involves a reference to purely material beauty in yet another way. Admirable mental qualities do, if our previous conclusions are correct, consist very largely in an emotional contemplation of beautiful objects; and hence the appreciation of them will consist essentially in the contemplation of such contemplation. It is true that the most valuable appreciation of persons appears to be that which consists in the appreciation of their appreciation of other persons : but even here a reference to material beauty appears to be involved, *both* in respect of the fact that what is appreciated in the last instance may be the contemplation of what is merely beautiful, *and* in respect of the fact that the most valuable appreciation of a person appears to *include* an appreciation of his corporeal expression. Though, therefore, we may admit that the appreciation of a person's attitude towards other persons, or, to take one instance, the love of love, is far the most valuable good we know, and far more valuable than the mere love of beauty, yet we can only admit this if the first be understood to *include* the latter, in various degrees of directness.

With regard to the question what *are* the mental qualities of which the cognition is essential to the value of human intercourse, it is plain that they include, in the first place, all those varieties of aesthetic appreciation, which formed our first class of goods. They include, therefore, a great variety of different emotions, each of which is appropriate to some different kind of beauty. But we must now add to these the whole range of emotions, which are appropriate to persons, and which are different from those which are appropriate to mere corporeal beauty. It must also be remembered that just as these emotions have little value in themselves, and as the state of mind in which they exist may have its value greatly heightened, or may entirely lose it and become positively evil in a great degree, according as the cognitions accompanying the emotions are appropriate or inappropriate; so too the appreciation of these emotions, though it may have some value in itself, may yet form part of a whole which has far greater value or no value at all, according as it is or is not accompanied by a perception of the appropriateness of the emotions to their objects. It is obvious, therefore, that the study of what is valuable in human intercourse is a study of immense complexity; and that there may be much human intercourse which has little or no value, or is positively bad. Yet here too, as with the question what is beautiful, there seems no reason to doubt that a reflective judgment will in the main decide correctly both as to what are positive goods and even as to any *great* differences in value between these goods. In particular, it may be remarked that the emotions, of which the contemplation is essential to the greatest values, and which are also themselves appropriately excited by such contemplation, appear to be those which are commonly most highly prized under the name of affection.

123. I have now completed my examination into the nature of those great positive goods, which do not appear to include among their constituents anything positively evil or ugly, though they include much which is in itself indifferent. And I wish to point out certain conclusions which appear to follow, with regard to the nature of the Summum Bonum, or that state of things which would be the most perfect we can conceive. Those idealistic philosophers, whose views agree most closely with those here advocated, in that they deny pleasure to be the sole good and regard what is completely good as having some complexity, have usually represented a purely spiritual state of existence as the Ideal. Regarding matter as essentially imperfect, if not positively evil, they have concluded that the total absence of all material properties is necessary to a state of perfection. Now, according to what has been said, this view

would be, correct so far as it asserts that any great good must
be *mental*, and so far as it asserts that a purely material
existence, *by itself*, can have little or no value. The superiority
of the spiritual over the material has, in a sense, been amply
vindicated. But it does not follow, from this superiority, that
a perfect state of things must be one, from which all material
properties are rigidly excluded: on the contrary, if our conclusions
are correct, it would seem to be the case that a state of things,
in which they are included, must be vastly better than any
conceivable state in which they were absent. In order to see
that this is so, the chief thing necessary to be considered is
exactly what it is which we declare to be good when we declare
that the appreciation of beauty in Art and Nature is so. That
this appreciation *is* good, the philosophers in question do not
for the most part deny. But, if we admit it, then we should
remember Butler's maxim that: Everything is what it is, and
not another thing. I have tried to shew, and I think it is too
evident to be disputed, that such appreciation is an organic
unity, a complex whole; and that, in its most undoubted
instances, part of what is included in this whole is *a cognition
of material qualities*, and particularly of a vast variety of what
are called *secondary* qualities. If, then, it is *this* whole, which
we know to be good, and not another thing, then we know that
material qualities, even though they be perfectly worthless in
themselves, are yet essential constituents of what is far from
worthless. What we know to be valuable is the apprehension
of just these qualities, and not of any others; and, if we propose
to subtract them from it, then what we have left is *not* that
which we know to have value, but something else. And it must
be noticed that this conclusion holds, even if my contention,
that a true belief in the existence of these qualities adds to the
value of the whole in which it is included, be disputed. We
should then, indeed, be entitled to assert that the *existence* of a
material world was wholly immaterial to perfection; but the
fact that what we knew to be good was a cognition of *material
qualities* (though purely imaginary), would still remain. It
must, then, be admitted on pain of self-contradiction—on pain
of holding that things are not what they are, but something else

—that a world, from which material qualities were wholly banished, would be a world which lacked many, if not all, of those things, which we know most certainly to be great goods. That it *might* nevertheless be a far better world than one which retained these goods, I have already admitted (§ 111 (1)). But in order to shew that any such world *would* be thus better, it would be necessary to shew that the retention of these things, though good in themselves, impaired, in a more than equal degree, the value of some whole, to which they might belong; and the task of shewing this has certainly never been attempted. Until it be performed, we are entitled to assert that material qualities are a necessary constituent of the Ideal; that, though something utterly unknown *might* be better than any world containing either them or any other good we know, yet we have no reason to suppose that anything whatever would be better than a state of things in which they were included. To deny and exclude matter, is to deny and exclude the best we know. That a thing may retain its value, while losing some of its qualities, is utterly untrue. All that is true is that the changed thing may have more value than, or as much value as, that of which the qualities have been lost. What I contend is that nothing, which we *know* to be good and which contains no material qualities, has such great value that we can declare it, *by itself*, to be superior to the whole which would be formed by the addition to it of an appreciation of material qualities. That a *purely* spiritual good may be the *best* of single things, I am not much concerned to dispute, although, in what has been said with regard to the nature of personal affection, I have given reasons for doubting it. But that by adding to it some appreciation of material qualities, which, though perhaps inferior by itself, is certainly a great positive good, we should obtain a greater sum of value, which no corresponding decrease in the value of the whole, as a whole, could counterbalance—this, I maintain, we have certainly no reason to doubt.

124. In order to complete this discussion of the main principles involved in the determination of intrinsic values, the chief remaining topics, necessary to be treated, appear to be two. The first of these is the nature of great intrinsic *evils*,

including what I may call *mixed* evils; that is to say, those evil
wholes, which nevertheless contain, as essential elements, something positively good or beautiful. And the second is the nature
of what I may similarly call *mixed* goods; that is to say, those
wholes, which, though intrinsically good *as wholes*, nevertheless
contain, as essential elements, something positively evil or ugly.
It will greatly facilitate this discussion, if I may be understood
throughout to use the terms 'beautiful' and 'ugly,' not necessarily
with reference to things of the kind which most naturally occur
to us as instances of what is beautiful and ugly, but in accordance
with my own proposed definition of beauty. Thus I shall use
the word 'beautiful' to denote that of which the admiring
contemplation is good in itself; and 'ugly' to denote that of
which the admiring contemplation is evil in itself.

I.   With regard, then, to great positive evils, I think it is
evident that, if we take all due precautions to discover *precisely
what* those things are, of which, *if they existed absolutely by
themselves*, we should judge the existence to be a great evil, we
shall find most of them to be organic unities of exactly the
same nature as those which are the greatest positive goods.
That is to say, they are cognitions of some object, accompanied
by some emotion. Just as neither a cognition nor an emotion,
by itself, appeared capable of being greatly good, so (with one
exception), neither a cognition nor an emotion, *by itself*, appears
capable of being greatly evil. And just as a whole formed of
both, even without the addition of any other element, appeared
undoubtedly capable of being a great good, so such a whole, *by
itself*, appears capable of being a great evil. With regard to
the *third* element, which was discussed as capable of adding
greatly to the value of a good, namely, *true belief*, it will appear
that it has different relations towards different kinds of evils.
In some cases the addition of true belief to a positive evil
seems to constitute a far worse evil; but in other cases it is not
apparent that it makes any difference.

The greatest positive evils may be divided into the following
three classes.

125.   (1) The first class consists of those evils, which seem
always to include an enjoyment or admiring contemplation of

things which are themselves either evil or ugly. That is to say these evils are characterised by the fact that they include precisely the same emotion, which is also essential to the greatest unmixed goods, from which they are differentiated by the fact that this emotion is directed towards an inappropriate object. In so far as this emotion is either a slight good in itself or a slightly beautiful object, these evils would therefore be cases of what I have called 'mixed' evils; but, as I have already said, it seems very doubtful whether an emotion, completely isolated from its object, has either value or beauty : it certainly has not much of either. It is, however, important to observe that the very same emotions, which are often loosely talked of as the greatest or the only goods, may be essential constituents of the very worst wholes: that, according to the nature of the cognition which accompanies them, they may be conditions either of the greatest good, or of the greatest evil.

In order to illustrate the nature of evils of this class, I may take two instances—cruelty and lasciviousness. That these are great intrinsic evils, we may, I think, easily assure ourselves, by imagining the state of a man, whose mind is solely occupied by either of these passions, in their worst form. If we then consider what judgment we should pass upon a universe which consisted *solely* of minds thus occupied, without the smallest hope that there would ever exist in it the smallest consciousness of any object other than those proper to these passions, or any feeling directed to any such object, I think we cannot avoid the conclusion that the existence of such a universe would be a far worse evil than the existence of none at all. But, if this be so, it follows that these two vicious states are not only, as is commonly admitted, bad as means, but also bad in themselves. —And that they involve in their nature that complication of elements, which I have called a love of what is evil or ugly, is, I think, no less plain. With regard to the pleasures of lust, the nature of the cognition, by the presence of which they are to be defined, is somewhat difficult to analyse. But it appears to include both cognitions of organic sensations and perceptions of states of the body, of which the enjoyment is certainly an evil in itself. So far as these are concerned, lasciviousness would, then, include in its essence an admiring contemplation of what is ugly. But certainly one of its commonest ingredients, in its worst forms, is an enjoyment of the same state of mind in other people: and in this case it would therefore also include a love of what is evil. With regard to cruelty, it is easy to see that an enjoyment of pain in other people is essential to it; and, as we shall see, when we come to consider pain, this is certainly a love of evil: while, in so far as it also includes a delight in the bodily signs of agony, it would also comprehend a love of what is ugly. In both cases, it should be observed, the evil of the state is heightened not only by an increase in the evil or ugliness of the object, but also by an increase in the enjoyment.

It might be objected, in the case of cruelty, that our disapproval of it, even in the isolated case supposed, where no considerations of its badness as a means could influence us, may yet be really directed to the pain of the persons, which it takes delight in contemplating. This objection may be met, in the first place, by the remark that it entirely fails to explain the judgment, which yet, I think, no one, on reflection, will be able to avoid making, that even though the amount of pain contemplated be the same, yet the greater the delight in its contemplation, the worse the state of things. But it may also, I think, be met by notice of a fact, which we were unable to urge in considering the similar possibility with regard to goods —namely the possibility that the reason why we attribute greater value to a worthy affection for a *real* person, is that we take into account the additional good consisting in the existence of that person. We may I think urge, in the case of cruelty, that its intrinsic odiousness is equally great, whether the pain contemplated really exists or is purely imaginary. I, at least, am unable to distinguish that, in this case, the presence of *true belief* makes any difference to the intrinsic value of the whole considered, although it undoubtedly may make a great difference to its value *as a means*. And so also with regard to other evils of this class: I am unable to see that a true belief in the *existence* of their objects makes any difference in the degree of their positive demerits. On the other hand, the presence of another class of beliefs seems to make a considerable difference.

When we enjoy what is evil or ugly, in spite of our knowledge that it is so, the state of things seems considerably worse than if we made no judgment at all as to the object's value. And the same seems also, strangely enough, to be the case when we make a false judgment of value. When we admire what is ugly or evil, believing that it is beautiful and good, this belief seems also to enhance the intrinsic vileness of our condition. It must, of course, be understood that, in both these cases, the judgment in question is merely what I have called a judgment of taste; that is to say, it is concerned with the worth of the qualities actually cognised and not with the worth of the object, to which those qualities may be rightly or wrongly attributed.

Finally it should be mentioned that evils of this class, *beside* that emotional element (namely enjoyment and admiration) which they share with great unmixed goods, appear always also to include some specific emotion, which does not enter in the same way into the constitution of any good. The presence of this specific emotion seems certainly to enhance the badness of the whole, though it is not plain that, by itself, it would be either evil or ugly.

126. (2) The second class of great evils are undoubtedly mixed evils; but I treat them next, because, in a certain respect, they appear to be the *converse* of the class last considered. Just as it is essential to this last class that they should include an emotion, appropriate to the cognition of what is good or beautiful, but directed to an inappropriate object; so to this second class it is essential that they should include a cognition of what is good or beautiful, but accompanied by an inappropriate emotion. In short, just as the last class may be described as cases of the love of what is evil or ugly, so this class may be described as cases of the hatred of what is good or beautiful.

With regard to these evils it should be remarked: First, that the vices of hatred, envy and contempt, where these vices are evil in themselves, appear to be instances of them; and that they are frequently accompanied by evils of the first class, for example, where a delight is felt in the pain of a good person.

Where they are thus accompanied, the whole thus formed is undoubtedly worse than if either existed singly.

And secondly: That in their case a true belief in the existence of the good or beautiful object, which is hated, does appear to enhance the badness of the whole, in which it is present. Undoubtedly also, as in our first class, the presence of a true belief as to the *value* of the objects contemplated, increases the evil. But, contrary to what was the case in our first class, a *false* judgment of value appears to lessen it.

127. (3) The third class of great positive evils appears to be the class of *pains*.

With regard to these it should first be remarked that, as in the case of pleasure, it is not pain itself, but only the consciousness of pain, towards which our judgments of value are directed. Just as in Chap. III., it was said that pleasure, however intense, which no one felt, would be no good at all; so it appears that pain, however intense, of which there was no consciousness, would be no evil at all.

It is, therefore, only the consciousness of intense pain, which can be maintained to be a great evil. But that this, *by itself,* may be a great evil, I cannot avoid thinking. The case of pain thus seems to differ from that of pleasure: for the mere consciousness of pleasure, however intense, does not, *by itself,* appear to be a *great* good, even if it has some slight intrinsic value. In short, pain (if we understand by this expression, the consciousness of pain) appears to be a far worse evil than pleasure is a good. But, if this be so, then *pain* must be admitted to be an exception from the rule which seems to hold both of all *other* great evils and of *all* great goods: namely that they are all organic unities to which *both* a cognition of an object *and* an emotion directed towards that object are essential. In the case of pain and of pain alone, it seems to be true that a mere cognition, by itself, may be a great evil. It is, indeed, *an* organic unity, since it involves both the cognition and the object, neither of which, by themselves, has either merit or demerit. But it is a less complex organic unity than any other great evil and than any great good, *both* in respect of the fact that it does not involve, *beside* the cognition, an emotion directed towards its object, *and also* in respect of the fact that the *object* may here be absolutely simple, whereas in most, if not all, other cases, the object itself is highly complex.

This want of analogy between the relation of pain to intrinsic evil and of pleasure to intrinsic good, seems also to be exhibited in a second respect. Not only is it the case that consciousness of intense pain is, by itself, a great evil, whereas consciousness of intense pleasure is, by itself, no great good; but also the *converse* difference appears to hold of the contribution which they make to the value of the whole, when they are combined respectively with another great evil or with a great good. That is to say, the presence of pleasure (though not in proportion to its intensity) does appear to enhance the value of a whole, in which it is combined with any of the great unmixed goods which we have considered: it might even be maintained that it is *only* wholes, in which *some* pleasure is included, that possess any great value: it is certain, at all events, that the presence of pleasure makes a contribution to the value of good wholes greatly in excess of its own intrinsic value. On the contrary, if a feeling of pain be combined with any of the evil states of mind which we have been considering, the difference which its presence makes to the value of the whole, *as a whole*, seems to be rather for the better than the worse: in any case, the only additional evil which it introduces, is that which it, by itself, intrinsically constitutes. Thus, whereas pain is *in itself* a great evil, but makes no addition to the badness of a whole, in which it is combined with some other bad thing, except that which consists in its own intrinsic badness; pleasure, conversely, is not *in itself* a great good, but does make a great addition to the goodness of a whole in which it is combined with a good thing, quite apart from its own intrinsic value.

128. But finally, it must be insisted that pleasure and pain are completely analogous in this: that we cannot assume either that the presence of pleasure always makes a state of things better *on the whole*, or that the presence of pain always makes it worse. This is the truth which is most liable to be overlooked with regard to them; and it is because this is true, that the common theory, that pleasure is the only good and pain the only evil, has its grossest consequences in misjudgments of value. Not only is the pleasantness of a state *not* in proportion to its intrinsic worth; it may even add positively to its vileness. We do not think the successful hatred of a villian the less vile and odious, because he takes the keenest delight in it; nor is there the least need, in logic, why we should think so, apart from an unintelligent prejudice in favour of pleasure. In fact it seems to be the case that wherever pleasure is added to an evil state of either of our first two classes, the whole thus formed is *always* worse than if no pleasure had been there. And similarly with regard to pain. If pain be added to an evil state of either of our first two classes, the whole thus formed is *always* better, *as a whole*, than if no pain had been there; though here, if the pain be too intense, since that is a great evil, the state may not be better *on the whole*. It is in this way that the theory of vindictive punishment may be vindicated. The infliction of pain on a person whose state of mind is bad may, if the pain be not too intense, create a state of things that is better *on the whole* than if the evil state of mind had existed unpunished. Whether such a state of things can ever constitute a *positive* good, is another question.

129. II. The consideration of this other question belongs properly to the second topic, which was reserved above for discussion—namely the topic of 'mixed' goods. 'Mixed' goods were defined above as things, which, though positively good *as wholes*, nevertheless contain, as essential elements, something intrinsically evil or ugly. And there certainly seem to be such goods. But for the proper consideration of them, it is necessary to take into account a new distinction—the distinction just expressed as being between the value which a thing possesses '*as a whole*,' and that which it possesses '*on the whole*.'

When 'mixed' goods were defined as things positively good *as wholes*, the expression was ambiguous. It was meant that they were positively good *on the whole*; but it must now be observed that the value which a thing possesses *on the whole* may be said to be equivalent to the sum of the value which it possesses *as a whole, together with* the intrinsic values which may belong to any of its parts. In fact, by the 'value which a thing possesses as a whole,' there may be meant two quite distinct things. There may be meant either (1) That value which arises solely *from the combination* of two or more things; or else (2) The total value formed by the addition to (1) of any intrinsic values which may belong to the things combined. The meaning of the distinction may perhaps be most easily seen by considering the supposed case of vindictive punishment. If it is true that the combined existence of two evils may yet constitute a less evil than would be constituted by the existence of either singly, it is plain that this can only be because there arises from the combination a positive good which is greater than the *difference* between the sum of the two evils and the demerit of either singly: this positive good would then be the value of the whole, *as a whole,* in sense (1). Yet if this value be not so great a good as the sum of the two evils is an evil, it is plain that the value of the whole state of things will be a positive evil; and this value is the value of the whole, *as a whole,* in sense (2). Whatever view may be taken with regard to the particular case of vindictive punishment, it is plain that we have here *two distinct things,* with regard to *either* of which a separate question may be asked in the case of every organic unity. The first of these two things may be expressed as *the difference* between the value *of the whole thing* and the sum of the value of its parts. And it is plain that where the parts have little or no intrinsic value (as in our first class of goods, §§ 114, 115), this difference will be nearly or absolutely identical with the value of the whole thing. The distinction, therefore, only becomes important in the case of wholes, of which one or more parts have a great intrinsic value, positive or negative. The first of these cases, that of a whole, in which one part has a great *positive* value, is exemplified in our 2nd and 3rd classes of great unmixed goods (§§ 120, 122); and similarly the Summum Bonum is a whole of which *many* parts have a great *positive* value. Such cases, it may be observed, are also very frequent and very important objects of Aesthetic judgment; since the essential distinction between the 'classical' and the 'romantic' styles consists in the fact that the former aims at obtaining the greatest possible value for the whole, *as a whole*, in sense (1), whereas the latter sacrifices this in order to obtain the greatest possible value for some *part*, which is itself an organic unity. It follows that we cannot declare either style to be necessarily superior, since an equally good result *on the whole*, or 'as a whole' in sense (2), may be obtained by either method; but the distinctively *aesthetic* temperament seems to be characterised by a tendency to prefer a good result obtained by the classical, to an equally good result obtained by the romantic method.

130. But what we have now to consider are cases of wholes, in which one or more parts have a great *negative* value —are great positive evils. And first of all, we may take the *strongest* cases, like that of retributive punishment, in which we have a whole, exclusively composed of two great positive evils—wickedness and pain. Can such a whole ever be positively good *on the whole*?

(1) I can see no reason to think that such wholes ever are positively good *on the whole*. But from the fact that they may, nevertheless, be less evils, than either of their parts taken singly, it follows that they have a characteristic which is most important for the correct decision of practical questions. It follows that, quite apart from *consequences* or any value which an evil may have as a mere means, it may, *supposing* one evil already exists, be worth while to create another, since, by the mere creation of this second, there may be constituted a whole less bad than if the original evil had been left to exist by itself. And similarly, with regard to all the wholes which I am about to consider, it must be remembered, that, even if they are not goods *on the whole*, yet, where an evil already exists, as in this world evils do exist, the existence of the other part of these wholes will constitute a thing desirable *for its own sake*—that is to say, not merely a means to future goods, but one of the *ends* which must be taken into account in estimating what that best possible state of things is, to which every right action must be a means.

131. (2) But, as a matter of fact, I cannot avoid thinking that there are wholes, containing something positively evil and ugly, which are, nevertheless, great positive goods on the whole.

Indeed, it appears to be to this class that those instances of virtue, which contain anything intrinsically good, chiefly belong. It need not, of course, be denied that there is sometimes included in a virtuous disposition more or less of those unmixed goods which were first discussed—that is to say, a real love of what is good or beautiful. But the typical and characteristic virtuous dispositions, so far as they are not mere means, seem rather to be examples of mixed goods. We may take as instances (a) Courage and Compassion, which seem to belong to the second of the three classes of virtues distinguished in our last chapter (§ 107); and (b) the specifically 'moral' sentiment, by reference to which the third of those three classes was defined (§ 108).

Courage and compassion, in so far as they contain an intrinsically desirable state of mind, seem to involve essentially a cognition of something evil or ugly. In the case of courage the object of the cognition may be an evil of any of our three classes; in the case of compassion, the proper object is pain. Both these virtues, accordingly, must contain precisely the same cognitive element, which is also essential to evils of class (1); and they are differentiated from these by the fact that the emotion directed to these objects is, in their case, an emotion of the same kind which was essential to evils of class (2). In short, just as evils of class (2) seemed to consist in a hatred of what was good or beautiful, and evils of class (1) in a love of what was evil or ugly; so these virtues involve a *hatred* of what is evil or ugly. Both these virtues do, no doubt, also contain other elements, and, among these, each contains its specific emotion; but that their value does not depend solely upon these other elements, we may easily assure ourselves, by considering what we should think of an attitude of endurance or of defiant contempt toward an object intrinsically good or beautiful, or of the state of a man whose mind was filled with pity for the happiness of a worthy admiration. Yet pity for the undeserved sufferings of others, endurance of pain to ourselves, and a defiant hatred of evil dispositions in ourselves or in others, seem to be undoubtedly admirable in themselves; and if so, there are admirable things, which must be lost, if there were no cognition of evil.

Similarly the specifically 'moral' sentiment, in all cases where it has any considerable intrinsic value, appears to include a hatred of evils of the first and second classes. It is true that the emotion is here excited by the idea that an action is right or wrong ; and hence the object of the idea which excites it is generally not an intrinsic evil. But, as far as I can discover, the emotion with which a conscientious man views a real or imaginary right action, contains, as an essential element, the same emotion with which he views a wrong one: it seems, indeed, that this element is necessary to make his emotion specifically *moral*. And the specifically moral emotion excited by the idea of a wrong action, seems to me to contain essentially a more or less vague cognition of the kind of intrinsic evils, which are usually caused by wrong actions, whether they would or would not be caused by the particular action in question. I am, in fact, unable to distinguish, in its main features, the moral sentiment excited by the idea of rightness and wrongness, wherever it is intense, from the total state constituted by a cognition of something intrinsically evil together with the emotion of hatred directed towards it. Nor need we be surprised that this mental state should be the one chiefly associated with the idea of rightness, if we reflect on the nature of those actions which are most commonly recognised as duties. For by far the greater part of the actions, of which we commonly think as duties, are *negative*: what we feel to be our duty is to *abstain* from some action to which a strong natural impulse tempts us. And these wrong actions, in the avoidance of which duty consists, are usually such as produce, very immediately, some bad consequence in pain to others; while, in many prominent instances, the inclination, which prompts us to them, is itself an intrinsic evil, containing, as where the impulse is lust or cruelty, an anticipatory enjoyment of something evil or ugly. That right action does thus so frequently entail the suppression of some evil impulse, is necessary to explain the plausibility of the view that virtue *consists* in the control of passion by reason. Accordingly, the truth seems to be that, whenever a strong moral emotion is excited by the idea of rightness, this emotion is accompanied by a vague cognition of the kind of

evils usually suppressed or avoided by the actions which most
frequently occur to us as instances of duty; and that the
emotion is directed towards this evil quality. We may, then,
conclude that the specific moral emotion owes almost all its
intrinsic value to the fact that it includes a cognition of evils
accompanied by a hatred of them: mere rightness, whether
truly or untruly attributed to an action, seems incapable of
forming the object of an emotional contemplation, which shall
be any great good.

132. If this be so, then we have, in many prominent
instances of virtue, cases of a whole, greatly good in itself, which
yet contains the cognition of something, whereof the existence
would be a great evil: a great good is absolutely dependent for
its value, upon its inclusion of something evil or ugly, although
it does not owe its value *solely* to this element in it. And, in
the case of virtues, this evil object does, in general, actually exist.
But there seems no reason to think that, when it does exist, the
whole state of things thus constituted is therefore the better *on
the whole.* What seems indubitable, is only that the feeling
contemplation of an object, whose existence *would* be a great
evil, or which is ugly, may be essential to a valuable whole.
We have another undoubted instance of this in the appreciation
of tragedy. But, in tragedy, the sufferings of Lear, and the
vice of Iago may be purely imaginary. And it seems certain
that, if they really existed, the evil thus existing, while it must
detract from the good consisting in a proper feeling towards
them, will add no positive value to that good great enough to
counterbalance such a loss. It does, indeed, seem that the
existence of a true belief in the object of these mixed goods
does add *some* value to the whole in which it is combined with
them: a conscious compassion for real suffering seems to be
better, *as a whole*, than a compassion for sufferings merely
imaginary; and this may well be the case, even though the
evil involved in the actual suffering makes the total state of
things bad *on the whole.* And it certainly seems to be true
that a *false* belief in the actual existence of its object makes
a worse mixed good than if our state of mind were that with
which we normally regard pure fiction. Accordingly we may

conclude that the only mixed goods, which are positively good *on the whole*, are those in which the object is something which *would* be a great evil, if it existed, or which *is* ugly.

133. With regard, then, to those mixed goods, which consist in an appropriate attitude of the mind towards things evil or ugly, and which include among their number the greater part of such virtues as have any intrinsic value whatever, the following three conclusions seem to be those chiefly requiring to be emphasized:—

(1) There seems no reason to think that where the object is a thing evil in itself, which *actually exists*, the total state of things is ever positively *good on the whole*. The appropriate mental attitude towards a really existing evil contains, of course, an element which is absolutely identical with the same attitude towards the same evil, where it is purely imaginary. And this element, which is common to the two cases, may be a great positive good, on the whole. But there seems no reason to doubt that, where the evil is *real*, the amount of this real evil is always sufficient to reduce the total sum of value to a negative quantity. Accordingly we have no reason to maintain the paradox that an ideal world would be one in which vice and suffering must exist in order that it may contain the goods consisting in the appropriate emotion towards them. It is not a positive good that suffering should exist, in order that we may compassionate it; or wickedness, that we may hate it. There is no reason to think that any actual evil whatsoever would be contained in the Ideal. It follows that we cannot admit the actual validity of any of the arguments commonly used in Theodicies; no such argument succeeds in justifying the fact that there does exist even the smallest of the many evils which this world contains. The most that can be said for such arguments is that, when they make appeal to the principle of organic unity, their appeal is valid *in principle*. It *might* be the case that the existence of evil was necessary, not merely as a means, but analytically, to the existence of the greatest good. But we have no reason to think that this *is* the case in any instance whatsoever.

But (2) there *is* reason to think that the cognition of things

evil or ugly, which are purely imaginary, is essential to the
Ideal. In this case the burden of proof lies the other way. It
cannot be doubted that the appreciation of tragedy is a great
positive good; and it seems almost equally certain that the
virtues of compassion, courage, and self-control contain such
goods. And to all these the cognition of things which would
be evil, if they existed, is analytically necessary. Here then we
have things of which the existence must add value to any whole
in which they are contained; nor is it possible to assure ourselves that any whole, from which they were omitted, would
thereby gain more in its value *as a whole*, than it would lose
by their omission. We have no reason to think that any whole,
which did not contain them, would be so good *on the whole* as
some whole in which they were obtained. The case for their
inclusion in the Ideal is as strong as that for the inclusion of
material qualities (§ 123, above). *Against* the inclusion of
these goods nothing can be urged except a bare possibility.

Finally (3) it is important to insist that, as was said above,
these mixed virtues have a great practical value, in addition to
that which they possess either in themselves or as mere means.
Where evils do exist, as in this world they do, the fact that
they are known and properly appreciated, constitutes a state of
things having greater value *as a whole* even than the same
appreciation of purely imaginary evils. This state of things, it
has been said, is never positively good *on the whole*; but where
the evil, which reduces its total value to a negative quantity,
already unavoidably exists, to obtain the intrinsic value which
belongs to it *as a whole* will obviously produce a better state of
things than if the evil had existed by itself, quite apart from
the good element in it which is identical with the appreciation
of imaginary evils, and from any ulterior consequences which
its existence may bring about. The case is here the same as
with retributive punishment. Where an evil already exists, it
is well that it should be pitied or hated or endured, according
to its nature; just as it may be well that some evils should be
punished. Of course, as in all practical cases, it often happens
that the attainment of this good is incompatible with the
attainment of another and a greater one. But it is important

to insist that we have here a real intrinsic value, which must be taken into account in calculating that greatest possible balance of intrinsic value, which it is always our duty to produce.

134. I have now completed such remarks as seemed most necessary to be made concerning intrinsic values. It is obvious that for the proper answering of this, the fundamental question of Ethics, there remains a field of investigation as wide and as difficult, as was assigned to Practical Ethics in my last chapter. There is as much to be said concerning what results are intrinsically good, and in what degrees, as concerning what results it is possible for us to bring about: both questions demand, and will repay, an equally patient enquiry. Many of the judgments, which I have made in this chapter, will, no doubt, seem unduly arbitrary: it must be confessed that some of the attributions of intrinsic value, which have seemed to me to be true, do not display that symmetry and system which is wont to be required of philosophers. But if this be urged as an objection, I may respectfully point out that it is none. We have no title whatever to assume that the truth on any subject-matter will display such symmetry as we desire to see—or (to use the common vague phrase) that it will possess any particular form of 'unity.' To search for 'unity' and 'system,' at the expense of truth, is not, I take it, the proper business of philosophy, however universally it may have been the practice of philosophers. And that all truths about the Universe possess to one another all the various relations, which may be meant by 'unity,' can only be legitimately asserted, when we have carefully distinguished those various relations and discovered what those truths are. In particular, we can have no title to assert that ethical truths are 'unified' in any particular manner, except in virtue of an enquiry conducted by the method which I have endeavoured to follow and to illustrate. The study of Ethics would, no doubt, be far more simple, and its results far more 'systematic,' if, for instance, pain were an evil of exactly the same magnitude as pleasure is a good; but we have no reason whatever to assume that the Universe is such that ethical truths must display this kind of symmetry: no argument

against my conclusion, that pleasure and pain do *not* thus
correspond, can have any weight whatever, failing a careful
examination of the instances which have led me to form it.
Nevertheless I am content that the results of this chapter
should be taken rather as illustrating the method which must
be pursued in answering the fundamental question of Ethics,
and the principles which must be observed, than as giving the
correct answer to that question. That things intrinsically good
or bad are many and various; that most of them are 'organic
unities,' in the peculiar and definite sense to which I have
confined the term; and that our only means of deciding upon
their intrinsic value and its degree, is by carefully distinguishing
exactly what the thing is, about which we ask the question,
and then looking to see whether it has or has not the unique
predicate 'good' in any of its various degrees : these are the
conclusions, upon the truth of which I desire to insist.
Similarly, in my last chapter, with regard to the question
'What ought we to do?' I have endeavoured rather to shew
exactly what is the meaning of the question, and what
difficulties must consequently be faced in answering it, than
to prove that any particular answers are true. And that these
two questions, having precisely the nature which I have assigned
to them, are *the* questions which it is the object of Ethics to
answer, may be regarded as the main result of the preceding
chapters. These are the questions which ethical philosophers
have always been mainly concerned to answer, although they
have not recognised what their question was—what predicate
they were asserting to attach to things. The practice of asking
what things are virtues or duties, without distinguishing what
these terms mean; the practice of asking what ought to be here
and now, without distinguishing whether as means or end—for
its own sake or for that of its results; the search for one single
criterion of right or wrong, without the recognition that in
order to discover a criterion we must first know what things
are right or wrong; and the neglect of the principle of 'organic
unities'—these sources of error have hitherto been almost
universally prevalent in Ethics. The conscious endeavour to
avoid them all, and to apply to all the ordinary objects of ethical

judgment these two questions and these only: Has it intrinsic value? and Is it a means to the best possible?—this attempt, so far as I know, is entirely new; and its results, when compared with those habitual to moral philosophers, are certainly sufficiently surprising: that to Common Sense they will not appear so strange, I venture to hope and believe. It is, I think, much to be desired that the labour commonly devoted to answering such questions as whether certain 'ends' are more or less 'comprehensive' or more or less 'consistent' with one another—questions, which, even if a precise meaning were given to them, are wholly irrelevant to the proof of any ethical conclusion—should be diverted to the separate investigation of these two clear problems.

135. The main object of this chapter has been to define roughly the class of things, among which we may expect to find either great intrinsic goods or great intrinsic evils; and particularly to point out that there is a vast variety of such things, and that the simplest of them are, with one exception, highly complex wholes, composed of parts which have little or no value in themselves. All of them involve consciousness of an object, which is itself usually highly complex, and almost all involve also an emotional attitude towards this object; but, though they thus have certain characteristics in common, the vast variety of qualities in respect of which they differ from one another are equally essential to their value: neither the generic character of all, nor the specific character of each, is either greatly good or greatly evil by itself; they owe their value or demerit, in each case, to the presence of both. My discussion falls into three main divisions, dealing respectively (1) with unmixed goods, (2) with evils, and (3) with mixed goods. (1) Unmixed goods may all be said to consist in the love of beautiful things or of good persons: but the number of different goods of this kind is as great as that of beautiful objects, and they are also differentiated from one another by the different emotions appropriate to different objects. These goods are undoubtedly good, even where the things or persons loved are imaginary; but it was urged that, where the thing or person is real and is believed to be so, these two facts together, when combined with the mere love of the qualities in question, constitute a whole which is greatly better than that mere love, having an additional value quite distinct from that which belongs to the existence of the object, where that object is a good person. Finally it was pointed out that the love of mental qualities, by themselves, does not seem to be so great a good as that of mental and material qualities together; and that, in any case, an immense number of the best things are, or include, a love of material qualities (113—123). (2) Great evils may be said to consist either (a) in the love of what is evil or ugly, or (b) in the hatred of what is good or beautiful, or (c) in the consciousness of pain. Thus the consciousness of pain, if it be a great evil, is the only exception to the rule that all great goods and great evils involve both a cognition and an emotion directed towards its object (124—128). (3) Mixed goods are those which include some element which is evil or ugly. They may be said to consist either in hatred of what is ugly or of evils of classes (a) and (b), or in compassion for pain. But where they include an evil, which actually exists, its demerit seems to be always great enough to outweigh the positive value which they possess (129—133).

INDEX.

Organic relation, unity, whole
    common usage 30-6
    my own usage 27-31, 32-3, 36, 93,
        96, 149, 184, 187, 189, 190, 202,
        206, 208, 212, 215, 220, 223
Ought
    to aim at 24-6, 100
    to do 26, 105, 115, 116, 117, 127,
        128, 140, 146, 148, 173, 180, 223
    to be or exist 17, 115, 118, 127, 128,
        148, 173, 180, 223

Pain 64, 65, 210, 212-4, 217, 222-3, 225
Particular 3-4
Perception 111, 112, 134, 136
Pessimism 51, 53, 156
Plato
    on Egoism 98
    on goods 178
    on Hedonism 88
    on value of Knowledge 199
    on universal truths 111
Pleasure 12-13, 16
    consciousness of 87-91, 109, 212
    as criterion 91-2, 108
    and desire 68-71, 73-4
    and 'pleasures' 79
    'quality of' 77-81
    value of, 39, 46, 50-4, 59-66, 71-2,
        74-5, 79-81, 83, 85-96, 144, 146,
        171, 173, 174, 188, 205, 212-14,
        222-3
Pity 217, 221
Positive science 39
Possible action 150-1
Practical, 216, 221
    Ethics 115-18, 140, 146, 149, 151,
        154, 180, 222
    Philosophy 2
Practice 2, 20
Praise 171
Preference 77-9, 131
Promises 157
Property, respect of 157
Propositions, types of 123-6
Prove 11, 65, 66, 74, 75-7, 99, 112,
    137, 141, 143, 145, 169, 181
Prudence, 168
    'Maxim of' 102-4
Psychological 11, 130, 140, 148
    Hedonism 18, 68, 69, 70, 73

Punishment 164
    retributive or vindictive 214, 215,
        216, 221

Reason 143-4
Representative art 193
Reward 174
Right 18, 24-5, 105, 146, 180, 216,
    218, 223
    dist. from 'duty' 148
    relation to expediency 167
    externally 176-7
    internally 179 n. 1
Romantic style 215-16
Rousseau 42

Sanctions 159, 164
Secondary qualities 206
Self-evidence 143, 144, 148, 181
Self-realisation 113, 114, 120, 188
Self-sacrifice 170
Sensation 134
Sensationalist 130
Sidgwick, Henry 145
    value of beauty 81-4, 85-7
    on Bentham 17-19
    rationality of Egoism 99-103
    'good' unanalysable 17
    Hedonism 59, 63, 64, 81-7, 91-6,
        108-9
    'method' of Intuitionism 59, 92-4
    value of knowledge 82, 86
    neglects principle of organic wholes
        93
    pleasure as criterion 91-2, 94-5
    quality of pleasure 77, 81
    value of unconscious 81-4
Sins 161
Spencer, Herbert 46, 48-58
Spinoza 110, 113
Spiritual, value of 205-6
Summum Bonum 183, 205
Stoics 41, 110
Synthetic 7, 58, 143

Taste, error of 192-3, 211
Taylor, A. E. 60
Temperance 157, 168
Theodicies 220
Tragedy 219, 221